GLOBAL
SOUTH
ASIA

Padma Kaimal
K. Sivaramakrishnan
Anand A. Yang
SERIES EDITORS

MUMBAI TAXIMEN

Autobiographies and Automobilities in India

TARINI BEDI

UNIVERSITY OF WASHINGTON PRESS
Seattle

MUMBAI TAXIMEN WAS MADE POSSIBLE IN PART BY THE NAOMI B. PASCAL EDITOR'S ENDOWMENT, SUPPORTED THROUGH THE GENEROSITY OF NANCY ALVORD, DOROTHY AND DAVID ANTHONY, JANET AND JOHN CREIGHTON, PATTI KNOWLES, KATHERINE AND DOUGLASS RAFF, DAVID AND SUSAN PASCAL, MARY MCLELLAN WILLIAMS, AND OTHER DONORS.

Design by Katrina Noble

Composed in Minion Pro, typeface designed by Robert Slimbach

26 25 24 23 22   5 4 3 2 1

Printed and bound in the United States of America

Photos by the author.

UNIVERSITY OF WASHINGTON PRESS
uwapress.uw.edu

LIBRARY OF CONGRESS CATALOGING-IN-PUBLICATION DATA
Names: Bedi, Tarini, 1973– author.
Title: Mumbai taximen : autobiographies and automobilities in India / Tarini Bedi.
Description: Seattle : University of Washington Press, [2022] | Series: Global South Asia | Includes bibliographical references and index.
Identifiers: LCCN 2021019317 (print) | LCCN 2021019318 (ebook) | ISBN 9780295749853 (hardcover) | ISBN 9780295749860 (paperback) | ISBN 9780295749877 (ebook)
Subjects: LCSH: Taxicab drivers—India—Mumbai—Social conditions. | Taxicab industry—India—Mumbai. | Automobiles—Social aspects—India—Mumbai. | Mumbai (India)—Social conditions.
Classification: LCC HD8039.T162 I456 2021 (print) | LCC HD8039.T162 (ebook) | DDC 388.4/132140954792—dc23
LC record available at https://lccn.loc.gov/2021019317
LC ebook record available at https://lccn.loc.gov/2021019318

To the Kaalipeeli Taxi

CONTENTS

ACKNOWLEDGMENTS

I have three deep and enduring debts: first is to the city of Bombay/Mumbai and its sea breezes, smells, sounds, humidity, bumps, and scrapes along the roads where I first learned how to drive almost thirty years ago. I never took driving or its mundane strategies of repair and technique as serious subjects of knowledge until I spent ten years in the worlds of Mumbai's taximen. Therefore, my second debt is to all the Mumbai taximen and their families from whom I learned what expertise that carries across generations looks like, and what it means to really *live* in a city of dreams, hopes, and crashing disappointments. I owe them more than I will ever be able to repay in many lifetimes, for sharing their lives, their homes, their work, their prayer, and their cars with me. Over the course of this research, I have learned many lessons from taximen and union men about how to work with dignity and care, how to honor even heavy obligations with joy and humor, and how to keep fighting the difficult political battles, no matter what. Last, but not least, I am most indebted to the *kaalipeeli* taxis—cars that are inseparable from the landscape of India's most boisterous big city.

I am thankful for the generous funding support for almost ten years of fieldwork from the American Institute of Indian Studies, the Wenner-Gren Foundation for Anthropological Research, and the National Science Foundation's Cultural Anthropology Program (BCS Award no. 1917969). I could not have accomplished a long and intensive ethnographic project like this without this financial support. I began developing this research into a book during two year-long writing fellowships at the University of Illinois at Chicago's Great Cities Institute (2014) and the Institute for the Humanities (2016). I am grateful to the directors of the institutes at the time, Teresa Cordova (Great Cities) and Susan Levine (Institute for the Humanities) for keeping and fighting for these important spaces on university campuses for thinking, dialogue, and writing. I am so grateful to my colleagues who were at the Institute for the Humanities with me and who provided important feedback on some early chapters: Robin Reames,

Cynthia Blair, Robert Somol, Nasser Mufti, and Tatjana Gajic. I am especially grateful to Nasser Mufti, who prodded me to think about anachronisms in the literary archive, and Rachel Weber, who made me think
analytically about urban obsolescence.

Over the years, I have had many opportunities to present my work and
develop my ideas at workshops and seminars in various parts of the world.
There are too many people to name and I am sure to forget someone in the
bleary-eyed state of the COVID-19 pandemic that I write this in but you
know who you are, and I thank you from the very bottom of my heart. One
event that made an enormous impact on how I began to think about the
ethics of care and how this attached to men's bodies was at the 2014 South
Asian Feminisms preconference organized by Naisargi Dave and Priti
Ramamurthy at the Annual South Asia Conference in Madison. The insights
from Naisargi Dave, Geeta Patel, and Kath Weston opened up important
ways for me to think about the care labor of men, and I would like to thank
them publicly for this. It was also at this event that I first met Lorri Hag-
man, my editor at the University of Washington Press. I am humbled that
she saw value in this project even in its incipient phases, and even more
humbled that she stuck with me and shepherded this book to its comple-
tion with precision and care. Thank you to the series editors of the press's
Global South Asia Series, Padma Kaimal, K. Sivaramakrishan, and
Anand A. Yang, for having faith in this book and for their patience with
how long this took me. The two anonymous scholarly reviewers who read
and then reread the full manuscript so closely and so generously were
invaluable. I owe then an enormous debt for making this a far, far, better
book. In the final stages of my writing, Joanne Muzak, my structural editor, helped me become a better, and more attentive, careful writer, and
Lakshita Malik and Cynthia Col developed a beautiful index.

Sneha Annavarapu and Bhoomika Joshi have been smart, energetic interlocutors on many things automobile and I would like to give a shout out to
both who make up our trio of what we now call *automobilistas*! Michele Freidner, I am ever indebted to you for introducing me to the world of sensory
anthropology, though this is only one of many hands you have on this book.
Lisa Björkman and Michele Freidner read many versions of many chapters
at our writing retreats in Chicago, which were rewarded by jaunts to
Chinatown, wine, and Lisa's gourmet coffee. Thank you for making that
desperate, midlife stage of writing a book less lonely and showing me that
solid scholarly critique and solid friendships go together! My upstairs
neighbor and friend, Daniel Sutherland, was writing his book alongside me

for almost two years, and this solidarity helped me keep to all my submission and revision deadlines. We each had our statues of Saraswati, the Hindu goddess of learning, knowledge, and wisdom sitting on our desks. I have no doubt that when both of these books written under her watch appear in solid form, that Saraswati will be proud and relived that she can move on to more important things.

My father died in the early stages of this research and readers might see how much this affected how I saw my fieldwork and my writing after this. My mother continued bravely on in this breakdown to give me a home and place to land my feet and heart in the city they both loved. Her small Mumbai flat, surrounded by the sounds of *azaan*, *bhajans*, honking, loudspeakers, and band-*baja*, is the epitome of Mumbai's urban milieu, and I am so grateful she has given me her love and the keys to this noisy refuge far above the city lights.

Dhruv and Maya have lived with this book almost as closely as I have. They have endured my absence both in physical and psychological terms with understanding and kindness. Maya's teenage cynicism that I should take my book and myself less seriously, as in "No one is going to read this anyway(!!)," was oddly liberating and reminded me that those who love us don't really love us because we have great followings, or fans, or big accomplishments. I have no words to describe how much their support and their presence has sustained me. It has given me overflowing appreciation of how much we depend on our kin no matter what kind of work we do.

MUMBAI TAXIMEN

INTRODUCTION

Traffic, Families, and Other Tangles

WAITING IN TRAFFIC IN A QUIVERING *KAALIPEELI* (A BLACK AND yellow car) without air conditioning, I am drenched in Mumbai's soggy summer.[1] Rashid and I are sitting in a humid deluge at a traffic signal in the suburb of Andheri West in the tangle of late morning traffic. Rashid is a veteran Mumbai *taxiwallah*, from a family of hereditary drivers and mechanics. The bumpy road we left strewn behind us has snaked knots and vibrations into the depths of my stomach. These vibrations pull the sweat behind Rashid's ear down his face and into his silvery beard.[2] An old plastic bottle of water, cruelly scalded from several weeks of the searing summer, rolls out from under the seat and onto my perspiring feet, only to roll back into hiding. The dredges of milky tea I had for breakfast tickle upward as an unpleasant, but familiar sense of car sickness.

Rashid runs his damp, yellow towel around his glistening face and neck. I move my face and body toward the window, looking into the city outside the car, desperately in search of a light breeze, hoping to soothe my vibrating stomach. Rashid lays the towel on the frayed, worn-out, velvet of the seat next to him and slowly leans forward. His hands shake as he reaches for his radio. The crackling of Rashid's old radio adds to an abundance of sounds swirling around us from the city and the car. The windows and steering wheel rattle from the clamoring vibrations of the waiting engine. Growls emerge from the depths of Rashid's car while a howling medley of horns from every other vehicle jammed around us rises over the road and the smoggy haze, turning into angry shouts at the dirty, gray sky. As I struggle with my rolling stomach, nausea, and irritation with the heat and traffic, Rashid remains focused and calm. How does he do this? I think to myself.

Taxi drivers like Rashid in many parts of the world live every day amid conflicts, change, and urban onslaughts that they do not control. Yet Rashid has kept coming back with his old, vibrating car to the jam, smog, haze, and noise for almost fifty years. As the taxi industry is changing all around him, he refuses to give up his hereditary taxi trade and refuses to join the new taxi industry that he is being told he should aspire to for a better life.[3] What does Rashid's story of driving in Mumbai teach us about how urban workers inhabit, debate, and refuse change? Like Rashid, how do they continue to see their driving as dignifying work, and how do taxi drivers live honorable, ethical, and sensually fulfilled lives? These are the puzzles that drive this book.

Rashid comes from a community of taxi drivers known as *chillia*, who have been driving taxis in Bombay since the early twentieth century. For almost a decade, I drove, lived with, and sensed the roads, the city, and the upheavals in Mumbai's taxi trade with chillia taximen, mechanics, and their families who reside in a suburb of northern Mumbai called Pathanwadi (Place of the Pathans). To tackle the puzzle of what brings drivers like Rashid back onto the roads every day, this book explores the driving, repair, care, and collective, urban, sensory knowledge that chillia live with and participate in.[4] Over nine years I observed the changes in Mumbai's taxi trade from hereditary driving, to taxi fleets, to ride-share taxis like Uber and the Indian Olacabs from the vantage of chillia drivers and mechanics. As chillia continue to live with the upheavals we now see in taxi industries in practically every part of the world, their stories remind us of how and why transporters continue to live with dignity and freedom even amid rapid change and attempts by both state and capital to devalue everything that gives them social value.

JOONA DRIVERS: SENSIBLE RELATIONS, SENSORY LIVES, AND SENSUOUS SCHOLARSHIP

Chillia are Sunni Muslims from the Palanpur region in the neighboring state of Gujarat. They call themselves the original drivers of Bombay. When I asked drivers what being "original" meant, most responded with claims to an originary and unique sensory knowing of the city and its topographies. In the words of Rashid's son, Tariq, "Original means *joona* (old), knowing my taxi and knowing the roads of *Bambai*." I heard many chillia make similar connections between original presence in the city and technological and topographical knowledge. Joona, while a temporal claim to the past, was also a claim to originality of knowledge. To be joona marked a sense of creativity and expertise in mechanics, technological repair, urban politics, and urban navigation, rooted in the present and promising a place for chillia drivers in the future. While drivers make claims to the city's future as joona drivers, joona is less of what anthropologist Arjun Appadurai (2004) calls an aspirational claim than it is a dignifying one. What it meant to be original in time and to have originality as creative knowledge often fused—that is, joona drivers have both qualities.

People everywhere can and do desire creativity and fulfilment from the dirty and difficult work that they do, without necessarily wanting to be doing or aspiring to something else (Millar 2018). For chillia, originality and mastery over cars, mechanical technology, and roads, and the capacity to sustain a hereditary trade over a century are dignifying claims. These are not just about making a living; rather, they are also about making a knowledgeable and fulfilled sensory, relational, and kin life. As anthropologist Paul Stoller (1997) reminds us in his study of professional sorcery in Niger, mastery of a professional trade is less about a mastery of texts than it is a mastery of sentient bodies and sentient relations. Despite what road authorities and road safety programs promulgate, being a good joona driver is less about mastering official rules of the road than it is about knowing the city in sensory terms. While taxi drivers routinely complain about the negligence of the urban state and the state of the roads and traffic, like Rashid on this soggy morning, they also accept the sensuousness of broken roads, mud, potholes, and traffic as part of the work of driving. As I show throughout this book, accepting the sensuousness of driving has both painful and pleasurable dimensions for drivers. Sometimes drivers are resigned to the city's onslaught on the body and the senses. At other times they express a sense of pride and pleasure in being able to navigate a difficult city with expertise. At still others, they accept sensuousness as an accumulation of knowledge that sits in the body of a single driver but is shared with others who travel the same routes.

For all these reasons drivers lend their bodies, as Rashid does, to the world of older, vibrating cars, to the changing structures of labor in Mumbai's transport industry, and to the uncertainties of road surfaces (Anjaria 2019) by accepting and working with the pleasures, pains, smells, tastes, sounds, and vibrations, touch, and bumps of the city and its roads. My fieldwork unfolded in these bumps and vibrations in the manner of what sensory anthropologists call *participant sensation* (Howes 2019; Laplantine 2015). For chillia drivers, what anthropologist David Howes (2003) calls *sensual relations* with cars, roads, and rhythms of the city are also social relations of making a life (Laplantine 2015) and of what social anthropologist Timothy Ingold (2000) calls *dwelling* in a city.[5] I use this dwelling perspective to show how people live by attending creatively and consciously to the socialities, technologies, and landscapes around them and how they deploy these as political claims to urban rights and urban modernities.[6] Chillia drivers introduced me to worlds where they dwell: to chugging, vibrating, and resurrected cars, mechanical and technical expertise, ragged roads, dust, polluted atmospheres, the unremitting bureaucratic and regulatory haggle over permits, licenses, labor rights, claims to different surfaces of the city, and the everyday routines of kin, domestic labor, obligation, care, and piety.

As the sweltering and nauseating ride with Rashid suggested, and as I observed in chillia cars, homes, and mechanics shops, social and political togetherness was what anthropologist François Laplantine (2015) calls a sensible togetherness; it was about living, suffering, feeling, touching, reflecting, and resting together. For Laplantine the sensible refers to the embodied, emotional, and physical means by which knowledge, thought, and social life are produced. For chillia, the sensible experiences of driving work are the basis of social life and social value. These experiences create what they call *jaalu* (a web), where obligations to others are both sensible and social. It became clear that chillia don't just live and work together but they also sense the city and their cars together. Their dirty, difficult, yet dignifying collective work is about making a living in economic terms, and about making a life in social, cultural, and sensible terms. Not least, while driving work is a way of life for chillia, it is also a way of inhabiting the city and in its broader ecologies and landscapes.

In conducting this research and writing this book, I draw theoretically and methodologically from what cultural anthropologist Paul Stoller (1997) calls *sensuous scholarship*. This sensuous approach allowed me to play a more descriptive role as ethnographer. Stoller argues that if we commit to discussions of sensory lives and sensuous bodies, then as writers of ethnographic prose we must also produce sensuous scholarship. Stoller challenges writers to "tack between the analytical and the sensible, in which embodied form as well as disembodied logic constitute scholarly argument" (1997, xv). The chapters of this book are arranged and written this way to give readers a sense of the smells, sounds, tastes, and touches, vibrations, joys, pleasures, and pain that make up the lives of cars and kinship in South Asian cities, or in Stoller's (1989) words, gives the reader a "taste of ethnographic things."

A sensory analysis best captures how my interlocutors made sense of how to live well, how to develop expertise, and how to live ethically with each other and with their cars. I focus as sensory anthropologists do on how lives are lived through the proliferation and acceptance, rather than the containment, of sensory experience. Rather than privilege some senses over others, I emphasize that driving work is multisensory (Howes 2019; Howes and Classen 2014). Western theory has historically enumerated and hierarchically arranged sensory experience. As cultural historian Constance Classen (1997b, 405) reminds us, early anthropology categorized vision, and to some extent audition, as "higher" senses associated with reason, science, and the West, while devaluing taste, touch, and smell as "lower" senses associated with primitive races (Gould 1985; Schiller 1965). As a result, the latter were elided as serious subjects of inquiry and observation. However, as this book shows, driving and repair work in Mumbai are multisensory labor where odors, tastes, tactilities, and their diverse manifestations are the basis for how people gain and share urban knowledge, live with, and learn about meaningful work.

A sensorial approach also allows me to pay attention to how value gets embedded in particular material objects such as cars (Munn 1992). As drivers and joona mechanics transform the technological makeup of joona cars through shared sensory labor, they show how important care and sensory knowledge of both cars and kin are in sustaining the value of driving work. The development of sensory knowledge that emerges between driving and repair, and how both are important to driving work and to Indian drivers' attunements to the automobile, is a recurring theme in the book.

Finally, this approach allows me to respond to the puzzle of what keeps Rashid driving, even when everyone tells him that his city's infrastructure, his car, and his hereditary trade are crumbling around him. I push an understanding of what I call *Indian automobility* out of systemic and infrastructural domains (Urry et al. 2005) into a sentient, sensory, and kinship understanding of work, life, and the city's surfaces and topographies. Through this I disentangle automobility from a paradigmatic and universal category to one that describes what François Laplantine (2015, 16) calls the modalities through which driving is enunciated and experienced in India. For Laplantine, to think in modal ways is to pay attention to modes— to modulations and to modifications (2015, 106). This book describes these modulations and modifications through ethnographic attention to the sensory rhythms of driving work, to the modifications of mechanical and repair work, and to the changing topographies of road surfaces.

INDIAN AUTOMOBILITY WITHIN THE GLOBAL
DEBATE OVER CARS, ROADS, AND TAXIS

When I began my research on Mumbai's taxi industry in 2010, I thought I was looking at big things such as infrastructure (Fisch 2018; Harris 2013), automobilities (Urry et al. 2005), and the history of Bombay's transport industry over a century. Then, as they often do for ethnographers, these big things landed in smaller, sometimes sadder places. Mumbai's self-employed taxi trade was in transition and upheaval from the day I got there. First came the entrance of fleet taxis owned by large infrastructure investors; then came the app-based companies such as Uber and its Indian competitor Olacabs, colloquially known as Ola. Then in 2020 the restriction of all movement by the global spread of COVID-19 hit the taxi trade, bringing it to a standstill. Each of these changes brought different political, bureaucratic, and labor actions that swung between antagonism, alliance, and misrecognition among those who represent these different trades of driving work. During the COVID-19 lockdown, taxis in Mumbai morphed from objects of circulation of people and things to a primary means of halting viral circulation. Many taxi drivers got permissions to ply the roads as ambulances, taking the COVID-infected sick to hospital.

While these contemporary upheavals have taken unique forms, taxis and taxi driving have long been the center of debates in India as they have in other parts of the world. Mumbai's taxi trade has always been in motion, and living with the specter of transition has been the distinct mode of living in the trade since the early twentieth century. Mumbai taxi drivers have lived in a near-permanent state of changing policies, regulations, and new mandates for cars and fuel. In Bombay, as in other colonial and postcolonial cities, transport politics were central to how the city has confronted its political and infrastructural modernity since the early twentieth century. This book looks at this longer history and its disruptions in order to understand the present. Through a focus on a driving occupation that has been in the midst of change since I first encountered it, I show how people come to live with, understand, debate, and refuse these changes. Therefore, this story of chillia drivers, while located in the specificities of Mumbai, joins the global debates taking place over cars, road infrastructures, taxis, and the gig economy.

Observations of driving in the West have long recognized connections between driving and individuated masculine subjects (Beckmann 2001; Seiler 2008). However, my focus on the connections between driving work and what feminist scholar Michaela di Leonardo (1987) calls kin-work examines the collective, sensory, intersubjective, and kin relationships rather than the individuated subjects produced through automobility. This collective and intersubjective approach to driving work and to life lived and sustained around the automobile moves our thinking about automobility from an individuated to a collective understanding and sensing of urban life.[7]

While Mumbai's taxi trade and driving in India unfolded within the universal proliferation of automobiles worldwide throughout the twentieth century, it was the specific modes of dwelling, caring, sensing, and performing ongoing maintenance and repair that were required of Indians that enabled the automobile to become a generalized form of transport in Indian cities. The chillia taxi trade illustrates that Indian automobility is both a universal experience of automobilization and a specific and expanding form of urban knowledge and work. This knowledge develops through sensory, embodied, and political realms where people who drive for a living collectively cultivate relationships to cars, technology, repair, driving, and the material and ecological environment.

To speak of an Indian automobility (as opposed to automobility simply *in* India), I attend seriously to the connections between automobility and the sensory and social lives of driving subjects.[8] Rather than simply accept that automobility in India (re)produces worlds that mirror those where the automobile was invented, I describe these worlds with the help of Indian realities. This includes Indian surfaces, socialities, and ecologies, as well as India's broader relations with the world throughout the twentieth and twenty-first centuries. The original, joona, sentient driver, and the older, vibrant, and vibrating car are both sites of this Indian automobility and of the socially thick stories of those who are very present in urban environments as labor but otherwise written out of urban and technological modernity. To this end, I follow how people make lives through driving work and how they participate in a city's economic, bureaucratic, and political shifts amid the noise, vibrations, emissions, dust, scrapes, and bumps.

SCRAPES, BUMPS, AND TANGLES OF THE ROAD

Rashid and I suddenly hear and feel one of these gentle bumps. A motorcyclist tries to scrape by us by smacking the back of Rashid's taxi to alert him that the light has changed and that it's time to move. "*Chacha* [paternal uncle], the signal has changed. Be careful." Rashid raises his hand to thank the younger man. The motorcyclist acknowledges the gratitude by folding Rashid's sideview mirror away from the roaring start of his bike before zooming closely by him and pitching, engine first, into the sweltering morning. Rashid relies more and more on the eyes of other, younger men to give him these intersubjective signals when the traffic signals are indiscernible to his aging eyes in the glare of the morning sun. On Mumbai's roads, it is common for the sense of sight to be shared this way among strangers who see for you against the sun, through the steamy fog of summer, or in the bashing, blinding rains of the monsoon. These other shared eyes land as smacks of touch on the back of the car to signal when it's time to move or move over. Rashid tightens his right hand into a fist and with a gentle thwack, folds his sideview mirror back into place. He then gingerly lifts his left arm to the hand gearshift on the steering wheel of his Premier Padmini taxi.[9]

When I first met Rashid, in 2010, his arm glided up to the gearshift with the grace and experience of a maestro magnificently claiming the strings of his instrument. This afternoon, almost a decade later, his long, gaunt arm trembles tentatively up to the gear, and I see how difficult it is for him to control the twitch in his head and shoulders. In 2018 he was finally diagnosed with Parkinson's disease. In these years of progressing tremors, Rashid's car has also acquired new internal quivers and jerks. It rumbles and moves violently even when it is still. Its forward motion creeps more tentatively and shakily than it did before, and so much more slowly than newer cars on the road. Despite this lack of speed, being in Rashid's taxi is an experience of other kinds of movement. When the car stops or starts, the seats slide back and forth off their springs like a surfboard trying to stay afloat on the waves of a riptide. The windows rattle almost as loudly as the shouting horns outside; they've clamored this way ever since they lost their ability to roll up and down. Their handles, which once controlled their smooth and regulated movement, have disappeared deep into the burrows of the doors, leaving rusty trenches, smaller but as deep and mysterious as the ditches in the road outside that make them jangle so loudly. The once grand orange and emerald-green velvet flowers on the covers have faded into worn, wilted daisies. The torn, front-seat covers flap nosily if the car moves faster than fifteen kilometers an hour.

I cannot see Rashid's feet from the rear passenger seat, but I feel him instinctively move his experienced, calloused foot off the brake. I hear the familiar chug as the clutch moves into place, and then feel my stomach lurch as parts of the car rattle in different directions. If Rashid feels the road move between the hardened callouses on his feet and in the pinch of his spine, I feel the road in the lurch of nausea somewhere between my stomach and my throat. Pinches, lurches, nausea, and pain—the road imprints itself on both of us as sensations of the body. The car wobbles forward as parts of the road tear out into debris from under us. A swarm of two-wheelers roar by the tangle to beat us all to get past the traffic light. The driver of an air-conditioned Honda rolls down his window to bellow expletives at the swarm: "Tere baap ka road hai kya [Is this your father's road]?" Everyone turns to him, acknowledges what he says, but otherwise does nothing.

In frustration, the driver slams on the horn, producing a horrifyingly high-pitched howl. I am convinced that the howling horns of Mumbai are less about being heard by anyone in particular than they are about making the noise-maker feel that they have had their say on the road. The pitch and duration of the horn marks hierarchies in class and a sense of rights to convert the anger you feel into the blasts of sound you throw out into the city; the horn signals the class of the vehicle itself, the size of the car, whether the driver is driving himself or someone else, and differing capacities of how visible or vulnerable the driver might be to the wrath of others, the onslaught of the rain, or bumps on the road. I can no longer see the Honda driver from behind his rolled up window, but I can feel his satisfaction at having spoken not in words but in howls that make their way from his frustrated body through the rubber and plastic of the horn and into the humid air. Almost immediately, a burst of carnivalesque howling and screeching horns jangle from every corner of the four-way stop. While the Honda's wheels have not moved even an inch, the man and the car still manage to howl out their presence into the city and onto the road. Everyone else responds by howling, "Maybe you are here, but I am here too!

A BEST bus inches into the tangle with its characteristic elephant trumpet of a horn. More noise, more howls, more horns, even less notice. A group of young girls in school uniform laughs and chatters as they weave across the jammed crosswalk. Their *dupattas* (scarves) are well pinned to their tunics except for one whose *dupatta* floats off her shoulders like a wave of crisp blue water and onto the face of the stray dog who has darted across behind her. As she runs back to recover it, the rather ineffectual and irate traffic policeman shouts at her to be careful. Police who direct traffic are the nucleus of the tangle. While they are officially there to unravel the snarls, they also have to protect their feet from the assault of countless wheels rolling at them from every direction. Like any other nucleus, they shrink into smaller and smaller slivers of space on the road until no one can see or hear them at all. This is what differentiates police who direct traffic standing in the tangle from those who survey traffic from the corners and sides of the road. The latter threaten drivers with violation tickets and are infamous for confiscating licenses and taking bribes. If the traffic directors are nucleated, the traffic surveyors are the expansive faces of the state. Everyone who uses the roads knows this difference between shrinking nucleus and expanding surveillance. Taximen know this best of all. As this book will show, the work of driving is about developing the knowledge of how to navigate between the surveillance and nucleation of these low-level representatives of the state.

Hearing and seeing nothing of this nucleated and almost disappearing policeman above the clamor of horns, and caring even less if she did, the young girl nonchalantly pulls the light-blue fabric off the dog's head. She stands for a few seconds in the tangle, redraping her *dupatta* before running across to join her friends. By now, the other girls shriek with laugher and wave their mobile phones about, taking pictures of the *dupatta*-clad dog. An auto-rickshaw driver pulls up alongside us, leans out, and spits a blood-red, tobacco-tinged stream onto the road. This is the everyday ritual of the traffic stop in contemporary Mumbai. The bus, the taxi, the fancy chauffeur-driven car, the rickshaw, the policeman, the crumbling concrete of a weary road, the errant *dupatta*, the hungry stray dog hopefully following the aroma of a schoolgirl's lunch, and the streams of tobacco-laced saliva co-conspire as *vibrant matter* (Bennett 2009) to shape what will happen each time the light turns red. Everyone tries as best they can within this tangle to claim, but also to give to others, some right to the road.

There are different kinds of taxis that are part of this tangle. Mumbai's roads are jammed with taxi fleets owned by corporate investors, the transnational Uber, and its Indian competitor Ola. Chillia drivers inhabit this changing structure of the taxi trade and share the road with and encounter these other drivers all the time. These encounters, antagonisms, misperceptions, and periodically, alliances, are sprinkled throughout the book. My fieldwork unfolded against the background of the entry, first, of fleet taxis and then of Ola and Uber. Therefore, I allow these contradictions to appear in the book as I encountered them in the field. I do not try to resolve or elide them. Instead, I allow these dilemmas and contradictions of different labor worlds that exist under different regimes of capital to illustrate how these lives unfold as claims over rights to the road and to life on the road. I take up this question of rights to the road, what drivers call *haq*, between different labor regimes who stand at a crossroads most explicitly in the book's conclusion.

Those who motor for a living are observers, participants, and orchestrators of these dynamics of the road. However, while roads are assumed as stable spaces of driving and automobility, for Mumbai's taxi drivers they are neither stable, nor universally experienced surfaces. Instead, roads in Mumbai, operate less as fixed matter and more as changing ecologies that materialize in the course of driving work itself. While ethnographers are also itinerant travelers on roads, we rarely make our travels the object of our analysis. We generally bump along the roads of our field as though our travels are incidental to our ethnographic analysis or our anthropological theory (Horta 2019). I deliberately make the socialities and material experiences of the road objects of my observation. Throughout I ask about what happens on a road? How does a road become something else depending on how it is used? When does a road become a mountain of debris and mud? How does a road connect people to other urban ecologies to imprint itself on the senses and bodies of those who drive for a living? What happens to the car, the people inside, the people who they run into and interact with, and the road itself? What happens when drivers move and what happens when they face a standstill?

It was useless to fight today's standstill, so Rashid and I settle back into the wait. We hardly talk when we are in the car. After many years, we are accustomed to riding in silence when we are alone together. Mostly, I sit in the front seat to at least attempt a similar vantage of "sight" and to try as best I can to disrupt uncomfortable relations of power between front and backseat. I learned early on that while the front seat lets one "see," it is also the seat at which the machinery of the car is sensed most strongly when in motion. The squeak of the gear box, the grunt of the clutch, or chafing of the wiper all coalesce in the front seat; they also coalesce as knowledge that can later be used when the car needs to be repaired. The front seat of a taxi is the seat of both driving and mechanical knowing, where the capacity to see the road is only one among many other capacities.

DEKH-BHAL, CARE, AND KIN

Rashid never let me drive. Part of this is that I was a woman conducting fieldwork among hereditary driving families, and women in these families do not drive. Therefore, to conform to practices of other women in the community, I never took the steering wheel. Rashid and others all knew and accepted that I drove in my other life. However, they declared that my need to drive was my *majboori* (helplessness), a cruel lot that marked that I was torn from my family and relations who could support me. Here, among chillia, I was temporarily freed from this cruel lot. However, unlike most adult chillia women, I came in and out of the neighborhood and interacted with male drivers with relative ease and without a burka. Usually, other than my drives with Rashid and some of the oldest drivers, my interactions with men in the community always took place in collective and kin contexts. For chillia, both men and women, life rarely unfolded alone, and therefore my conversations and observations always included the presence of many people. Looking back at nine years of field notes, apart from lone drives after a passenger drop-off, I could not find one occasion when either I or my chillia interlocutors were ever alone in Pathanwadi. Further, as a woman, and a woman who came to the community with my own growing daughter and lived with different families of drivers at various times, I participated in daily activities with chillia women. This is where I observed how domestic and driving lives intertwined and felt the sensory pleasures and burdens of both in ways that I might not have been able to do had I focused entirely on men who drive. Even in a trade where the majority of driving and mechanics is conducted by those who identify as men, women were profoundly present. While women are present on India's roads as drivers and passengers, the multiple roles that chillia women played in the hereditary taxi trade without actually being on the roads was striking to me. As social anthropologist Pascale Bonnemère (2018) reminds us, while it may appear that women have no part in male initiation rituals simply because they are absent from ritual spaces, in fact men cannot be "made" without interventions and relational ties with others who act in other physical spaces.[10] These various forms of labor make up what chillia collectively called *dekh-bhal* (looking after).

Dekh-bhal is a Hindustani term that circulates in several South Asian languages. Gujarati, which is what most chillia speak, is no exception. It roughly translates into *dekh*, which is also the sensory act of looking, seeing, or watching, and *bhal*, which means action that is careful and considerate. In this sense, dekh-bhal in the Hindustani dictionary has capacious meanings that are both sensory and material. In sensory terms, it is the work of looking at, looking after, and watching over (Craven 1893; Fallon et al. 1886), surveying, reviewing, inspecting, and supervising (Prasad 1890). In material terms, it can mean to "tamper with" (D. Forbes 1857) and to inspect. What braids the sensory and the material is that dekh-bhal signals sustained, lifelong work. In the end, to do dekh-bhal is to do work that is conducted well, with care, and carefully (Fallon et al. 1886), even if the work requires supervision, management, control, and violence (Craven 1893). This explains why dekh-bhal refers broadly to the work practiced in kinship contexts where care, looking after, and social cohesion intertwine with social control, filial and gendered burdens, and breakdown. For chillia drivers and mechanics, dekh-bhal is directed both at cars and at drivers— maintenance of other kinds of kin, but kin nevertheless.

While dekh-bhal is kin-work in the sense that it is directed at other people, it is also a general form of looking after the things and environments that surround the people we are responsible for. Depending on its usage, dekh-bhal can signal both maternal and paternal forms of care. Further, like all practices of looking after, dekh-bhal can be obligatory, pleasurable, loving, burdensome, and unappreciated in equal measure. And as this book will describe, the technical vocabulary of care associated with the maintenance and repair of cars and the kin-work of making a life lived around automobiles are intertwined. While dekh-bhal is a specific linguistic and sensory orientation to care in South Asia, in practice it alludes to political scientist Joan Tronto's (2013) insight that to care is "to maintain, continue, and repair" the world. This is the broader definition of care that I work with through this book.

This care requires nurturing and repairing both relations and cars. It involves the physical and mental work of taking care of, of fixing, cajoling, cleaning up after, and maintaining bodies and souls. It also involves dirty, messy work, and work that is not spatially relegated to the home. To understand the collective life of the taxi trade and all the repair, maintenance and care work that it involves, I take Tronto's argument seriously in that economic life is lived alongside practices of care. However, in trades like chillia driving, dekh-bhal as a form of care is less connected in a straightforward way to people's psychological or emotional orientations than it is to their social and performative ones. This social understanding of care is what anthropologist Felicity Aulino (2019) calls "rituals" of care, where caring is less about sincerity of feeling than it is about performing, in a ritual way, what is socially expected. When obligations break down or expectations cannot be fulfilled, people experience guilt and disappointment. This is the contradictory place of caring in the lives of chillia drivers. Given that the chillia driving and mechanics trade is occupied by bodies that identify as male, there is a distinction between women's and men's practices of care. However, care is not just about gender; it is also about race, class, religion, and piety. While the term *care* and all that it signifies has gendered dimensions, dekh-bhal is an orientation to care work that operates between masculine and feminine bodies, and between caring human bodies and all the other things they are responsible for as they make a life.

In Rashid's domestic sphere, his wife, Salma, is responsible for stretching money from the rattles and roars of driving as far as it can go. Salma uses these stretched earnings to feed and care for two sons and one daughter, one-daughter-in-law, three grandchildren, and Rashid's elderly, widowed, and almost immobile mother. While Rashid conducts his labor for money, his participation in his community's hereditary driving and mechanics trade also cements male kinship obligations that have long been sustained through the trade of driving. While Salma does none of the driving, fixing, or maintenance of cars, she is fundamental to the other work of dekh-bhal or maintaining a life in Pathanwadi. Salma earns some money conducting Koran lessons for children in the neighborhood, all of whom are connected to taxi-driving families and many of whom are related by blood or marriage to either her or Rashid. This means that Salma is usually the first to hear of and to help resolve conflicts among kin over money or over the use of a car. She is the first to hear about discussions drivers have about new opportunities for financing the purchase of new cars that are consonant with Islamic rules against interest, or about whether someone is thinking about leaving the hereditary trade to join a corporate-owned taxi fleet or the app-based taxi services Uber or Ola. Salma's deep knowledge of the Koran, through which she leads the women's *taalim* (religious education) in the damp basement of the local mosque or in the packed front room of her own house, give her a high social standing in the neighborhood. This kin-work is deeply intertwined with being a *taxiwallah* in Pathanwadi. While Rashid moves around the city doing driving work, Salma hardly ever leaves Pathanwadi. She spends a great deal of time both inside and outside her house, arranging religious activities for women and children, providing counsel to younger women, or arranging marriages between chillia in Mumbai and those in their village around Palanpur in Gujarat. Salma's capacity to generate goodwill through her spatial emplacement and her dekh-bhal might be seen as an expression of "fixity," what cultural anthropologist Sarah Besky (2017) sees as the social capacity to fix and maintain social connections in the same way that one might maintain physical infrastructures. Sentient, sensing bodies of hereditary drivers like Rashid and Tariq, and their pain, perspiration, and debilitation, intersect with a practice of care, looking after, and watching over that women like Salma do every day.

Rashid and Salma, despite the large family that surrounds and makes demands on them, share an affectionate and communicative relationship. They lie down side by side after lunch and *namaaz* (prayers) for an afternoon nap in the back room of their two-room house and talk intimately about their day and their worries, while I sit with their daughter and daughter-in-law stitching clothes on sewing machines in the front room. This sustained and intimate kin-work, together with the circulating and mobile work of motoring, has undergirded and enabled what drivers in Pathanwadi call *khandani dhandha* (family business) and the dekh-bhal that it entails to continue to adapt to various changes for over a century. By looking at the expressions of dekh-bhal, I attend here to the fleshy and sensuous lives of men, their bodily engagements and bodily breakdowns, and the connections between the feminine and masculine attunements to care in hereditary professions of taxi driving.

JAALU AND THE ENTANGLEMENTS OF CARS AND KIN

That there are significant connections between maintenance of domestic spheres and accumulation of capital has been richly observed in several contexts.[11] This book traces the sensory labors of dekh-bhal and hereditary driving that have shaped Indian automobility over the twentieth and twenty-first centuries. While these labors are led by knowledgeable workers with vast technological and urban expertise, they do not always map onto liberal understandings of what work is and can do for individual prosperity. The relations in the chillia trade suggest that it is possible to detach the commonly assumed connections in Western understandings of labor between technological expertise and both liberal and neoliberal labor subjectivity (Peck 1992, 1996). Instead, this is work that is rooted in social, pious, and kinship relations that sometimes constrain, and at other times enhance, freedoms, flourishing, and innovation of many kinds. These relations are multiple, and each chapter delves into questions of what relationality does in different ways: between male and female kin and their different capacities to act and build urban lives and livelihoods; between drivers, mechanics, and their cars; between those who manufacture and those who drive, maintain, and fix automobiles; and between those who drive and all the people and things they are entangled with in their own cities and beyond. Given the centrality of cars, driving, and all the maintenance and dekh-bhal that surrounds the automobile for the chillia, the work of maintenance also stretches from domestic spaces to taxi stands, roads, mechanic shops, gas stations, and union offices.

While I was located ethnographically in the chillia residential neighborhood of Pathanwadi, my research followed drivers in and out of the neighborhood. Therefore, while Pathanwadi presented a central spatial node in the relations I was most interested in, the book moves around spatially to reflect how drivers see, experience, and shape the spaces of the city as part of the work of driving and to understand how they create what they call the *jaalu* of the chillia taxi trade. *Jaalu* is the Gujarati term for a web; it is *jaalu* in the singular and *jaal* in the plural. That chillia drivers regularly use the singular term *jaalu* to mark their entangled experiences in the trade, even when speaking of spatially and materially expansive relations, seemed significant—as though the taxi trade as they know it is a singular entanglement of many people and things. My sensorial orientation attunes to the jaalu as life and work inhabited through social, material, and ecological enmeshment.[12]

The intersection between driving work, the jaalu, and masculinity is significant. While it is common for women in Indian cities to drive, taxi driving as work, and as trade, is a staunchly a male profession. Since 2012, in the midst of incidents of rape and sexual assault of women on unauthorized public transport (Dey 2019; Gilbertson 2018) and in Uber taxis (Crowell 2015; Steele 2014), fleet taxi companies with women-only drivers have entered the industry in various Indian cities. On one hand, these companies are advertised as secure options for female passengers, and on the other hand as symbols of labor freedom and emancipation for women in a traditionally male-dominated profession. These taxi services are well-received, useful additions to the taxi industry in Mumbai and elsewhere. They follow a widely accepted need in India for gender-segregated transport. This gender segregation is already commonplace on Mumbai's commuter trains, all of which have a ladies-only compartment, and on the local buses, which have several front seats reserved for women. However, as workers, while men are able to move in and out of different arrangements within the taxi trade—that is, between the kaalipeeli industry, the fleet taxi industry, and the app-based taxi services—so far, women drivers (with a few recent exceptions) remain confined to driving in the women's taxi services only. Therefore, the taxi trade remains heavily male dominated; even as some women are moving into taxi driving, the trade is defined by the far greater capacities that men have to move between different kinds of work in the taxi trade even when they are in subordinate or less powerful positions to other men. This book is attentive to how the relations, (auto)biographies, and burdens of men intertwine through the work of driving and repair and, in turn, how these relations make what are considered good, respectable men.

For all these complex significations between driving work and male respectability, when I drive around the city with Rashid both of us are content with the agreement that I don't drive and only interact with this laboring car of his as a passenger. If Rashid wants to pick up a passenger, I stay in the front seat and we explain to the passenger what I am doing. The passengers rarely ask any questions, and if they are alone they simply get on their phones for the journey and ignore us both. If there is more than one passenger, they usually chat with each other, and direct a question to me on occasion. When Rashid picks up more than two passengers, I usually get out of the car and find my own way home since I do not want to interfere with his business and take up more space than the taxi can afford. Many passengers ask Rashid to "turn on GPS" as soon as they jump in. He always shakes his head and gives the same response, "No GPS, but don't worry, the map is in my head." On this particular morning, he is taking me from Pathanwadi to a meeting on the other side of town. After he drops me off, he plans to ply around South Mumbai's business district for most of the morning. Then he has an agreement with a regular customer, a chartered accountant, who will pay him to ride back to the suburbs at 2:00 p.m. When it comes to passengers, therefore, this book contains only observational data rather than interviews. I was singularly interested in the labor aspect of the taxi trade; indeed, since this labor dimension became dispersed and wide, the voices of (real) passengers are conspicuously absent in this book. Taxi passengers are given voice in the media, and passenger experiences (largely grievances, though not always) are the most widely reported aspect of the taxi trade. Further, while I begin here with a soggy and humid taxi ride as passenger, this is so because the act of motoring undergirds everything in this book. However, unlike some excellent ethnographic work on urban driving and automobile travel, I do not focus just on driving but rather on *driving work* and its stops, starts, and chugs more broadly.[13]

Rashid's taxi chugs again, but this time to a halt to await its turn again at the same signal. A fresh stream of perspiration swells out from behind his ears and settles into his thick, gray beard. Rashid's body continues to twitch and tremble as he sits quietly, almost meditatively, waiting just a few steps ahead of where we began at the same tangled intersection, for the same signal to change to green again. This afternoon is characteristically provocative for how I think about transport labor, particularly the labor of those who motor for a living in cities of the Global South. Driving is a profession where understanding the tangle, or what sociocultural anthropologist Caroline Melly (2017) calls the "bottleneck," of traffic is important. However, it also begs an understanding of tangles of other kinds—the ways in which movement, stillness, and slowness intersect and constitute each other, and mostly how those who negotiate the tangle of motoring for a living are also implicated in, and part of, the tangles and accumulations of respect and obligations of other kinds.

Rashid is a well-respected man in the chillia taxi trade, and his family has benefited from his standing in the community as an honest, upright, and knowledgeable man. In recent years, he admits that he is reconciled to live through breakdown both of his body and his self-employed, hereditary taxi trade. Over the years I have known him, Rashid and his taxi have both slowed down, but have also developed new kinds of uncontrollable motion more or less together. They share a world of these quivers and jerks, a singular *mutuality of being* (Sahlins 2012) as they bump across the roads of the city, fighting for the right to be there, while each is judged by the other's limits. For almost twenty years, Rashid has fixed, repaired, and decorated his car. Over the last four years, however, he has bothered neither with the maintenance of his own body nor with that of his taxi. He knew that by June 2020 his car would have to be retired and demolished since it would have passed the limit of how long a taxi is allowed on the roads. "Why bother when this is going to be nothing but ruins?" says Rashid, resignedly. Rashid does not yet know what he will do in the aftermath of this ruination. As the involuntary movements of his body have become more pronounced, Rashid's wife and children plead with him to see a doctor. "Do some dekh-bhal and fix your body problem, *Abba* [father]," I have heard them say many times in my presence, god knows how many times else. Rashid refuses. "I have been moving all my life, so if I have to die, it makes sense that Allah would have mercy on me by giving me a disease that moves me instead of one where I am still all the time. Let my body move as much as it can and one day it will move me to heaven. But not yet, since I still have a responsibility to provide for my family. Maybe when this car stops moving my body will too."

Rashid's wife, Salma, was worried about him being on the roads like this, but quietly acquiesced to this response without further argument. His invocation of familial duty was something she chose not to argue with. Rashid brought in daily earnings driving from seven in the morning until lunchtime. At one thirty, he would come home for lunch, afternoon prayers, and rest. This time of rest was when his moving, twitching body sank gratefully into the rolls of soft fabric of his bed. On Tuesday and Wednesday afternoons, his oldest son, Tariq, drove the same rattling car until late evening. Tariq's hands were steady and still, and somehow, the car offered up a different kind of motion when he was at the wheel. Over the last two years, as Rashid's body has become increasingly frail, I have sat more often in the car with Tariq. Whether Tariq's younger, steadier body makes him a "better" driver is difficult to say. What is significant perhaps is that Tariq's driving presents a different kind of sensual relation to the roads. I feel less of the tickle of nausea when Tariq is at the wheel, but I also feel less of the breeze and hear less of the whizzing. Tariq's body vibrates with the car but it does not quiver like his father's does, particularly when he is fatigued. The matter of quivering and how much dekh-bhal can be extended to the car or to a tired body on any given day plays an important part in the decision of when the car should be taken out and by whom. In this way, the relations and obligations of kin intertwine as sensual relations (Howes 2003) in Rashid's family. The car was purchased secondhand, in 2009, through an accumulation of pooled resources and it belongs to both men. If Rashid shakes and knows the quivers of the car, Tariq's steady hands know its persistent and comforting chug.

Rashid's maternal first cousin, Altaf, takes the car out in the afternoons every other day of the week, for which he pays Rashid a small, monthly rental fee. When I counted, I found that the income from this rattling vehicle supports and feeds a total of eighteen people across three different households. The rattling labor of this vehicle is intertwined with the various labors of making a life in Pathanwadi and the autobiography of the car intersects with the biographies of the families who drive it. It is also intertwined with the many other worlds beyond the neighborhood of labor unions, roads, vehicle manufacturing, traffic safety, licensing, permitting, policing, financing, protest, and mechanics that together make up the everyday life of laboring in an industry of driving. This book introduces readers to some of these worlds as they are encountered by drivers.

I call these many settings *worlds* in two senses. First, there are different worlds in the ontological sense.[14] These are the material and environmental worlds such as cars, debris, emissions, dust, noise, and air that surround driving work that make their mark unpredictably but continually on the sensory domains of driving and repair. Second, they are many worlds in the social, political, and epistemological sense. These are the political, legal, and bureaucratic worlds of taxi unions, taxi fleets, app-based taxis, road rules, urban planners, and police. These worlds shape the work of chillia driving and are shaped by it. However, they also have their own structures, forms, and rhythms, through which they order urban knowledge and change. Chillia drivers also see these as operating via different relational, temporal, and sensorial regimes. I examine how driving work encounters and produces these different worlds. While these different worlds and rhythms are enmeshed and intertwined, I find there is no singular way that contemporary driving work is absorbed into capitalist or neoliberal logics. In fact, chillia drivers remind us that there remain many ways of imagining how wealth, worth, life, and driving work are governed and lived today.[15]

I present these worlds as I encountered them via the drivers. The worlds of driving and repair work, the jaalu, emerged as deeply sensory, intimate, relational, and enmeshed, and I write about them this way. Others, such as the work of unions and technocrats, operated through relational but less intimate modalities, and I write about them differently, as in chapters 3 and 6. Tacking between the different forms of ethnographic voice is deliberately intended to take readers in and out of the different rhythms of the taxi trade and to illustrate how the taxi trade reflects the different temporal regimes of life in a city. Further, while these worlds of the senses and of bureaucracy operate differently, I encountered their convergence via shared disdain over the newer taxi services, like Ola and Uber. Often this disdain was expressed through deliberate failure to recognize such services as taxis at all. For example, chillia drivers and union representatives of the older taxi trade talk about app-based Ola and Uber drivers by discounting the value of these other kinds of mobility and speak of them as temporary interlopers and outsiders to the trade and to the city. This discounting allows them to make their own claims of local expertise, knowledge, and place in Mumbai's past and its future. In practice, these are worlds with different temporal arrangements that have to share and cooperate in the immediate context of laboring on the roads. At the same time, refusal to acknowledge the other is a deliberate political and social strategy that reflects the dilemmas and contradictions of different labor and knowledge-making practices that coexist under different regimes of capital that we now see everywhere, not just in the taxi trade.

NOSTALGIA

The music system in Rashid's taxi crackles before it bursts into song. It plays a song from the soundtrack of the 1957 Bollywood film *Naya Daur* (New era), "Ude Jab Zulfain Teri," rendered so exuberantly by India's beloved playback singers Mohammed Rafi and Asha Bhonsale and starring Dilip Kumar and Vyjanthimala.[16] Rashid's body seems to relax to the music as his right thumb taps on the steering wheel to the lilt of the music. There are so many beautiful songs on this soundtrack, so I am not sure if Rashid just loves this song or whether he recognizes the irony of the story of the film's storyline and how close this 1957 film comes to reflecting his own life. *Naya Daur* is the story of the competition of man versus machine. Reportedly, the scriptwriter, Akhtar Mirza, wrote the screenplay after hearing a speech by Mahatma Gandhi. Gandhi was a famous critic of technology as a tool of colonial oppression (Gandhi [1938]1944). In an era where technology was taking away jobs of ordinary Indians, Gandhi warned that man would always remain superior to machines ("The Making of *Naya Daur*" 2017). *Naya Daur* tells the story of a *tongawallah*, a professional driver of a horse-drawn carriage in a post-independence Indian village. It tells the story of the threat to the business of *tongawallahs* from a new bus service started by the son of a rich landlord. This new capitalist feels that transport is the best place to invest in postcolonial, urbanizing India. The film focuses on the conflicts between *tongawallahs* and the owner of the bus service. Both parties finally decide to race to identify the winner in the transport industry. While the tonga is no competition for the bus in terms of speed, the enormous support by the people for the *tongawallah* gives him a surprise victory. Perhaps Rashid plays this soundtrack because he simply loves the songs; they make him tap in joy on the weary steering wheel and transport him to a world of love and abandon where a journey means the carefree careening through cool winds of rural India, as the actors in the film do. Or maybe it helps him understand and come to terms with the conflicts he faces in Mumbai's transport industry today. Both possibilities of Rashid's ruminations, of joyful abandonment and of reconciliation to conflict, led me to understand how capital and the state intersect with somatic experiences of the road and those who move along them.

Just two months later, on my return from a trip to Turkey, I exit into the comparatively sterile summer at Chicago's O'Hare airport. The Chicago taxi driver whose car I fortuitously get into is a Syrian immigrant who came to the United States almost forty years ago. He loads my suitcases into the trunk and cheerfully hops into the driver's seat, equipped with a cushion that raises his tiny frame high enough to see through the windshield. In the short time we have each committed to the mundane rituals of getting into a taxi with luggage, he has gleaned my Indian origins. He tells me with a poignant nostalgia that he misses and dreams of Damascus of the 1950s and 1960s because those were the days where the city was full of music and of Bollywood films and music in particular. "Do you mind if I play these old Bollywood songs for the ride home?" he asks. I agree and close my jet-lagged eyes to another familiar song by Mohammed Rafi and Asha Bhonsale, "O Haseena Zulfonwali Jaane Jahan," from the film *Teesri Manzil* (Third floor). "These songs remind me of home," he says. "They remind me of a time when Damascus was the center of the world and when Indian music and jazz played everywhere in the streets. But for me this music of Mohammed Rafi is my favorite, I don't understand all the words, but I know from his voice that he sings of love and beauty and of what happens when it is all lost."

Indeed, old Bollywood songs, across time and space, seem to sustain the souls and the labor of those who motor in so many places. The tangle between nostalgic sounds of music and the clamoring of howling horns are integral to these soundscapes.[17] That sound and the other senses are fundamental background to urban memory and to particular kinds of urban experiences is not a new observation.[18] However, when I talk to friends and family informally about old Bollywood music in taxis, a common response is that, as passengers, they judge the "manners" or "politeness" of drivers and, by extension, the experience of the taxi and the ride, by whether or not they have loud Hindi music playing. In short, many of Mumbai's middle classes associate silence and smoothness with a good ride, and the alternative—loud music and the jangle of windows and engines—with a bad one. I have always associated taxis with the delights of old Bollywood music and with soundscapes of the city; I have also always associated driving in Mumbai with rolled-down windows and the smell of the salty, sea breeze laced with the pungent smell of drying *bombil* (fish, also known as Bombay duck).

Growing up in Bombay and then returning for fieldwork to Mumbai almost two decades later, the taxi is the place that I associate with my knowledge of lyrics to Bollywood music, where the driver would invariably crank up his radio to accompany the ride. This was, of course, long before disciplinary practices of control over the taxi, the vehicle, the driver, and the passenger experience within the taxicab's space became part of Mumbai's discourse on "infrastructural" modernization. Indeed, this was also a time long before Bombay became Mumbai (Hansen 2001). When I feel this nostalgia, I recognize that it is not that I want to go back in time, but rather that I want to continue to feel the sensory world that loud music, open windows, and salty breezes entailed. Across the gaping social divides between me and my interlocutors, it was a shared understanding of how cities and senses intertwine as memory that became a significant place of ethnographic entry.

While my Syrian taxi driver in Chicago invoked a geopolitically tinged nostalgia for a place now in both political and material ruin, my nostalgia was of the more common sort. It is the nostalgia that urban theorist Svetlana Boym (2001) so beautifully captures as the jumble between yearning for a different place, which is really a yearning for a different time, and a yearning for a way to find a new home in a different world. Nostalgia in a changing world (and planet), as anthropologist Kath Weston (2017, 433) argues, is temporally complicated—it is a way to find a way back, but also a way forward. Often, as for me, the nostalgic and biographic spheres of ethnographers and their interlocutors are entangled. Some readers of earlier pieces of this work have warned that this nostalgia has made me less critical and more sympathetic to the older, kaalipeeli taxi trade than I should be, and less open to the possibilities that new entrants into the taxi industry might provide. On one hand, this is valid criticism and I have considered for years how to strike this balance between the accidentally entangled biographies and the cultural critique that anthropological fieldwork demands (Carsten et al. 2018).

There is no doubt, as Boym (2001) suggests, that nostalgia can be contradictory. These contradictions are central to this book. I prefer to own up to a "reflective nostalgia" (Boym 2001), which can be critical, humorous, and emotionally poignant at the same time. Reflective nostalgia is my way of claiming, with Boym (2001), that longing and attachments to other times and critical reflection need not be opposed to each other. I found that my interlocutors were experts at handling these contradictions.

I own up to the charge of nostalgia as fundamentally important to both my methodological and empirical inspirations. Several years ago, a German stranger sitting next to me on a flight to Frankfurt, as I was on my way to fieldwork in Mumbai, was befuddled by my response to his question of "What research do you do?" His face squinted into a ball of wrinkles and, in response to my answer, he blurted out, "Taxis? I am sorry, but that is the strangest subject for a woman. Why would anyone want to do that?" A conversation stopper for what became a long, transatlantic flight for both of us, but it was a valid question: Why does anyone choose to work on anything? It is rarely an accident.

While I have done research before in Mumbai (Bedi 2016), something was different for me this time around. In the tangle (pun intended) of empirical, theoretical, and analytical directions that this book began to take, my own life became unavoidably implicated. This was not only in how I began to collect and think about my ethnographic data but also in what happened to my social and emotional (in)stability in the field. In 2011, just as my field-work for this book was taking shape, I lost my father to a rapidly moving and ravaging illness. My father had already lived as a physically disabled man for twenty-five years before his death. It is difficult for me to grasp that he was as old as I am now when he was stricken by a debilitating stroke that paralyzed one side of his body that never recovered. For twenty-five years he dragged, and pulled, and wheeled the weight of this uncooperative body around a city that never provided space, support, or transport even for the class-privileged disabled body. The recent, renewed, and more intense debil-itation of his body and the mundane but terrifying burden of dekh-bhal helped me come to terms with how kinship relationships are articulated in times of impending death. It also forced me to acknowledge how these rela-tions sadly break down through experiences with debilitation, especially the debilitation of male bodies. This might well explain why my reflections on the connections among debilitation, dekh-bhal, and masculinity chafe against the stories of technological invention and the making of men. It was this shared, bewildering, and frightening experience of watching the bodily debilitation of male breadwinners, and the recognition that neither bodies nor cars duly cooperate on the roads of Mumbai, that initially drew me to understand the taxi trade and its familial and gendered obligations through the lens of Rashid's Parkinson's-afflicted body and through the car and kin that surrounded him.

What has been even more poignant for me is that my nostalgic inclina-tions have found collective spirit in various places and with so many other people. This is precisely how Boym (2001) differentiates between "melan-cholia," which is confined to planes of individual consciousness, and "nos-talgia," which sutures relationships between individual and collective memory. When I have presented my work in public and a photograph of the Premier Padmini car floats onto a presentation screen, Indians in my audience who came of age in early postcolonial India begin to reminisce joyfully. I have seen tears well up in people's eyes and smiles of affection for this car and for the lost times that it seems to signify. Many people have even come to me afterward to thank me for reminding them of happier times, of a car, of a city, and of a life they associate with a lost home. I realized that so many Indians have a Padmini story just as they do a taxi story—and in many cases these memories overlap. They recount fond mem-ories of their first romantic encounters in a kaalipeeli or of taking a kaali-peeli to the movies or for *kulfi* (an ice-cream desert) at Chowpatty beach. Some of the fondest memories people recount are of when the family's

Padmini, the pride and joy of the household, broke down on a family out-
ing and someone had to get out and fiddle around with the engine, while
everyone else got out to push the car up a hill or through the pounding
monsoon rain. In these cases, it was the cooperation between drivers and
passengers that drove the Padmini home. Almost everyone had a Padmini
breakdown story, which was simultaneously a story of the collective work
of kin. I realized through these stories that the Padmini, like many early
cars in India, was technologically incomplete.[19] This was due to rigid cus-
toms and duties on imported technologies and foreign exchange constraints.
Particular parts were deliberately missing in the production process and had
to be adapted and adjusted from other things; this encouraged local mechanics and engineers to expand their ingenuity and made the cars open to a
variety of adaptations to locally available resources.

These stories of incompleteness and technical possibility were particularly important to taxi drivers. Lavishing care, affection, and upgrades to
this vehicle was a matter of necessity that involved those who drove and
those who rode, and one that inevitably required the collective, relational
work of everyone. I know this well, as my own English grandmother came
to Bombay with what I used to think of as her Punjabi Padmini. The secondhand car took us to the movies, to school, and to the shops; and wherever we went, we often had to push and pull the car all over the city. When
she was too old to drive anymore, the Padmini stood immobile and rust-
ing at the back of our apartment building for years. Stray cats, pigeons,
crows, and sometimes even the building's off-duty watchmen rested inside
it on hot, sunny afternoons. When the building's association finally ordered
its removal, claiming it was attracting rodents and rotting food, she sold it
sorrowfully for scrap in the late 1990s. The cats, the pigeons, and all the
watchmen who had dwelled and slept in the shell of the car stood at the gate
together with the rest of us as we stoically watched the Padmini being towed
away. While I have never been able to recall by heart the registration plates
of any of the cars I have driven or owned since, my grandmother's Padmini
and its license plate number are still seared, clear and laser-like, nostalgi-
cally, into my memory: PNU 38.

For all these reasons, as an ethnographer who conducts research in a city
I once called home, but struggles with what to call it now, I recognize how
my work was enabled, enriched, and destabilized by nostalgia, and the presence and loss of my own kin, my own Padmini, and my own home. Thinking particularly closely about kinship relationships, loss, deaths of various
kinds, and yes, nostalgia, were vital to the kind of ethnography I did here

and to the kind of book this has turned out to be. In this nostalgia, in many ways, this project began for me long before it seemed to begin. It was my music-loving father who infused my childhood with the joys of Moham-med Rafi's melodious singing playing on car radios. It was the permanent debilitation of his body by a paralyzing stroke three weeks after my thir-teenth birthday, and after which he was never able to drive me anywhere, that I first began to take kaalipeeli taxis alone around Bombay. It was my father's advice that when I got into a taxi at night, I should always try to find a chillia driver, identifiable by the white pajama-kurta and special chillia *topi* (cap), as he believed them to be the most trustworthy and knowl-edgeable drivers in Bombay and the least likely to lose their way or rip me off. It was he who hired Rahim *bhai* (brother) as his private chauffer. Rahim belonged to the chillia community, and had been a former taxi driver for almost twenty-five years before he went into what he called "service."[20] It was through Rahim bhai that I first came to Pathanwadi, a community of taxi drivers, mechanics, and taxi leasers, and which became the earliest and primary site of my fieldwork. This remained the site from which I observed the volatile shifts in Mumbai's taxi trade beginning in 2010 and leading into the present.

My association with Rahim bhai, who claimed relational ties with almost all the drivers I worked with, allowed me access to a community where deeply embedded kin and labor relationships are the most significant mark-ers of trust and respect. The deaths of both Rahim bhai and my father, to different but equally ravaging cancers, in quick succession consolidated rather than weakened my position in Pathanwadi, possibly because it allowed for new solidarities to emerge in the frightening spaces of loss and death. I started my research in solidarities of grief when I moved to live with Rahim's family. This unifying experience of death, even across our vast dif-ferences of class was significant; the pain of loss, or what my interlocutors call *pida*, actually manifests in particular places, and often in the same places that driving makes its mark—on the lower back, or buried behind the sternum where the hard, old steering wheel of the Premier Padmini car hits the body of the driver each time he bumps to a sudden halt. Pain that makes its way through the body as imprints of the road or as sensations of loss or failed obligations of dekh-bhal emerges all through this book as a sensory realm of knowledge in hereditary driving work.

While I have for years referred to this as "my taxi book," in fact this book is an attunement to the Bombay taxi as a *vehicle* in all its forms: a thing driven; an economic, sensory, and political connection; a history of urban time and technology; a union; a family history; a lever of politics; and finally, a contest over rights to the urban road. By moving empirically between these domains, this book moves analytically between the entanglements of (auto) biographies and (auto)mobilities to understand the cultural, sensory, material, technological, and labor biographies of motoring in India (Kopytoff 1986).

1 DHANDHA

Chillia Taximen of Mumbai

THROUGHOUT THE TWENTIETH CENTURY, AND INTO THE CONTEM-
porary period, taxis have been central to Mumbai's transport politics and
to its aspirations to urban modernity. The taxi trade has historically been
organized around groups of self-employed labor from specific ethnic
groups. Drivers and mechanics who identified as chillia were central to the
expansion of the trade. Because chillia began as taxi drivers in the early
twentieth century and continue to drive today, it is important to connect
the shifts in the trade over time to the conditions that chillia drivers face
today.

Chillia families began migrating to Bombay in the early twentieth century from the Palanpur region in the neighboring state of Gujarat. They
began as drivers of horse-drawn Victorias, also called *gharries*. While
chillia identify as low-caste Muslims, they are not entirely dispossessed of
land and resources in Palanpur. Their experiences of urban migration are
not undergirded by experiences of rural dispossession. Instead, they are
marked by a desire to be part of Bombay's urban world and a sensibility
that urban life heightens, rather than diminishes, their social worlds and
cultural attachments. This is an urban world of cars, mechanics, technological expertise, and mastery over urban landscapes. It is a world of new
political engagements, urban religious community, and the expansion of
kinship and economic possibilities. Not least, it is the sensory world of
dust, potholes, bodily pain, waiting, traffic, police, bureaucracy, and competing sensory claims to the shifting surfaces of the city.[1]

TWISTS AND TURNS IN BOMBAY'S TAXI INDUSTRY

British colonial Bombay was the first Indian city to develop a systematic
taxi trade in the late nineteenth century when horse-drawn carriages or
hackneys, similar to those driven in London, began to ply the colonial
city's streets as taxis ("Taxicab in Bombay" 1909). Bombay was also the first
Indian city to adopt a motorized taxi trade in the early twentieth century.

Automobiles imported from France and the United States first appeared in colonial Bombay between 1908 and 1909 ("Walk or Ride?" 1918). Indian transport labor was an early adopter of these new machines and technologies. However, early cars were incomplete technologies. This meant that the material work of sustaining and making cars run required dedicated and unpredictable labors of mechanical attention and care, making driving work and mechanical/technological work closely intertwined. This intertwining has persisted. Regular breakdowns along the road of these incomplete machines gave rise to regulatory systems to monitor the health and reliability of vehicles. Out of this regulation of taxis and taxi labor grew a more generalized mode of colonial, urban governance. Regulations focused on a variety of mobile bodies from horses and drivers to imported cars and later Indian cars. The colonial state's relationship to taxi drivers became structured through this management of breakdown and the monitoring of the health and safety of vehicles, horses, and drivers. It became a continuation of what postcolonial theorist Homi Bhabha (1997) described as a "civilizing mission by other means," but focused particularly on transportation and transport labor.

By the late 1940s and early 1950s, the taxi trade buttressed early postcolonial India's indigenous automobile production.[2] During this period, new regulations discouraged capitalist taxi owners and speculators in the transport trade and encouraged owner-operators to buy Indian-made cars. This meant that state transport authorities and cooperative banks provided special financing incentives to those who owned, drove, and maintained vehicles themselves rather than to those who hired employee drivers or mechanics. This rise of taxi cooperatives, taxi unions, and individual ownership of taxicabs and small enterprises were intertwined with postcolonial India's Soviet-style, socialist, economic planning. For drivers this meant enhanced power and more incentives and financial support to purchase their own cars. The Bombay Taxi Association was founded in the 1920s and connected drivers to sources of cooperative credit. Many leaders of this association were also leaders of associations that worked on behalf of other transport labor such as dockworkers and tramway workers. The Bombay (now Mumbai) Taximen's Union was established in 1962. Both the association and the union continue to operate today.

In the late twentieth century, India moved from a state-led, developmentalist economy to a market-focused one.[3] In Indian cities, representatives of the urban state (civic bodies, planning bodies, and municipalities) became focused on improvements of urban infrastructure. This was due in no small part to the fact that infrastructural projects were sites for quick landing and circulation of large investment capital, resulting in a state of what architect Rahul Mehrotra (2012) calls "impatient capital." Transport and road infrastructures became predominant targets of these initiatives. This is how discussions over modernizing taxis and upgrading roads began to coincide. It resulted in an initiative called "taxi modernization" that began in 2006 (Bhayana 2007). This is what began a rapid slew of new policies that continue to impact the contemporary taxi trade.

TAXI MODERNIZATION: THE SINGAPORE MODEL AND OLA-UBER

Taxi modernization, led by a coalition of planning authorities and private-sector consultants, drew on the city of Singapore as a model (Chua 2011) to transform Mumbai's taxi industry. The main effort was to rid the industry of owner-operator taxis in favor of taxi fleets owned by large private investors who would invest in new, luxurious cars that use modern technologies such as GPS (Global Positioning System). Mumbai's urban planning is distinctly fragmented.[4] Competing political parties control different urban agencies, and different interests compete for funds. Taxi modernization mobilized interests of a broad coalition of city planners, consultants, car manufacturers, investors in transport and other heavy infrastructure, middle-class citizens, business elite, and transport authorities. These coalitions also called for modernizing other city infrastructures. To be world class became associated with "looking" new, and it generated policies and judgments rooted in what critical geographer Asher Ghertner (2015) calls "rule by aesthetics."

In Singapore, liberalization of the taxi industry began in 2003. Until then, the industry was organized around cooperative societies of independent owner-operators. Liberalization encouraged corporate investors to enter the taxi market and phased out owner-operators and their cars (National Taxi Association 2010). Taxi service operator licenses were issued to companies rather than to individual drivers. Encouraged by the Maharashtra state transport government, labor leaders from Mumbai's taxi trade traveled to Singapore to learn about Singapore's liberalization. They were expected to replicate "best practices," particularly with regard to helping the expansion of fleet taxis in India.

The mandate on retirement of old kaalipeelis was influenced by regulatory strategies drawn loosely from Singapore's taxi operator licensing scheme that privileged taxi fleets. In the 1990s, Mumbai's regional transport authority created a limited supply of taxi permits and issued no new permits after 1997.[5] This instigated two interrelated processes: taxi fleets either had to entice independent drivers to join the fleet (with their permits), or they had to entice drivers to sell their permits so fleets could hire other drivers. When both strategies failed to entice enough drivers, the State Transport Authority (STA) set age limits on existing taxis to further regulate the market in favor of fleets. Drivers with older cars who could not or did not want to purchase new ones were encouraged to sell permits to the STA. By 2010 the STA acquired several thousand such permits and began auctioning them to the highest bidder. Permit auctions were loosely inspired by the open bidding system for vehicle registration and ownership in Singapore, which is also carried out through monthly auctions where potential car owners bid for vehicle registration numbers. However, in Mumbai, auctions applied only to taxi permits and not to other private vehicles. Fleets with less capital opted out of auctions to pursue individual drivers for permits and labor. Fleets with more capital successfully procured permits, but needed drivers. Therefore, the regulatory context altered the contours of taxi-driving in Mumbai. At the same time, drivers continued to control how and when permits moved across the industry. Permits were a way for drivers to bargain politically and economically, which allowed them to refuse joining taxi fleets and slowed down expansion of the fleet taxi trade. A move from a self-employed, owner-operator taxi trade to one based on corporate fleets meant that the labor relations of motoring began to shift—and this shift was particularly felt by those in the hereditary taxi trade.

Mumbai's taxi drivers never traveled to Singapore. However, in their critiques of the fleet taxi model, they routinely spoke as if they had. Venture capitalists and investors in fleet companies regularly traveled between Mumbai and Singapore. These groups saw drivers' resistance as their inability to understand the benefits of modernization—an idea that fit well with their notion that the working classes cannot adapt to change. For these groups, where fragmented urban governance made it difficult for big infrastructural visions to be realized quickly, new taxicabs signified progress and speed. As a manager in one of Mumbai's new fleet companies patiently explained to me, "We want our taxis to look like Singapore. New cars with trained drivers will make us look modern and provide passengers with comfortable, modern service." In this context of looking, seeing, and the privileging of vision, Singapore's taxi liberalization seduced Indian planners.

Then, around 2013, technology-based taxi services Uber and the Indian company Olacabs entered the fray. Fleet taxi companies that had started out with hope began to suffer under the burden of owning and maintaining their own cars and managing employee-drivers. They also struggled under the weight of interunion battles and a shortage of drivers with permits willing to drive for them. Many young men found Ola and Uber more attractive options because they promised to help them become car owners. In this tangle between hereditary taxi drivers, fleet taxis, and app-based mobility, the matter of planning and transport modernization changed. What mattered now were new political alliances and claims-making on the part of transport labor and those who represented them. The question of what kinds of cars and drivers have rights to the road in modern cities also came to the fore. The most recent September 2019 amendment to the Motor Vehicle Act and its magnification of road safety and increased fines for traffic safety violations has made the question of roads, road use, and driver conduct even more salient for those who use roads most.[6] Together, both historical and contemporary tangles between drivers, unions, investors, and transport and regulatory authorities have shaped the chillia taxi trade.

CHILLIA: EVOLUTION OF AN URBAN LABOR CATEGORY

Chillia identify as Sunni Muslims of the Momin caste.[7] In Gujarat the bulk of Momins are found in Banaskantha District, in and around the area of Palanpur, which was a former princely state of India. By 1800 the importation of horses from the Persian Gulf became significant to maritime trade in western India. Prominent families, particularly princely families, kept stables as marks of their cosmopolitanism and upper-class status (Mohiuddin 2002). Stables were important places of employment for Muslim labor, otherwise employed in marginal farming and petty trades. Many employed in stables took their knowledge of horses with them and followed other family members into Bombay's transport trade as drivers of horse-drawn Victoria taxis. By around 1911, Victoria taxis began to share the road with motorized taxis. Finally, when Victorias disappeared, many Palanpuri carriage drivers moved to the motorized taxi trade together.

The needs of the trade in colonial Bombay manifested spatially. Palanpuri drivers settled residentially in and around spaces where they could park their Victorias and harness horses. Most lived in and around South and Central Bombay in areas that provided stables and watering spots for horses (Dwivedi and Mehrotra 1995). Close spatial arrangement, where families and extended families migrated to drive horse-drawn taxis, made it desirable for men to migrate with their families. Women and children were surrounded by extended kin and remained integrated within networks of support and piety that carried over into Bombay. Care and grooming of horses required several members of the community. Drivers benefited from the assistance of close relatives with these duties. When drivers moved to motorized cars, many families responsible for servicing carriages and grooming horses started small spare-parts businesses, tire, and mechanic shops. The social, economic, and cultural dependence on others from the same community meant that residential communities made up entirely of taxi labor emerged. These close spatial arrangements have persisted throughout the twentieth and twenty-first centuries. Pathanwadi is one such community where working-class Muslims produce and debate their urbanity and cosmopolitanism rooted in the labor they do.

The city has a particularly strong hold over the imagination of Indian Muslims, and city and urban life have historically been vital in producing new Muslim subjectivities. For example, by the nineteenth century, Bombay was a rich mosaic of Muslim communities who traveled from around the world and became consumers in what historian Nile Green (2011) calls a *religious economy*. Consumption in this religious economy intersected with the rise of new Muslim working classes and customary community boundaries. This religious market influenced the spatial topography of the city through shrines and religious festivals anchored in particular neighborhoods. These cultural foundations of the labor economy among Bombay's Muslim communities undoubtedly influenced how Palanpuri Momins came to, and persisted in, the taxi trade.

"Momin" broadly translates as "true believer." During the early decades of the twentieth century, Muslim weavers and other similar occupational groups in several parts of India mobilized politically against higher-status Muslim elites under a single community that called themselves Momins.[8] For Palanpuri Momins in colonial Bombay, this low-status position, what they see as a "caste," intersected with circumscribed possibilities of labor and work in the city. Undoubtedly, the question of caste among Indian Muslims is complicated. While caste among Hindus has been studied widely (Beteille 1997), systems of social stratification among South Asian Muslims has received less systematic attention (Ahmad 1973; Ali 2002). The most well-studied aspect of social hierarchies among Muslims is the division between Ashraf, high-status immigrant ruling classes, and Ajlaf, low-status converts from mostly artisanal and trade backgrounds. While these broad categories are important, systematic understanding of how social hierarchies inflect Muslim social life is only possible if we look at social worlds within which real Muslim groups operate in local situations. Caste among Indian Muslims is broadly articulated through linguistic, regional, ethnic, and class registers.[9]

It was particularly telling that when I set out to visit the Palanpur region, where most of my informants still have strong family roots, I was instructed not to refer at all to the term *chillia* for fear that I would be misunderstood: "No one in Palanpur will know what you are talking about; at home we are Momin, in *Bambai* we are chillia."

Indeed, Palanpuri Momins who migrate elsewhere are not known as chillia; it is only Bombay migrants who are. As Palanpuri Momins migrated into Bombay in the early twentieth century, in search of employment, they used ethnic and kin networks to monopolize three important trades in the city. In the words of Yusuf, a veteran chillia driver, "For chillia in *Bambai*, you can say our dhandha is H-M-T: Hotel-Motor-*Tabela*. H-M-T."

The term *hotel* in the Indian context refers to an eatery rather than a boarding place. Many chillia men run and work in small eateries that cater to working-class neighborhoods. These restaurants and the community that runs them are so closely identified with each other that restaurant patrons refer to the restaurant itself as chillia.[10] *Motor* refers to taxi driving and all its mechanics, maintenance, and auxiliary functions. *Tabela* is the horse and stable industry—more recently, cow and buffalo stables of Mumbai's dairy industry. These narratives suggest that only Palanpuri Momins associated with the taxi, restaurant, and stable trade may claim to be chillia. This caste identification was important to gain entry into these trades and for Palanpuri Momins to consolidate themselves as small capitalists by establishing khandani dhandhas (family businesses). However, it also set boundaries for entry by others and operated as social control over those already in the trade. The connections between particular kinds of work, being a good taxi driver, having a good, honest dhandha, and being a good chillia man became intertwined. Social control in this case was particularly exerted on men, and it was difficult for most chillia men in Pathanwadi to reject the taxi trade outright. In cases where men were ambivalent about joining the trade, they would defer their entry into the taxi trade by trying out a religious education at a madrassa or working for chillia in the restaurant trade.

The precise historical point at which *chillia* became a term of self-identification for Palanpuri taxi drivers in Bombay is unclear. Based on narratives of taxi drivers today, it was tied to interactions Palanpuris had during the course of plying their trade. For example, taxi driver Ismail offered his understanding: "In my great-grandfather's time we chillia all drove horse buggies. During that time, most of the buggy drivers were from our caste from Gujarat. We only spoke in Gujarati and Gujarati has a lot of *cha, cha, chi, chi* in the language so people just started to call us '*cha, cha chillia.*' And that name has stuck."

Yasser, Ismail's brother-in-law, explained the genealogy of the chillia identity somewhat differently: "The family name of people of our caste was 'Shailiya.' But during the British period, there were many Parsis in Bombay who used buggies and cars driven by the Shailiya. Mispronunciation of Parsis created the bastardization of the surname and it became 'Chiliya.'"[11]

Abdul, Ismail's brother, repeated the story of mispronunciation of the family name, though in his understanding it was the British who mispronounced the name, not the Parsis. Collectively, these narratives suggest that chillia and its associated identities were a product of the later colonial period in urban Bombay. In the context of shifting and cracking colonial power, different urban communities were staking claims to emerging possibilities for the generation of capital. These late colonial shifts in capital and social relations impacted how Palanpuri Momins were urbanized through their participation in Bombay's labor force and their interactions with colonial Bombay's urban elite. The identification has stuck and been co-opted as a term of urban identity and a way of drawing on different resources in the city than were needed in Palanpur. Chillia is therefore a colonial formation perpetuated in the postcolonial period as a caste, which produced a sense of genealogical connections with the taxi trade. Articulated first as a labor identity, it began to encompass other forms of moral and cultural difference and distance from other workers and other urban communities. As in the case of Qureshis, a butcher community in Mumbai, in addition to regional productions of caste, caste among Indian Muslims also operates as a flexible social structure that adapts to, absorbs, and responds to shifting forms of capital and new social, religions, and moral orders (Mirza 2019). Chillia as a category emerged and shifted in these ways.

Historically, identification as chillia was a discursive strategy of distancing from other taxi-driving communities who also organized their working lives around ethnic and religious connections. For example, by the early postcolonial period three minority communities dominated Bombay's taxi trade: Palanpuri Momins, Konkani Christians from Mangalore, and the Sikhs. By the 1960s, most Sikh drivers moved into heavy motoring like truck driving. Due to different structures of migration, and higher literacy than others in the taxi trade, Mangaloreans gave up on motoring and moved into white-collar occupations.

Further, chillia also differentiate themselves from other working-class Muslims, even other Momins and from weaver or julaha castes (Haynes and Roy 1999; Pandey 1990). In the context of twentieth-century western India, the main ethnic divisions among Muslims were between Kokani Muslims, who are descendants of early Arab (and Persian) migrants and merchants along the western coast, and Momin Muslims from the weaver or julaha castes (Momin 1973). As the economic influence of Kokani Muslims grew along the western coast of India, they claimed a higher social status because of their direct lineage with Arabs. While Kokani Muslims were endogenous, they were socially ranked according to occupation. In western India, Momins of the weaver castes were integral to the textile industry in eighteenth-century Surat. They provided significant piece goods for the British and Dutch East India companies and for local merchants who distributed commodities for local consumption (Nadri 2009). It seems plausible that many Gujarati Momins who identify as chillia in Bombay trace their heritage back to these weaving professions in eighteenth-century Gujarat. However, both their work and the terms used for their castes shifted by the twentieth century based on political and social movements among non-elite Muslim groups in other parts of India (Ghosh 2010), as well as on migration out of Gujarat into the city of Bombay.

Arguably, for Palanpuri Momins, different work produced different needs for resources and customary differentiation from other working-class Julaha castes. Historian Nile Green (2011) uses historian E. P. Thompson's (1963) notion of "custom" to think about the nexus between caste, class, and community. Green argues that customary idioms of labor were never static entities. Rather, idioms articulated through caste provided Muslim communities a "diverse pool of resources" (Thompson 1963) that could be called on when needed. In this sense, caste identifications operated as social, cultural, and political connections in the labor market. Connections that promised the most resources emerged most prominently; and when they were no longer useful, these identifications either shifted or were replaced. As sociologist Syed Ali (2002) argues, caste among Indian Muslims is a related set of *elective* rather than *imperative* resources that undergird economic and social relationships.

While chillia as an urban labor identity utilized a range of possibilities available at the time, many chillia economic choices draw from commitment to Islamic principles. The Koran provides a set of values and guidelines for economic conduct as well as sufficient space for Muslims individually and collectively to choose among economic options that reflect Koranic outlook, values, and norms. Chillia specifically conform to guidelines that limit the absolute freedom (McAuliffe 2002, 8) of members of the community to pursue purely individual economic objectives. Further, the everyday, trusted, hard work that driving and mechanics entails allows chillia to live an economic life consonant with Islamic economic guidelines that say that wealth should only be accepted if it comes from striving and effort. The khandani dhandha, dekh-bhal, and the life of the jaalu are important articulations of these commitments to trust and collective striving.

ECONOMIES OF TRUST AND URBAN EMBEDDEDNESS

Today, to delineate moral difference from other urban workers, even from other taxi drivers, chillia drivers call on a shared narrative that chillia are singularly trustworthy; they are drivers on whom urban citizens can lay complete *bharosa* (trust) in their travels around Mumbai. Stories of passengers leaving expensive suits, wallets, phones, and briefcases full of cash, all of which are returned to the rightful owners by chillia drivers in good time, circulate widely in Pathanwadi. Stories about recouping of property from taxis and the trustworthiness of taxi drivers are also recounted by union leaders, transport authorities, and other drivers. For chillia drivers, trust is not just a noble part of the taxi trade, but a significant mark of respectable masculinity, and economic, ethnic, and religious identity.

As communal tensions in Mumbai are rife with narratives of Muslim men as criminal, oversexualized, and untrustworthy, the narrative of the trustworthy chillia man has persisted.[12] I suspect that it persists, albeit even if recast, precisely because of these other negative stereotypes. These publicly circulating ideas leave little room to envision Muslim men's labor in the city outside their work in Mumbai's infamous "underworld" or as allies of "terrorist" groups across the border in Pakistan. Either way, the narrative of trustworthy chillia in Bombay's taxi transport is key both to the production of this community's identity and to their capacity to mobilize claims not just to protect but also to actively shape their self-employed, hereditary trade. It marks chillia as good Muslims, more trustworthy and committed to the city than other working-class Muslim labor.

Chillia identity and its moral affiliations with trustworthiness took on a potent value in the aftermath of the 2008 terrorist attacks in Mumbai. Members of a terrorist group affiliated with the *Laskhar-e-Taiba* (Army of the Good) in Pakistan, allegedly with the assistance of local allies, carried out a series of shootings and bombings across Mumbai that lasted for several days. After these attacks, it became particularly important for chillia to distance themselves from other Muslim communities for whom allegiance not just to India but also to Mumbai was questioned. Chillia refer denigratingly to other Muslims who are later migrants and who live around them as *mian-log* (Muslim people). This term, applied particularly to North Indian Muslims from Uttar Pradesh and Bihar, co-opts the derogatory nature of this reference used by Hindus to describe poor and working-class Muslim men. The chillia denigration specifically implies that *mian-log* engage in activities (like violence) that go against Islam.

For example, Rehanna, who runs a grocery shop that her husband owns in Pathanwadi, makes a revealing but representative moral argument: On the morning after the celebrations of *badi raat* (night of deliverance), a holy day in the last week before the end of the month of Ramzan, I was sitting with Rehanna, whose brothers are taxi drivers. Rehanna clicked her tongue disapprovingly as she recounted the celebrations of the previous night. "These *mian-log* do a lot of bad things on *badi raat*—things that are against Islam. They eat and drink all night, they make a noise, and drive all over the city of Mumbai creating chaos. See our chillia boys, what did they do? They spent the entire night praying to Allah and to their ancestors; they are quiet and don't make a lot of *dikhawa* [show]."

Pathanwadi has a large mosque where different communities worship together on important religious festivals, and Mehta Chawl, where most chillia live, has its own small mosque funded by chillia families where daily prayers and worship take place. Chillia see this separate space connected to a shared piety that differentiates them from other mosque-attending Muslims. They see *mian-log* as less committed to Islam, but also less committed to the city and to hard work. Chillia also see *mian-log* as more rural, peasantlike and less urbane. While chillia drivers cooperate with other Gujarati Muslims in the upper-middle-class housing societies around Pathanwadi, for the most part, working-class Muslim communities keep a significant social distance and neither socialize with nor visit each other's homes even on religious festivals.

Many Muslim migrants from Uttar Pradesh and Bihar in Pathanwadi have also entered the trades of taxi and auto-rickshaw driving. However, the chillia trade is entirely closed to them. These newer migrants are more precariously positioned in the taxi trade since they do not own their own taxi permits. They cannot show longer-term residence or domicile in the city, which is required for taxi permits. This draws these communities into the fleet taxi trade or into driving with Uber and Ola, as they require less documentation and are less dependent on a jaalu. Therefore, the distinctions of piety between different Muslim communities also find expression as political-economic and urban rivalries in Pathanwadi.

Finally, customary ethnic boundaries also produce urbane and cosmopolitan sensibilities and subjectivities connected to the automobile. These are produced out of a sense of enduring connections to urban mobility and early automobility in the city. For chillia, this connection is part of the community's place in Bombay's urban modernity. In the early days of taxi motorization, several models of British and American cars entered the taxi market. Chillia drivers frequently narrate family histories of motoring through these different models of cars. Chillia drivers purchased Padminis either by pooling resources of extended families or getting special loans from the Bombay Mercantile Bank, a Muslim-owned cooperative bank that provided loans with no interest. Many chillia still drove Padminis when I started my research. The history of its acquisition, the acceptance in the community that the purchase conformed to Islamic rules against interest, and the embeddedness of this car in daily lives interlaces chillia autobiographies.

The story of the destruction of Rahim's taxi illustrates this well.

CHILLIA TAXI DRIVERS AND TAXI MODERNIZATION

I sat on the speckled floor of taxi driver Rahim's house. Rahim, otherwise both so agile and imposing, looked beaten, drained, and defeated on this rainy July evening. He limped despondently past the bright curtain that shaded the dark front room of this two-room house in the small Mumbai settlement of Pathanwadi. A profound sadness hung heavily over all of us, much heavier than the violent Mumbai monsoon that battered and banged ceaselessly against the tin roof. "Padmini *mari gayu*," he said softly in Gujarati. "My Padmini has been killed." He lay down and closed his sharp eyes—eyes that could find every hidden street, gully, and *naka* (crossroads). Finally, looking up, he spoke to the dusty fan circling above his head, "My taxi has been cut into many pieces, but my heart is broken into many more." His oldest daughter, Nafisa, who Rahim always praised as the "best cook in the world," stood at the stove, stirring the creamy milk and sugar with her strong hands into a large vessel of tea. Watching Nafisa stir, I could see that even those experienced hands trembled ever so slightly. Nafisa was usually stoic and contained. While she often spoke in philosophical ways about sadness in her life, she rarely sobbed or cried publicly like her father did.

The characteristically contained tremble of her hands this evening seemed to signal a desperation and a hope that the scalding cup of her father's favorite *adrak chai* (ginger tea) would burn away his memories of this dreadful day. "Abba, your pain is my pain and I know you don't want to see me in pain. How can I take away this pain in your heart?" Nafisa implored as she knelt down to place the cup of tea at her father's feet. Rahim lovingly touched Nafisa's head and wiped a hint of moisture from her damp eyes before he broke into uncontrolled sobbing.

It felt like we were there to offer condolences for a tragic loss in the family. Taxi drivers, car mechanics, and several young boys who washed taxis in this taxi-driving community every morning sat solemnly on the floor or stood in the doorway in sympathetic silence. Periodically, they glanced out onto the empty sliver of pavement where Rahim had parked his taxi for twenty-five years. One less car to repair, one less car to wash for these men who relied on the daily cash that Rahim and other drivers gave them for scrubbing, shining, and tuning Padminis. Rahim and all the other boys and men who stood around him were chillia. That evening, Rahim had returned from Mumbai's Motor Vehicles Department, the state's main licensing and regulatory body. At his annual visit to get his taxi's license renewed, he was forewarned that it no longer complied with new regulations on age and would need to be handed over to the state to be destroyed. Rahim's youngest son, Syed, drove the same car for the evening shift, and his brother-in-law, Aziz, drove the car on Fridays when others went to prayers at the mosque. This shared car had a long and hardworking relationship to Mumbai's roads, as did the men who had driven it. Syed and Aziz sat next to Rahim and angrily complained.

SYED: "All these years the RTO [Regional Transport Office] officials took our bribes and gave a passing certificate; now all of a sudden they are trying to enforce the law?"

AZIZ: "What was the real age of this car? What is age anyway? Is it the body of the car, or is it the inside of it? We have put in a new engine, a new taillight, new brakes, and a new CNG [compressed natural gas] tank."

SYED: "But they have decided it's too old, only because it looks old, and has no place in the new Mumbai; they want us to either buy new cars or give up our family business and join a fleet taxi company. Where will we get the money to buy a new car? After being a public servant my whole life, who wants to become a *ghulam* [slave] of the private sector? What happens to workers?"

To ensure that Rahim's old vehicle would never again benefit from upgrades or repair that had marked its life for two decades, three low-level employees of the state government violently yanked the doors off the car before a small crane came down like many sharp bullets to shatter its roof. The car, showing either its own defiance or the well-known sturdiness of the Padmini, did not fall easily into a pile of wreckage. Instead, it simply crumpled in various places, just enough for the authorities to be satisfied that they could leave it for dead. For several months after this crumpling, Rahim's Padmini still stood as a car that once was, among many of the other ruins on the grounds of the Regional Transport Authority. I visited these ruins many times and took photographs for Rahim even though he often could not bear to see them. Each week, the film of dust on the car's body became thicker, and bits and pieces of metal and wires were extracted by men who earned money through recycling the materials all over the city.

While Rahim's taxi had traveled around Mumbai for several years as a machine that supported several families in the taxi trade, its extracted parts now made their way through recycling operations, gaining their value as metallic debris. Holding his head, Rahim said softly, "My family, we were *Bambai*'s original taxi drivers, but there is no place for anything original. The police, the RTO, this *sarkar* [government], and even our own union people have decided that only what is modern can be on the roads, never the old. We are old taxi drivers and our taxis are old cars. There is no place for us in this new Bombay."

Rahim has driven a Padmini kaalipeeli taxi since 1982. His father and grandfather also drove taxis for over five decades before returning to their native village near Palanpur, in the neighboring state of Gujarat, so they could die auspiciously in their small, ancestral home. In the early twentieth century, his great-grandfather was the first to migrate to the city as a teenager when he followed his maternal uncles to colonial Bombay to drive a horse-drawn hackney. This long, hereditary association of chillia with Bombay's taxi trade led to claims that they were Bombay's original or joona taximen. As Syed lamented above, throughout the twentieth and early twenty-first centuries, chillia drivers adapted to regulatory, economic, political, and technological shifts in the taxi trade. This resilience undergirded chillia persistence in the trade even when other ethnic communities associated with taxis moved into other professions.

When I entered this community in 2010, rampant debates circulated over the future of the taxi trade. Drivers like Rahim faced intersecting forms of

destruction—of their taxis, of labor structures, and of circuits of reciprocity that had persisted in various forms for over a century. When taxi modernization first began and when drivers were required to replace older
kaalipeelis, chillia vociferously debated these changes. They denigrated the
government for being in bed with car manufacturers trying to hold up a
lagging car market by tapping into the taxi trade and with corporate investors and urban elite groups calling to "modernize" cars, regulate and ratio-
nalize roads, and manage motoring labor.

Veteran chillia drivers had three choices: to buy new cars in order to
keep driving, to give up their taxi permits to the state and leave the trade,
or to sell their permits to a corporate fleet who would employ them. Additionally, for chillia drivers who pooled resources to purchase vehicles to
avoid Islamic religious restrictions against loans and interest, the purchase
of new cars was doubly complicated. While car loans and mortgages have
become commonplace in India over the last decade, the accumulation of
interest that these credit economies require go against Islamic prohibitions
of *riba* (interest). The early refusals of taxi modernization were rooted in
claims that new cars would drive chillia into conventional credit economies that involve the giving and taking of interest, which is against
Islam. For observant chillia, the Koran provides a range of guidelines on
how to live a just economic life and how to engage in socially and economically meaningful work. Chillia in Pathanwadi adhere routinely to
the prohibition of usury or riba in their everyday lives, though this prohibition took center stage when taxi modernization began. Many Muslims consider riba equivalent to interest; usury, like gambling, is believed
to be misappropriated wealth, and aiding this misappropriation is considered not only anti-Islamic but also societally unjust and disruptive
(Maurer 2005; McAuliffe 2002). This commitment to economic justice
and to earning wealth through honest means is a way of life for chillia.
However, in their refusals of taxi modernization it became a collective,
calculative resource as they faced both the market and the state. In the
marketplace, the reiteration of honesty and trustworthiness is a way for
chillia to claim resources, customers, and credit that is less available to
others. Similarly, by invoking piety, and their inability to take conventional loans to purchase new cars, chillia also make claims on the state to
slow down and redirect the trajectory of taxi modernization.

Through these claims to Islamic piety, chillia viewed contemporary taxi
modernization as a way to disenfranchise minorities and erase Muslim
labor in a city that has seen both spectacular anti-Muslim violence and

everyday forms of exclusion of Muslims from public life (Hansen 1999, 2001). The reality is that chillia are poor Muslims in a city where Muslims are violently excluded, circumscribed, and policed. Labor relations in Mumbai have long been shaped by exclusions of caste, religion, and nativism.[13] These dynamics are vital to why different drivers are affected differently by taxi modernization.

Although an abundant scholarship on Muslims in Mumbai discusses brutalities of Muslim lives in India in relation to their violent relationships with the Hindu majority, it fails to fully foreground contemporary Muslims' lives in political-economic and labor terms.[14] For instance, at points of extreme uncertainty over the fate of the kaalipeeli taxi trade, and when a sense of betrayal by both the Indian national and Mumbai urban state were heightened, many chillia men talked about being left no other economic choice but to "become *antankvadis*" (terrorists).[15] This declaration of potential violence by chillia taxi drivers has little to do with the material affinity for violence of these men. In fact, in all other parts of their lives, chillia specifically denigrate other Muslims who engage in such violence, since economically benefiting from terrorist acts is also widely understood as anti-Islamic. Rather, this declaration is a scathing critique of the structural and economic violence that discourages Muslims from participating fully in economic life, generating modern capital on their own terms, and controlling the work they can do as a collective or a *khandani dhandha*.

TAXI DRIVING AS *KHANDANI DHANDHA* AND
NETWORKS OF WORKING-CLASS CAPITAL

Dhandha, in the taxi trade, is work that is about the body and its relationship to other bodies. The term is used widely in several South Asian languages. In contemporary dictionaries of Hindi, Marathi, and Gujarati, dhandha translates to encompass the terms *occupation, vocation, trade, business*, and *work* (Bernsten 1982–83; Caturvedi 1970; Sastri 1976–81). In contemporary Mumbai, it describes those engaged in business, particularly a small business. Dhandha is also applied to self-employed labor more broadly. However, not all businesses are dhandhas; nor are all forms of self-employment (Aggarwal and Bedi, forthcoming). As early as the late nineteenth century, British colonial administrators recognized the importance of dhandhas among those they governed, which led them to create guides for their administrative employees that translated the capaciousness of the term. In these dictionary/guides, dhandha is defined conventionally as work, labor business, occupations, and trades, but it also refers to something that accumulates *dhan* or wealth (Forbes 1857) and fortune or as a way of life (Sangaji and Shakespear 1899). Drivers today describe their dhandhas as both work and as a form of living (Millar 2018). Historically, dhandha is used both by those who conduct this business and by those who surveil and govern the workers. The work that dhandhas entail is capacious but also boundary marking in terms of who can participate in a transaction and when. These various meanings of dhandha are undergirded by the relative importance of economic and social accumulation, and the socially reproductive and relational work that supports dhandhas.

The ubiquity of references to dhandha in colonial texts, and the realities of how driving dhandhas are governed today, suggests that dhandha occupies different moral registers for different people.[16] Since dhandhas are not conventionally waged work, with regularly timed wages or structured hours, the work is seen by the public and by governors as illicit, licentious, or excessive.[17] Dhandha also takes place in spaces where workers, even those who are poor and whose lives are precarious, have some autonomy over their time. This autonomy is fundamental to how chillia drivers engage with each other and the city. For taxi drivers, whose trade is conducted across road and street networks, rather than from fixed spaces in the city, carrying out a dhandha is particularly fraught with instability and must be constantly negotiated.[18] Driving dhandhas are structured through erratic and arbitrary enforcements by the police, passengers, and others who share the road with them as well as by legal guidelines of the Motor Vehicle Act.

Drivers' autonomy—their capacity to set their own timings and to refuse rides—has led representatives of the urban state and the public to argue that taxi dhandhas must be reined in. Police regularly complain that drivers circumvent the law and must be subject to proliferating and ambiguous regulations. This makes taxi dhandhas places where social regulation and bureaucratic state regulation intersect in otherwise "unregulated" economies. While the taxi dhandha is not waged work in the conventional sense, drivers do not experience their work as informal or unregulated work. Rather, the chillia taxi dhandha is a heavily regulated form of work but it is regulated socially and bureaucratically. Usually, social regulations are quite complex and formalized via long-term promises and obligations rather than through legal or documentary systems. Dhandhas also mark a gendered and generational division of labor, where spaces of work and the spaces of kin-making overlap and expand each other. Dhandhas can only be profitable if the social networks grow. And while these social networks grow, dhandha advances and thickens, and people engaged in dhandha develop new social and technical skills together.

Dhandha does not always preclude distinctions between employer and employee or worker and business owner. However, the social categories of labor and owner usually coalesce around groups of kin, fictive kin, neighbors, and friends who both own capital collectively, but who also labor together. This makes dhandha a distinct form of capitalist enterprise, in that those who own and benefit from the capital earned and those who conduct the actual embodied labor are often isomorphic. In purely economic terms, dhandhas are a source of livelihood and a way to create, accumulate, and circulate capital. In the Koran, wealth can be acquired in a wide variety of ways. However, the most "noble" form of wealth is acquired through earned rather than unearned acquisition and through effort and meaningful contributions. Money and other forms of value that are noble and consonant with Islamic practices are those that have to be created "meaningfully." Trade is a permitted and encouraged economic activity, according to Islamic principles, since it is considered both meaningful and socially beneficial. This might explain the importance of dhandha, and especially khandani dhandha, in the making of pious chillia subjects. Khandani dhandhas, work done as a family, require an investment of effort and meaning, both of which are encouraged by the Koran as ways of acquiring wealth (Maurer 2005; McAuliffe 2002).

A key reason that chillia resist joining taxi services such as Ola, Uber, and fleet taxis is because they are not dhandhas but individuated forms of competition, where drivers are incentivized to hit certain targets of time on the road or driving distance. They see this kind of work not only as losing control over time but also as antithetical to the social cohesion of dhandhas that the Koran teaches them to honor. The Koran emphasizes vibrant, economic activity, and Muslims are strongly encouraged to seek and earn in the economic sphere. While it makes clear that wealth can be acquired and is both encouraged and celebrated, the Koran cautions that wealth must not accumulate. Rather, wealth must always be kept in circulation. It should also be distributed to ensure social cohesion by preventing the concentration of wealth in the hands of a few (McAuliffe 2002). The khandani dhandha of the kaalipeeli taxi trade is an ideal type of work for the realization of the goals of circulation emphasized by the Koran; the business of small capital operates through a cash economy and the sharing of risk rather than a reliance on debt. Further, it is socially meaningful work because it is conducted through the jaalu of kin and mutuality.

MUTUALITY AND SPACE

Chillia living as neighbors in Mumbai commonly claim that their families also lived next to each other and cultivated adjacent plots of land in Palanpur. Veteran drivers Hafiz and Karim and their sons made these claims regularly. When I traveled to Palanpur with Karim's family I found that while the families did have plots of land, they were not adjacent in the strict geographical sense of the word but scattered across a landscape that spanned two different village units. Therefore, *adjacency* marked a social and relational rather than a geographical fact. Chillia drivers in Pathanwadi are closely connected to Palanpur, visit their villages at least once a year, and have an intimate knowledge of geographical boundaries of people's land. However, by and large, everyone accepts claims of village adjacency as integral to sustaining dhandha in the city. When claims to adjacency are absent or change, this marks shifts or breakdown of social relations of dhandha. For drivers who live and work closely together in Mumbai, this claim of adjacency in their native village is an articulation of their closeness in the city and their obligations to each other. Over the generations, their shared labor of driving for a living in Mumbai intertwined with claims to a shared ancestral village and to adjacent land, which makes for good marital alliances and shared business interests. It both enables and constrains how they inhabit the broader landscapes of the city around them. Pathanwadi, where I was located for most of my fieldwork, is one such urban landscape.

Pathanwadi (place of the Pathans) is a dense, residential space occupied by an array of working-class Muslims from practically every part of India. It encompasses a heterogeneous cluster of residential settlements. Each cluster is identified by its own name. Boundaries are marked by work and by linguistic and regional origins of residents. When I mentioned to friends in Mumbai that I was living and working in Pathanwadi, the first and almost universal reaction was to ask whether I felt safe there. Although this was a curious and disappointing question, it was not unsurprising in the context of contemporary Mumbai. Working-class settlements are often perceived as impenetrable and unsafe. More importantly, Muslim neighborhoods (much like Black neighborhoods in the United States) are misconstrued, from the outside, as spaces of hopelessness, illicit economic, political, and social activity, rather than as spaces of legitimate accumulation of capital and life-making. In Muslim areas of Mumbai, the production of political economy is shaped by both these external misrepresentations and the realities of economic life within.

Within the broader urban space is a settlement called Mehta Chawl, which houses only chillia taxi drivers and mechanics. To the untrained eye, these houses and the matrix of narrow, muddy lanes that curve, loop, and disappear around them are indistinguishable from each other. But for those who live here, there are clear demarcations of residential spaces based on profession and trade. Differentiation based on work and livelihood historically created spatial enclaves that house only butchers, or only weavers, or only taxi drivers. Residential settlement expands social connections—the jaalu, the web—that undergird everyday working lives. This historical arrangement remains vital to the inclusion and exclusion regularly practiced in contemporary Mumbai. For chillia, this residential arrangement provides access to the taxi trade as well as social control over those who are in it. Chillia drivers, like industrial and informal labor in colonial Mumbai (Chandavarkar 1994), find it difficult to abandon the trade and move elsewhere. They also find it hard to leave the kaalipeeli trade and join fleets, Ola, or Uber unless this move is negotiated collectively.

Rafi was among the youngest drivers here. He leased a kaalipeeli car from his second cousin's husband in Pathanwadi. In 2014 Rafi was to be married in a few months to a distant relative from his village of Badargarh. He had suffered harassment from police over his older car and lost a lot of money in bribes. Saying he wanted to save enough money to begin to support his new family, Rafi took permission from his leaser, an older man from his village, to work with a fleet. The fleet company leased Rafi a spanking new Toyota. When he first brought the car back to Pathanwadi, it stood out like a sore thumb at the *naka*. Rafi's fleet manager had given him strict warnings that, no matter how many mechanics he knew, the car would have to go through standardized maintenance and inspection procedures each week. Rafi was warned, "Don't touch anything inside the body of the car; just keep your hands on the steering wheel and your eyes on the road." A month later Rafi began to feel out of place at the *naka*. He said his car was too "*sthir* [still] and untouchable." Two months later, he admitted that he was tired of taking his Toyota back to the fleet's mechanic twenty-five kilometers away for small repairs. Further, since he had to drive eleven hours a day to make enough to pay off the higher cost of the lease, he had missed all the special *taalim* (education) programs at the mosque. He also missed preparations surrounding the *badi raat* celebrations. He no longer felt like a khandani chillia (of the family). Two and a half months later, Rafi gave up on the fleet and went back to driving a kaalipeeli. He said he preferred to wait with other chillia drivers as they navigated the most appropriate moves collectively: "If chillia drivers have to give up their kaalipeelis, then we will have a meeting of the chillia community to get agreement, to negotiate, and get the details on the company [fleet company] that we will all support. We will not do this alone, but collectively, because that is what has kept the chillia taxi trade fair in the past and will in the future."

Most chillia in Pathanwadi own their taxis and their taxi permits. Those who are lessee taxi drivers like Rafi lease from others in their own neighborhood, and always from other chillia. Therefore, the uncertainty of being a self-employed lessee driver seen in other contexts, such as New York, for instance (Hodges 2007; Mathew 2005), is largely mitigated. Those who lease from other chillia speak highly of the relationship with their leaser. They refer to their leaser by kinship terms such as brother, uncle, brother-in-law. Usually, the leaser is a taximan himself who owns more than one car—one he drives and the other that he leases.

On one hand, in the taxi trade, as observed in other labor contexts in South Asia, kinship is a register of control and discipline. On the other hand, kinship is malleable and negotiable and is a discursive and a structural domain (Haynes and Roy 1999; Neve 2008). Chillia invoke kinship when someone new wants to enter the community and enter the trade. In Pathanwadi everyone invokes close kinship, extended kinship, and fictive kinship ties in order to enter and remain in the taxi trade. Kinship therefore has moral, tactical, and strategic dimensions that undergird monetary networks within the trade. It provides social control over prices the lessor charges his lessee, as well as over how the lessee treats the vehicle. Bilal, for example, is powerful in Pathanwadi. When speaking about Bilal, many drivers say, "Bilal bhai [brother] is my *real* uncle's son." The term "real" connotes that there might be some consanguineous relationship, but that is not a necessary fact. Whether Bilal actually has so many cousins or *real* cousins is beside the point, rather it is more important that cousins are obligated to each other. Not least, they are the first and most desirable prospects for marriage alliances for their children. This in turn strengthens economic and social dependence. Over the years of my fieldwork, and especially as Bilal's advisory role in the chillia community grew, I began to notice slippages and shifts in how different men saw their relationship to him.

Bilal himself came to be a respected man, a senior adviser, a source of marital alliance—a *person*—only in relation to the kinship terms applied to him. The invocation of varied kinship in labor contexts is what anthropologist Marilyn Strathern (2005, 2020) marks as the difference between categorical and interpersonal kinship. The former are categories of kinship provided by language and society, while the latter emerge through interpersonal relations. However, interpersonal kinship claims continue to use the categorical kinship terms available to mark obligation and ties. The blood relation or the categorical claim of being someone's *real* brother does not have as much meaning in an interpersonal claim. For those who claim to be Bilal's real cousins, shared origins in land and blood are important. However, the labor claims to mutual dhandha are what actively shape their interpersonal kinship to him in Pathanwadi. These claims to kinship through labor claims must be continually renewed or else they might ultimately disappear.[19] Further, for some drivers who receive considerable financial help from Bilal, both categorical and interpersonal claims are trumped by sensory ones. In the words of Hafiz, who has purchased a new car through Bilal's help, "With all the help he has given me, Bilal bhai *feels* like my brother." It no longer mattered where Bilal came from or who he was; what mattered was what his presence and support felt like—for Hafiz, he *felt* like a brother.

In 2015 when many drivers were debating retirement of the cars, the talk was that Ismail, an original chillia driver, had retired his kaalipeeli to buy a new car. Soon after the car came home to Pathanwadi, Ismail took his family and the new car to Badargarh for an entire month. Ismail's daughter told me, "Abba decided to go away, to get away from all the *talk*." She was correct; there was a great deal of talk and this trip was a tactical move to avoid the immediate aftermath of the purchase. While Ismail was away, questions such as what kind of loan he had taken, and whether he had violated Islamic tenets to do so, circulated around Pathanwadi. Once Ismail's return from the village was imminent, speculation turned to sympathy with Ismail's situation. Rahim, who was married to Ismail's sister, said empathetically, "Ismail bhai has been driving all his life, so if buying a new car is the only way he can stay in the taxi business that is what he must do." Bilal sympathetically consented, "He must have *majboori* [unavoidable circumstance]. He has to support his family and his wife. He must have taken a loan without interest. He is my brother, so I must understand. If he has bought a new car, we can learn from him."

About two years ago, Ismail's wife, Tasneem, suffered a debilitating stroke that left her alert but unable to care for her daily needs. Sadiya, his daughter-in-law, who was also his wife's niece, carried out the day-to-day care and dekh-bhal of her mother-in-law, while Ismail and his sons kept the car running all day to support the household and Tasneem's rapidly mounting medical expenses. As the financial and care demands intensified in Ismail's household, Ismail admitted that he was tired of living in a state of uncertainty over his older kaalipeeli; he had no desire to join any of the fleets because he wanted his "own timetable." He felt strongly that ownership of his car allowed him control over his time, which driving a fleet taxi would not afford. When his wife fell ill, he knew he would need money for the car and for her medical bills. The previous year, he procured a loan from a small, cooperative bank close to his village where interest payments were not required if the entire loan was paid off within twenty months. The creditor in Palanpur also offered financial help for dekh-bhal of his wife, which he also accepted. By June 2015 he had enough to return his principal for both the car and healthcare expenses so he returned to Badargarh to pay off the loan. He now had a new car (still a kaalipeeli but new model of car) and, in his words, could "Carry on my dhandha and dekh-bhal of my wife without being forced into being a *ghulam* [slave] for someone else." Ismail became an important adviser to other chillia drivers. He had expanded financial circuits by providing new avenues of financial credit for those who wanted to remain in the trade without being forced into the fleet business. These were circuits between capital in the village (Momins in Palanpur) and chillia borrowers in the city.

CHILLIA AND CONTEMPORARY TAXI MODERNIZATION: *GHULAMI* OR AUTONOMY

"In any of these new jobs you can say you have created an entrepreneur but really what you have created is slaves; I am free from this self-selected bondage and I can always choose to stay that way." This claim to dignity and freedom was made by veteran driver Bilal at a 2017 taxi strike in response to what he understood to be Prime Minister Narendra Modi's encouragement for all drivers to join Uber and Olacabs. These refusals of bondage had been proliferating among chillia drivers from the start of the taxi modernization project and became more vociferous with the entry of Ola and Uber.

When fleet taxis entered the market, the focus on new modern cars was accompanied by other disciplinary techniques focused broadly on "conduct" (Foucault 2007) and particularly associated with reforming the laboring body. Fleet taxi drivers had to wear standardized uniforms and learn English to meet the needs of passengers connected to circuits of global capitalism. They were also expected to become proficient with technologies most closely associated with modern mobility—particularly GPS. Khaki uniforms worn by lessee drivers had long been used to distinguish them from owner-drivers, who wore plain clothes. For most of Bombay's postcolonial period, taxi drivers regarded uniforms as marks of bondage to an employer and associated white or plain clothes with autonomy—a visible symbol of ownership of their work and their cars. The new mandate for all drivers to wear uniforms disrupted customary distinctions between owners and lessee drivers and the embodied symbols long associated with ownership and dignity in the taxi trade. Chillia, as owner-drivers, have always worn clothing that marked them as chillia: distinctive, long, white shirts, white pajamas, and a prayer cap or *topi*. They see the requirement to discard these markers of identity as another form of control over their labor.

Further, the commodification of taxi permits unleashed another moral discourse. It created ambivalence among chillia who saw commodification in conflict with pious Sunni religious practices. However, they also recognized that the permit was the main capital that drivers hold. How they chose to use this capital was an important form of refusal to consent to dominant notions of resource allocation. As Rahim said,

> If I have to give up driving my taxi, I will tear up my permit and throw it away. Why should I give it to anyone? See, if I retire my taxi and give my permit to the government, they will pay me two lac rupees for my permit and then sell it to one of these private people for ten lacs. Why should I do that? The permit is our only bargaining chip right now; it is our only *dhun* [fortune]. They say if we sell them our permits, we can come and drive their taxis. Do you really think private companies are interested in drivers? They are only interested in our permits, which are in short supply. If I sell my permit to the private company, even if I drive his car, what do I have that is mine? He can get rid of me whenever he wants, and he gets to keep my valuable permit. Am I mad to become a *ghulam* [slave] of the private company after all these years?

Transport workers commonly use the metaphor of *ghulami* (slavery) to denounce their working conditions (Terra 2014). The rejection of ghulami allows drivers to challenge the logics of discipline that employers impose on them and, in the process, gain the support of public opinion (Bellucci et al. 2014). They also use the metaphor to distinguish their freedom from that of drivers who drive taxis for a local *maalik* (boss) who pays them daily commissions in return for driving one of his multiple cars. Increasingly, chillia reject ghulami to distinguish themselves from those who drive for platform-based taxi services such as Uber and Ola. Here ghulami shifts from a labor relation that depends on a concrete, emplaced, exploitative boss to one at the mercy of abstract global capital and an impenetrable algorithm that takes away drivers' ability to choose their routes through the city. However, the desire for freedom from ghulami does not necessarily also translate into a desire for freedom from social control and obligation. Instead, declaration of freedom from being a ghulam is at the same time an acknowledgement and embrace of social enmeshment in the community.

Brothers Jaffer and Altaf have resisted joining fleets or Ola and Uber to preserve their autonomy. Reflecting on their position in the changing landscapes of the taxi industry, Jaffer asks me, "Do you know what it means to work in your khandani dhandha?"

I shake my head, listening, but say nothing, which encourages both men to keep talking. Jaffer nods knowingly, "Khandani dhandha frees us from ghulami. But does it mean we are free and alone from everything? No, it also puts us in a jaalu with everyone else in the trade, in the city, with what is happening on the roads, and those who are *aas-paas* [nearby/close]."

Altaf reiterates, "Yes, Jaffer bhai is absolutely correct. This is a dhandha that gives freedom but it is freedom that comes from being *jud ke* [together], otherwise it cannot work. That is why those of us in this khandani dhandha cannot drive in fleet taxis or Ola-Uber; that is ghulami; who wants to be a ghulam driving alone on the roads of *Bambai* for someone else?"

"What do you mean that being together gives you freedom?" I push.

Jaffer looks at me amusedly, as he often does when he feels that I misunderstand the value of social togetherness and cohesion. All through my fieldwork, both men and women sighed in sadness when telling their neighbors that I was alone in Mumbai, that I had traveled for hours alone on a plane to be in India, and that my siblings, parents, and cousins lived in different cities. Jaffer goes on to explain, "Just driving to make a living is ghulami because you drive for someone else; but driving in khandani

dhandha is freedom. I am doing the work that my family and my community has done for many years. The car is my family car, so it is also a part of
me. I can carry on my family business; but more than that, this khandani
dhandha gives me control over when I want to stop driving and come home
to rest. I can drive when I want and stop when I want. That is freedom."

I prod Jaffer more by asking him how he decides when to stop.

He responds proudly, "Nobody tells me when to start and when to stop.
You might think, Jaffer bhai has so many people in his house, so on the roads
I would feel free and so if I am free then I would keep driving until dark;
but driving on the roads does not make a man free; being able to come home
to rest and letting someone else drive the car makes him free. When I rest,
someone else will take this car and he will make money and stop when he
wants. Then he is free when he gives the car to his son or his brother. See,
freedom has to be given; you cannot take it from someone who does not
want to give it to you."

Indeed, obligation and freedom are not mutually exclusive for Jaffer. The
matter of a shared freedom from ghulami and autonomy is particularly
important for mobile labor (Joshi 2008). At various historical moments,
transport labor has had different relationships to capital than industrial or
agricultural labor since their common position as small-scale entrepreneurs
and their mobility gave them greater autonomy and maneuverability (Bellucci et al. 2014). Jaffer and Altaf and many others refer to their freedom as
workers as something that they are now habituated to: "We have the *aadat*
[habit] of being free [from ghulami]." This habituation to freedom has
deterred most chillia drivers from joining other burgeoning taxi industries
in the city, despite the fact that they also perceive their own self-employed
trade under some threat.

CONCLUSION: CHILLIA AND CAPACITIES FOR REFUSAL

The caste category of chillia emerged alongside Palanpuri migration into
Bombay and their participation in the taxi dhandha in the early twentieth
century. This caste identification rooted in Islamic piety, mutuality, and
hereditary knowledge have shaped chillia motoring subjectivities and their
political and cultural claims over time. This capacity to make collective, historical claims distinguishes chillia from other workers in the nonindus-
trial sector and from others in the more precarious transport sectors.

Chillia have refused to join fleet taxi companies and Ola and Uber on
grounds that it is bondage and slavery that contradicts Islamic principles.

This refusal has persisted even as they were subject to various forms of destruction. The immediate result has been that long after they were supposed to be absorbed into the corporate-owned fleets, chillia drivers continue to drive their own cars on their own terms. These strategies of refusal have more recently been intertwined with proliferating anxieties over shrinking consumer demand for older kaalipeelis. These anxieties are no longer undergirded simply by the losing of market share to fleets; they are driven by the entry of technology-driven transport options like Uber and Ola. In 2006, when the fleet taxi model was introduced and the debate over the "age" of cars began, the city's planners and middle classes were convinced that transformation was within reach. Fleet taxis had some success recruiting recent migrants as employee-drivers. They also drew on some of the practices of the existing taxi trade, such as customary notions of social cohesion and friendship among those they recruit.

Many in Mumbai's social and technocratic elite are impatient about why kaalipeeli drivers do not just change, or as one Ola executive said to me, "[Why not] leave behind the past and move into the twenty-first century? Because they will lose their jobs one day and then they will regret." Many argue that the postindustrial landscape in the Global South is characterized by a crisis of work, survivalism, and disposability of the poor (Bauman 2014; Davis 2004). However, taxi driving per se is not in crisis, as the options for drivers to join fleets and other platform-based rides proliferate. Instead, the crisis for chillia drivers is the threat to the dhandha of taxi driving, which generates capital but that also accumulates and collects other forms of value, particularly freedom. Chillia drivers assert that new taxi services fail to provide opportunities for social accumulations and autonomy. They are not dhandhas and are seen as work that operates under regimes of bondage (time, direction, electronic payments) rather than work that provides freedom by way of social accumulation. Chillia are watching to see what happens—anxious, but yet refusing and unwilling to consent.

2 ECOLOGIES

Driving Work and the City

ON THIS AFTERNOON IN JULY 2016 (SEE FIG. 2.1), BILAL, HABIB, Fayyaz, and Tariq, sit, rest, sleep, read the papers, and exchange information about car registration away from the chaos of the city, in quiet companionship and close to the shade of trees. The motoring work that chillia have been engaged in for decades is intertwined with the twists and turns of the taxi trade throughout the twentieth and twenty-first centuries. The relational economy of the chillia trade allocates human, cultural, and physical resources among this community, and their hereditary connection to the trade has produced a thick social environment that makes work possible. However, if jaalu and the khandani dhandha of taxi-driving and the care and maintenance of driving work unfold within thick social environments, they are also practiced within the broader political and material ecologies and environments of the city. These ecologies and practices are palpable, and present for drivers. They are the very basis of the driving experience rather than the background to driving work.

Dhandha encounters and shapes the contemporary city's ecology and environment, and for those who drive and repair for a living, roads, streets, air pollution, water supplies, cars, and the city itself are not simply settings in which they drive but dwellings in which they live and work. I draw this *dwelling perspective* from anthropologist Timothy Ingold (2000). For Ingold, attention to dwelling is founded on the premise that whatever humans do arises within the contexts of their involved activity, in specific relational contexts, and in their practical engagement with their surroundings (Ingold 2000, 2011). Taxi-driving work entails working with material and political environments and adjusting to different forms, rhythms (Laplantine 2015), and relations with the city's ecologies.

Driving and repair work materialize through a wide range of practices and rhythms of work and are intertwined with dust, water, debris, and other ecologies that surround them. Drivers dwell in these ecologies and make lives and livelihoods here. But these ecologies also dwell in and with drivers; and their rhythms and temporalities shape how driving work unfolds.

FIG. 2.1. Drivers and taxis at Pathanwadi Naka

In this chapter, I explore these various surroundings and dwellings and the sensory, social, and material worlds that they engender. The khandani dhandha of driving work unfolds through what philosopher of science Isabelle Stengers (2005) calls an *ecology of practices*. Stengers argues that there is no social identity or practice independent of its environment, and that these ecologies produce an experimental togetherness among practices, as those who practice are also learning and gaining knowledge of what works for them. Ecologies of practice also produce and foster a milieu in which people learn, experiment, build relations, and make lives.

For drivers, these ecologies of practice unfold within Mumbai's multiple urban ecologies.[1] The city's island location along the coast of the Arabian Sea, determines the possibilities of movement. The sensorial dimensions of driving are shaped by seasonal shifts in the air, the debris, the mud, the roads, the smells, the pollution, the noise, and the heat.[2] These in turn oscillate based on the rhythms of the day and religious and political climates. Taxi drivers dwell in all these ecologies and these ecologies are all fundamental to the decisions drivers make about when and how to conduct their work.

DWELLING IN THE AIR, HEAT, AND SHADE

Hafiz and Karim sit on the hoods of their old kaalipeelis reading newspapers on a late May morning. Karim had returned from an early morning shift, driving his taxi from 4:30 to 10:00 that morning. Karim suffered from a hacking cough for months that would not go away. The smoggy afternoons and evenings sitting in an open, idling car made his chest heave so much that he had to stop his car to catch his breath—"There is choke in this city and most of it is in the air; once the rains come it will be better," he said. The heavy monsoons from June until early September each year cleanse the smoggy choke for Karim and bring him some relief from the heat. But they also pummel the city's roads into lumps of debris, spray through the open windows, drenching the seats and Karim himself, and splay the city's sludge all over the car so that Karim has to wash himself and his car more often.

Kaalipeeli taxis have no air-conditioning and therefore have to travel with the windows rolled down and open to the world outside. This lack of air-conditioning is built into the licensing systems for these metered taxis, and Karim has little choice or money to install an air-conditioner in his kaalipeeli. While Karim is physically located within the confines of a closed automobile, he encounters the city, its air, and its environment as an open space. There are no barriers between the outside of the city and the inside of the kaalipeeli. Both the car and the driver subject themselves to what anthropologist Harris Solomon (2016) calls *porosity*, which he defines as a form of exchange of substance between bodies and cities, and to what feminist theorist Tiffany Lethabo King (2016) calls *fungibility* to denote how laboring bodies suffer the environmental and political onslaught of their work at the same time that this onslaught allows for alternative possibilities of life-making.

In the summers the early morning drive is easier for Karim as he idles less and feels less assaulted by fumes and pollution in the morning air. "I like to smell the *bombil* (Bombay duck) drying on the beaches or the fish from the morning's low tide rather than the evening's diesel fumes. It's [fishy] smell reminds me that there is a *samundar* [sea] somewhere," he says.[3] Mumbai has distinct morning and evening smells, and drivers structure their days around which of these smells takes the least toll on their bodies, or around those that are redolent but comforting, like drying fish. "I prefer to wake up early than to choke," says Karim. "And this way, my nephew, who has three young children to support, can take the car for the full day.

I need less money and less choke; he needs more money and, since he is young, he will take a bit more time until he starts to suffer from this choke of *Bambai*. This sharing of less choke and more choke works for all of us." The question of how to make a life and a living when respiration is at stake each day is a common discussion among drivers. Writing about air pollution in Delhi, critical geographer Asher Ghertner (2020) asks how we might think about urban citizenship imagined through the atmosphere in places with heavy air pollution that has different effects on different bodies. Ghertner is concerned with the judicial and state articulations of these differences in what he calls an *atmospheric citizenship*. Drivers, however, perceive the atmosphere less in these politico-legal terms and more as smells and matter that settle somewhere in the body to produce coughs and feelings of choke. This perception shapes their everyday decisions about how they are to live and work in this atmosphere. While the air makes its presence felt in Karim's lungs, and the cough marks this presence, the air is also a material entity in which Karim and other drivers are immersed, and they use the sensations of this immersion to make everyday decisions about their work. Temporal and self-regulation become key practices in this sensory labor. These are the rhythms that drivers feel they can devise anew as the seasons change since the atmosphere, even as it is all-encompassing, is uncontrollable.

In this atmospheric recalcitrance and unpredictability, drivers regulate their temporalities of driving through whiffs, breaths, and respiration, rather than solely through attention to infrastructural blockages or traffic flows. While traffic blockages and atmospheric pollution are no doubt connected, for drivers, they are experienced differently in sensorial terms, and they devise different sets of practices for each one. As Karim explained, he and his nephew swap driving shifts based on who is better equipped to take on these assaults on respiration; this is traffic regulation and driving shifts organized and rooted in the obligations that the generations have to each other and to their relative vulnerabilities to the city's ecologies. Karim is obligated to support his deceased brother's son by allowing him more driving time; his nephew is obligated to face the city's onslaught more fully by taking the later shift.

It helps that early morning and late night rides have nighttime surcharges, so Karim makes more money with less time spent driving. Less idling, less fuel used, better aromas, and less pressure on his body—for all these reasons Karim admits that it is unlikely he will ever go back to driving in the days again.

During the time Karim began to shift his schedule, I was living in his household, where I slept in a back room with his wife, Nadia, his daughters-in-law, Saima and Farida, and two of their infant children. In the early hours of the morning, I would hear him rustle awake in the front room with the Muslim call to prayer from the *azaan* at the nearby mosque. He would cough uncontrollably a few times, then splash his hands and face from the large plastic bucket where the family stored their daily water before settling down to his prayers on the raised corridor outside their house. Most mornings Nadia would prepare him a warm saltwater gargle, which he noisily tossed around the back of his throat to catch the overnight settlement of the debris from the previous day's leftover city dust and smog and to insulate against what would come at him that morning.

On this particular morning, as the throaty swish of Karim's gargle recedes, it is replaced by the swish and slush of water that their neighbor, the fourteen-year-old water boy, Rehman, collects at the communal tap in several small bottles. Rehman uses this water to fill the radiators of the six taxis parked nose downward on a tenacious slope nearby. These are the six cars that will traverse the morning city today, and Rehman gets them well hydrated for the ride. The *azaan*, Karim's coughing, and the swishing and slushing at the water tap makes Farida's baby stretch and open his mouth to give out a gentle wail. Farida sits up sleepily, places the baby in the cradle of her crossed legs and rocks him back to sleep moving her right leg up and down vigorously to provide motion under the baby's head. As Karim murmurs his prayers outside, prayers from other homes and corridors rise as a rhythmic buzz into the dark morning. Jagged conversation of sleepy people in line awaiting their turn to use the shared public bathroom punctuates the buzz of shared prayer. The groaning rumble of a bus stopping and then starting up at a nearby bus stop is met by the raspy chorus of barking stray dogs on an adjoining street. The dogs complain and howl like this every morning as they grudgingly give up their nighttime rule over the roads as cars, trucks, buses, bicyclists, and morning walkers take over. I make my way into the line at the public bathroom with Nadia. In front of us, each of the car bonnets lets out a birdsong of scraping metal as Rehman lifts and sloshes the water into the depths of the machines. A faint, satisfied gurgle emanates from the thirsty radiators as Rehman pulls the bonnets back into place. The cars are ready.

Karim finishes his namaaz and then, as a man of habit, eats exactly two and a half pieces of dry rusk toast dipped in his milky morning tea. After rusk and tea, Karim walks over to open the trunk of his car and places his rolled prayer mat into a small nook at the back of the trunk under the CNG (compressed natural gas) tank. Suddenly, several drivers burst from inside the nearby houses and push their prayer mats into a small space in the trunk. As everyone is on their way to wait and pick up at airports and train stations—the most common and lucrative fares during the morning shift—they need to keep the trunk and the inside of the car as clear as possible to accommodate extra luggage and groups of people. Since older kaalipeeli taxis have been converted to use CNG fuel, rather than built for it, the large CNG tanks are installed as strange, cylindrical appendages that take up space in the trunks. Premier Padminis have spacious trunks and are able to accommodate some luggage beside their CNG tanks. However, most of the other models of taxis, where the CNG tank takes up almost the entire trunk, have metal luggage carriers on their roofs and use the trunk only for small, soft items that can be wedged around the tank. When large families of passengers who are new to Mumbai arrive with hordes of luggage at stations and airports, they ask the driver to remove the appendage to make more space. For drivers, this suggestion signals that the passengers are not from the city, which also signals that they will depend on them entirely for directions and the best routes to their destination. The drivers gently educate the passengers about the fuel tank, which leaves most passengers asking more and more questions about why a fuel tank exceeds the body of the car this way.

This morning drivers greet each other and settle into their cars. The ignitions crank up together and Rehman waves all six cars down the narrow slope to make sure they don't bump into the walls of the houses that abut it. Suddenly, they are gone, leaving drops of quickly evaporating water in their wake. Karim, along with five of his cousins and brothers-in-law, have set out into what they delightedly call the *fresh* morning. What makes for fresh air is a subjective and calculated sensory reflection. On a few occasions, I accompanied Karim on these fresh morning rides. The city looks and feels different in the mornings. Mumbai mornings are not devoid of smog. In fact, during the mornings, the undisturbed, sleepy smog of pollution mixes with the fog of humidity to hang low over the city. However, this is a languid, quiet smog rather than an aggressive, proliferating one—or at least that is how it feels. The smog has many colors—gray, pink, and orange—that change by the minute as the sun rises. Mumbai smog is anchored in the sky and then dips at certain places onto buildings and slum settlements along the highway. It is a smog that the eye can see quite clearly; it is almost solid and like an object itself, but it does not assault drivers as does the more unseen onslaught of pollution and vehicle emissions that move around the city, inside the car, and inside the body during busier parts of the day. The exuberance of the changing colors, and the fact that it can be seen and identified over the horizon, makes the morning smog feel less wily, more predictable, and fresher. Since there are fewer people around, it feels as though the morning sea breezes can ripple through the city unobstructed to touch those who traverse the morning city. In this touch of the breeze, mornings are less sticky and humid. Karim says that when he does not perspire, he himself feels fresh. The freshness of the morning signals many things that materialize as sensory attunements of the environment and the body in the course of the drive.[4]

However, while the morning air feels fresh and the morning road is less jammed with moving traffic and people, the early morning road topographies are dotted with clusters of pavement dwellers sleeping together and early morning vegetable and flower vendors who sit in groups arranging, cleaning, and plucking silently at flowers and leaves. As Karim drives past Dadar station, a center of pavement dwelling and vending life, his body stiffens in anticipation of a sleepy child stretching too far into the road space or a vegetable basket flying across the windshield. He also knows that when we get to Dadar's vegetable and flower market the faint fragrance of roses and jasmine will mingle with the pungent aroma of thousands of bunches of fresh cilantro, and the more distant smells from the sea.

Today, like most early mornings, Karim spends his shift traveling through the smog, and the *bombil*-jasmine-cilantro inflected air, giving rides to passengers between the international airport and the city, and between the city and the Bombay Central and Victoria Terminus train stations for those catching trains in and out of Mumbai. The atmospheric milieu and the city landscape in which kaalipeeli taxis ply their trade reflects a distinct form of dwelling in the city. The ecologies of practice that kaalipeeli drivers engage in are significantly shaped by these dwellings. Kaalipeelis mostly move between and around Mumbai's southern core of the Island City and what are called suburbs, rather than between suburbs themselves. The term *suburb* is applied to regions of the city outside the southern core of the Island City. However, it means something different in Mumbai than it does in the Anglo-American contexts where suburbs are characterized by low-density, large, detached homes and a predominance of automobiles over pedestrians and other non-automobile transport. In terms of landscape and land use, suburbs in Mumbai are still very much a dense city. Many suburban areas actually reflect an even greater density than the southern core of the city. In the past twenty years, the center of gravity in commercial and cultural terms has shifted north from the older downtown areas of South Mumbai. In addition to taxis, the suburban areas are also served by three-wheelers called auto-rickshaws, which are cheaper forms of transport and are preferred for the shorter distances within suburban areas. While kaalipeelis can ply between suburban areas, they face heavy competition from the cheaper auto-rickshaws, which are confined to suburban journeys and are not allowed into the southern, Island City. Further, kaalipeelis are also not allowed to ply outside the city limits, which are marked by the boundaries of the jurisdiction of the municipal government. Therefore, the movement of kaalipeelis marks the boundaries and borders of the city of Mumbai, while the borders of the city and what other transporters are allowed to do within these borders shape how kaalipeeli drivers practice their trade.

The borders of travel also mark the potential ecologies drivers might encounter. In other words, how much smog, or how intense the smell of drying or rotting *bombil* depends on how much of the route unfolds along the Western or Eastern Express Highways (map 2.1) or near the murky, smelly, salty Arabian Sea. These smells of the city meld with the smells of passengers. This morning, while Karim traverses humid, fishy air in the southern Island City, he brings home a car that smells of musty luggage from travelers' suitcases, stale breakfasts eaten in haste as passengers scuttle sleepily from one form of transport to the other, and the musky smell of sweat from traveling clothes slept in for one day too many.

By ten that morning, Karim is done for the day and his car is ready to be cleaned before his nephew takes it over. As he awaits the cleaning, he sits with Hafiz as he routinely does, reading the paper in silence on the bonnet of his car. Both Hafiz and Karim place small towels between their bodies and the hot, burnished metal of their cars. When the long wait for rides in the afternoon heat makes drivers drowsy, these towels are deftly rolled into pillows and placed on windshields or seats of the car for quick naps. Lines of kaalipeelis with their doors open and with the cracked, hardworking feet of reclining, resting drivers peeping out of one end or the other are a part of the urban landscape of hot Mumbai afternoons. Driving in Mumbai is mobile work, but, at the same time, many of the sensory pleasures of movement are derived from the periods of rest that surround and punctuate it. These rhythms between movement and rest are vital to how driving work unfolds.

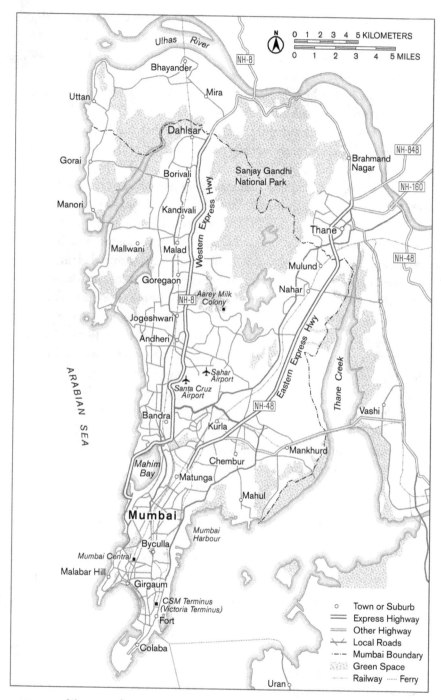

MAP 2.1. Western and eastern express highways, showing the roads and boundaries of the city. Map by Ben Pease.

Rest does not come easily, however, and the pursuit of rest and waiting entails labors of its own. The work of driving a kaalipeeli in Mumbai involves a lot of waiting and sitting around outside. Finding a place to wait is not easy. Drivers have to plan for and envision a place to go between rides to rest or to wait. They look for street corners, official taxi stands, or sheltered, tree-lined slivers of road. These are spaces where they can avoid being fined by the traffic police for stopping. They are where they can rest their bodies between the battering, noisy, smoggy rides through the city, find some shade to eat in and nap for a while, or say their prayers. The searing sun and the urban heat are absorbed into Mumbai's built urban landscape (Budhiraja et al. 2020). They are also absorbed into the metallic containers of cars that move around the city all day. The search for shade from the blistering heat and humidity in Mumbai draws out a circuitous search for the shade of trees or the sea breeze from the murky Arabian Sea. For Karim and Hafiz, driving work demands this uniquely thermal orientation to the city where considerations of heat, shade, dampness, and humidity are always part of their decisions about roads and routes.[5] Hafiz admits that he accepts afternoon rides when the sun is hottest only if they take him in the direction of shaded parts of the city where he can sit, rest, and complete his namaaz under the shade of trees, before the bumpy evening ride home. He searches for the baobab, peepal, or karanj trees in Dadar, Shivaji Park, Borivili, Navy Nagar, and Colaba—south, central and northern points of a city where publicly accessible shade is a scarce form of relief from the heat. For transport planners, routes within the city are marked by roads, maps, and speed. For drivers who sit in hot, open cars all day, the route is marked by the trees and breezes that promise shade, relief, and rest. The spaces of waiting are also spaces of rest, and drivers prefer to rest where they are likely to know others who rest there (fig 2.2). Rest for these men is less about leisure than it is about work. Rest, and the ecologies, sensualities, and socialities that surround it, mark ways of dwelling as a taxi driver in the city. It is no accident that the demands made by taxi drivers on the government are not only for better roads, but for better places of rest—taxi stands.

TOPOGRAPHIES: ROADS, *NAKAS*, DEBRIS

This morning, Hafiz and Karim are parked in the bazaar not far from home. Several other kaalipeelis are parked around them. While Hafiz's kaalipeeli is still an older Premier Padmini, Karim's is a newer but secondhand Hyundai Santro. Based on new mandates about how long a taxi can legally ply

FIG. 2.2. Drivers at rest

the roads, both these models were waiting for their imminent retirement (see chapter 3). Hafiz will have to retire his car by 2020 and Karim a few years later. While they are not related by blood, Hafiz and Karim refer to each other as brothers, and most people who speak of them refer to them this way too. They have driven taxis since the 1970s, but the cars they drive today represent different material and economic relationships to India's postcolonial history. Hafiz drives a Premier Padmini while Karim drives a Hyundai Santro. These cars mark different biographies of driving and sensing the city.

The Padmini is a symbol of the development of India's early automobile industry. It was a car shaped by the limits and priorities of postcolonial India's industrialization. The Padmini was an Indian car that had to search for drivers in a country where private car ownership was a rarity. Padminis were manufactured in Bombay by Premier Automobiles, which played an important role in India's progressively nationalizing automobile industry. By the 1970s, Padminis became what the automobile industry calls an "indigenous" car. This was a car that had most of its parts produced and assembled in India and that became a symbol of Indian nationalism.

Hyundai, a Korean-based company, marked the world's turn to India to catch an expanding consumer market that the Indian automobile industry could no longer meet. Hyundai entered India in the 1990s, during India's liberalization phase. Padminis, and later Santros, both became important vehicles in the taxi trade. Once they became established as city taxis, both models lost their appeal for other buyers. According to representatives of the manufacturers at these two companies, the public saw these as "working-class cars"—symbols of downward mobility. Manufacture of these models was terminated in 2000 and 2014, respectively, and now both face imminent retirement due to their age (see chapter 3).

There are two intertwined forms of laboring, aging, and weathering of bodies going on here—of cars and drivers. Hafiz's and Karim's taxis are also working bodies that emit smells, crash, and bump around the roads in different ways. They are both machines from which livelihoods of motoring and mechanics are extracted in the midst of the debris around them. This work of cars and people unfolds in the broader ecologies of atmosphere, smell, shade, and heat that surround them. It also unfolds in topographies and surfaces of the city that are significant to taxi-driving work but not easily classified in infrastructural terms as roads or streets—this is the *naka*.

Until last year, Hafiz and Karim and other chillia drivers parked in a straight line on a small pathway just off the main road of the market in Pathanwadi after they returned from their shift or else to rest before going out again. This was the space where the handover of taxis between one shift and another was practiced. Drivers referred to this area of parking and rest as a naka, while spaces of driving and movement were referred to as roads. Nakas are places where a road ends; but they are also places where another road begins. Therefore, a naka is where movement either stops or where one enters a road. Often, the term *naka* also denotes a crossroad or a place where two roads stop to meet. For those who are regulars at a particular naka, the naka is a place of rest and recovery from driving work; for those who do not belong, the naka is a place of conflict. Therefore, nakas are thoroughly malleable spaces. They are surfaces and topographies that suture connections between roads and streets and that take on both form and function through the specific practices, rhythms, and politics of what happens there. The interstitial surface between nakas, streets, roads, and all the materials they share and exude, such as debris, dust, and socialities, are all places where drivers and driving dwell and where driving work unfolds.

This naka led to a dense slum settlement. The precision with which each driver slid his car into a vertical parking spot at the naka made it operate and look like an official taxi stand, which meant that traffic police generally allowed the cars to park as though it were de facto a government-sanctioned stand. Over the last few months, however, the slum settlement had been demolished and a twelve-story apartment building inched its way up through the uneven gravel and into the hazy Mumbai sky. Future residents of this new building would need a paved road for their cars to enter the naka and exit onto the road. An unpaved naka would not do. In preparation for this paving, the unpaved naka, where taxis had once stood in precise parked lines, was haphazardly dug up. The debris from this digging had made its way all the way to the paved road. The mounds of debris that extended out of the naka and onto the roads made it increasingly difficult to tell where the naka ended and where the road began—at least in textural and topographic terms (Boek and Baloji 2017). I began to see how new practices and patterns emerged in these textural and topographic shifts between naka and road.

The pothole is the most commonly discussed problematic road topography in Mumbai (Lakshmi 2014). This is the hole in the road that disrupts the smooth ride. It is the broken and unintentionally emergent area below the surface of the road that has come to represent all the other holes in the bureaucratic, technical, and administrative domains of Mumbai's road infrastructures. As urbanists of postcolonial cities have noted, the figure of the "hole" operates as a master trope to express the dismal quality of living in a city in today's postcolonial urban context (Boek and Baloji 2017, 143). There is no doubt that the work of driving in Mumbai entails slumping in and out of potholes along the road. Much of the battering and hammering of drivers' bodies can be traced to the stumbles in and out of these topographical interferences.

Topography is an important sensory mediator of driving work, and drivers often speak of their bodily pain and injury in topographical terms. For example rubble, road debris, and accidentally dislodged stones that hit windshields at fast speeds are connected to back pain, headaches, and eye injuries. However, pain and hammering are not the only topographic or textural encounters for Mumbai's taxi drivers. Topographic and textural disturbances are not always depleted of all content or possibility (Boek and Baloji 2017). Topographic disturbances do not stand in for, nor are they always experienced as degradation, decline, and empty of possibility.

Sitting amid the debris, stones, and digging at this construction site, the varying textures of this urban topography enabled different kinds of topographical engagements for drivers even as they sat off the road at the naka.

Attention to texture, what anthropologist Jonathan Anjaria (2019) calls "surfaces," suggests that infrastructures in Mumbai are not simply underlying, a priori, social or political systems; nor are they empty failures of urban living. Rather, they are textures that are also seen, experienced, produced, and sensed by those who drive for a living. Anjaria (2019) argues that thinking with "surfaces," rather than with infrastructural objects such as roads or topographical disturbances such as holes, provides a multilayered understanding of urban ecology and landscape.[6] Relatedly, archeologists of ancient roads systems argue that despite universal assumptions of engineering and stability, roads have historically operated as both infrastructural sites and as an amalgam of various surfaces (Hendrickson 2010).

The prevailing ideas of paved infrastructural systems, and of engineered and preserved road surfaces, come from Roman Italy and Europe.[7] However, in practice, in most parts of the world, political and social possibility have always resided in the shifts between surfaces. In contemporary Mumbai, these seemingly haphazard surface topographies are everywhere, and are seen as holes that must be blocked or patched. However, for those who live and work in and on these surfaces, the "surface is where the action is," to use historian Joseph Amato's words (2013), since it undergirds most sensory life and is the place where work and life dwells. Bicyclists, because of their less-protected proximity to road surfaces, do have a more textured encounter with the urban landscape than motorists do (Anjaria 2019).

For Hafiz and Karim, who drive older kaalipeelis, textures and surfaces are palpable in the impressions they make on their cars and on their bodies. They are palpable along the route as potholes, ditches, and uneven surfaces. But they are most palpable when drivers remain in place, and as they watch and participate in how these textures, surfaces, and topographies come to be in the first place. These surfaces materialize in movement on the roads, but they also materialize in place at the naka and through the intertwining of various kinds of material and environmental debris and the practices that drivers mold around them. This is why the naka as a space and as a surface is such a significant place of dwelling. The surface of the naka, and those who share in it, are social s(kin).[8] It is a surface that is malleable and where things, politics, and sociality touch and enter the bodies and machines that dwell there.

For instance, at this naka, the rubble from construction of both road and building is scattered everywhere like bundles of fuselage, a mixture of stone, bitumen, cement, concrete, old plastic bags, leaked petrol, and leftover rainwater. As a result, taxis encountered unfamiliar, uneven, and scraggy terrain. They no longer lined up in precision as they once did. In fact, they were now parked just as they moved on the roads: out of line and out of linear visual order. As I have discussed in my introductory chapter, driving on Mumbai's roads is characterized by congregational and entangled movement rather than the linearity one finds in Western driving contexts and where cars move in straight lines along straight roads. Many of Mumbai's roads have traffic lanes painted onto them, though in most places these markings are scraped over or are faded reminders that linear thinking and driving along protected, laned, and demarcated road spaces are neither universal desires nor practices for those who spend the most time on Indian roads.

The line, or in the case of driving—the lane—is a form of representation that signals broad landscapes of movement; however, when one zooms into these representations in the cartographic sense, the line disappears and one sees no lines but only surfaces (Dorsch and Vinczent 2018; Ingold 2007). This tension between representational life—staying in line by keeping in lanes on the road—and the actual life of driving on surfaces is where the ecologies of practice of Indian automobility collide with straightforward, progressive narratives of modernity and order. While this tension between surfaces and linearly ordered lines is played out on the roads all the time, nakas and other places of rest and refueling, like gas stations, do sometimes operate as places of linear order largely because these are spaces where cars need delineated spaces to be opened up for fuel or repair.

The naka alongside the construction site used to be where the congregational and entangled arrangements of the road came apart to allow ordered space for repair and mechanical care. However, given the new terrain at this naka, the surface arrangements of the moving road carry over to the resting naka, which brings the haphazard vehicular arrangement between naka and road together. The cars are left to maneuver around mounds of fuselage until they find their comfortable angle of rest in this space that is neither entirely road nor entirely naka. It is a surface that materializes not out of conscious roadbuilding projects, road imaginaries, or engineering but out of the ecologies of use, the work of digging, and the accidental shifts of debris between roads and naka discarded from other kinds of building.[9]

Those who use Mumbai's roads most encounter this kind of debris as a material form of accidental terrain everywhere. Mumbai's landscape is full of debris that molds itself in a variety of topographical formations. Sometimes this terrain is a road, sometimes a naka, and sometimes a taxi stand. What it becomes and how it is used shifts incrementally, depending on the season, the value of surrounding land, or the moods of the municipality. Drivers talk about the Padmini kaalipeeli as the hardiest car in this moody, accidental terrain. Its wheels and undercarriage can brave accidental debris on the surfaces of the road, and its body is toughened against accidental encounters with other bodies who share the road, famously called *thoks* in Mumbai (see chapter 5).

As the naka struggled to become a road, the Padminis opened themselves up to thoks as they moved closer to each other. The taxi stand had become a montage of kaalipeelis, with noses at a variety of angles, looking out onto the debris from various heights. The traffic police who left taxis alone when this was an unpaved naka now showed up periodically to threaten drivers with parking tickets. Sitting in the same place that they had been in for twenty years, Hafiz, Karim, and their taxis had unwittingly become part of this tangle between streets, nakas, and roads, and the shifting presence of authority at these places.[10] This unwitting entrance into the tangle did not mean that Hafiz or Karim were passive victims of this shift. To the contrary, they were active participants in this shift from naka to taxi stand, and from rubble to road. Sometimes they participated in these shifts through their collective work of kin, and sometimes they used these collectives to keep other people out. Kaalipeeli drivers who dwell on the surfaces of the city because they sit and wait around at the nakas and stands to be hailed directly by passengers actively differentiate themselves from fleet taxis that rely on call centers and the app-based Ola and Uber drivers who rely on smartphone apps. They see these taxi drivers as men directed via technological intermediaries rather than as dwellers who share the city, the naka, and the roads. Therefore, these taxis are not allowed to rest at nakas; if they park close to kaalipeeli stands, they are shooed away. The drivers of these other taxis admit that they see nakas as places of conflict rather than as places of rest. This tension over rights to particular surfaces of the city signals the surface politics of who belongs on these surfaces and who is allowed to belong fully in the social skin that is joona taxi driving.

To the casual observer, the leftover debris at the naka, the refuse of digging and building, signals a cityscape in disarray. The spaces where debris rises and grows are seen as neglected, dirty spaces, characterized by inattention and lack of care. However, in this space of the naka clawing itself into a road, chillia drivers and others have expanded complex networks of practice in these places of waiting and debris. Access to the mounds and the areas of parking around the debris are reserved for chillia drivers. During busy seasons, like Eid, Diwali, and the wedding

season, when there are many visitors to the markets and nearby buildings, younger chillia men stack a few inches of this debris to build make-
shift speed bumps along the entrance to deter other cars from entering
the area. It is not uncommon to hear the disgruntled exasperation of
visiting drivers trying to get their cars and tires disentangled from the
sharp stones of this debris. One also sees young scrap pickers going
through the debris looking for pieces of glass, metal, or discarded plastic
bottles and plastic bags that make their way into the debris from the surrounding market with great regularity. Since chillia drivers have come to
know this debris well, they routinely direct these young pickers to particular spots that they know to be particularly rich with what could be
resold as scrap. Over the years, this interstitial space between naka and
road has become a point of intricate material, social, and environmental
coalescence between people trying to make a living amid accidental digging and debris.

DUST, WATER, *DHOOLI*

As Habib and Karim read their papers, two young boys, Ali and Hamza,
scuttle through the zigzag of cars at the naka carrying soapy buckets of
water, bright yellow washcloths, and scrubbing brushes. Ali soaks his wash-
cloth fully in the bucket and slathers each car with the yellow, soapy slush.
Hamza dips his cloth lightly into the water, squeezes soapy suds onto the
road, and then carefully wipes the medley of grime that has accumulated
from various part of Mumbai on windows and windshields of each car. Dust
from the fumes of sticky, black carbon has settled into a grimy charcoal that
sticks to taxis like it belongs there. Dust, as Joseph Amato (2000) has argued,
has always been the pervasive ecological background to life and living. Dust
is central to many of life's routines and regimens of cleaning, removing,
building, and repairing. Dust is spatially recalcitrant, moving everywhere
around the urban landscape, unmindful of social and material boundaries
of inside or outside. It makes its way into domestic spaces where it neces-
sitates and fundamentally shapes the gendered work of cleaning, scrubbing,
and sweeping to keep it at bay. It is inescapable for those who move around
the city's landscape. For drivers, dust clings to the skin, beard, hair, and
clothes and penetrates the body, scraping the throat and irritating the eyes.
In Mumbai, dust mixes with rain and humidity to become grime and sludge.
In Indian cities this dust and grime are everywhere (Shulman 2009). In
Mumbai, the longer you spend in the city, the more you absorb and collect

these accumulations. Those who move from place to place accumulate and absorb every variety of this city debris.[11]

Taxis are central repositories of these myriad accumulations. On Hafiz's taxi there is the gray and white crust of pigeon excreta that comes from parking too long under laburnum trees; on Karim's car there is the jet-black grime that emanates from diesel engines of cars and trucks and settles into the cracks of the door and onto the hands and clothes of drivers. This is the grime that Karim's daughter-in-law, Saima, says she has a difficult time rubbing out of his clothes when she washes the household's laundry. Her husband, Karim's oldest son, Jalal, also returns at the end of his driving shift with grime and sweat etched deeply into his clothes. Saima soaks, beats, and scrubs their kurtas out of obligation, love, and some frustration until she is able to proudly remove these environmental marks of the city entirely. Karim's wife, Nadia, insists this has settled into his lungs as a permanent cough. Karim agrees that he feels the grime in his throat and lungs, but as he watches Hamza sluice the grime off the body of the car, he marvels at how much of the grime the car absorbs that would otherwise blow into his throat. On both cars there is the lighter yellow dust from the crumbling gravel of roadbuilding that flies around cars and breezes through their windows. And then, there is the ashen, grainy cement dust from the ever-proliferating building construction sites across Mumbai.

If hereditary motoring is sustained through thick social and economic accumulations, it also unfolds amid these other ecologies of accumulation. These accumulations are perfunctorily referred to here as *dhooli*—an endless form of environmental, chemical, and organic accumulation that young men get paid to wipe, scrub and clean off cars across Mumbai day after day. Ali and Hamza periodically scamper over to a tap of water by the building's construction site to empty dirty water and refill buckets. As they wait for the buckets to fill, they run their hands through the cool water, touch the coolness to their faces, and sprinkle water playfully at each other. The boys feel both the coolness of the water and the heat of the city through their skin (Tuan 1995). Neither of them is old enough to drive. Though like others their age, while they wash at the naka, they encounter Mumbai's roads through accumulations of dhooli long before they sit behind a wheel. They can tell when a taxi has waited too long in the salty sea breeze at the gateway of India, or idled in a traffic jam around spilled chutneys of snack shops in Thakurdwar, or when it has trudged through the muddy roads of Aarey Milk Colony. This morning, they can smell the musty luggage of Karim's early morning passengers and promise him they will sweep the crumbs of sleepily eaten food off the backseat. All these accumulations and knowledge end up in buckets at the construction site at the naka.

Apart from a familiar nod acknowledging their youthful energy and their polite and respectful demeanor, the construction workers and building engineers largely ignore the boys. They are focused on their drilling and metallic scraping, which periodically engulfs the naka with a thick dhooli of its own. On the higher floors of the building, the metal dust seems to catapult into the heavens, while on the lower floors it drops like a luminous waterfall onto the brick and cement trucks below. Sometimes, it flops as unwelcome flotsam onto the two jeeps of the building engineers. These men occasionally ask Hamza or Ali to dust off their cars. While the boys initially felt that this was reciprocal work they had to do in return for use of the water tap, they were surprised to be offered money for their services. At first, they embarrassedly declined the payment because they were unaccustomed to participating in a paid economy outside the taxi trade, but on some insistence from the engineers, they acquiesced. The engineers assumed the boys were brothers or else understood from their casual observations of their choreographed work that they were somehow enmeshed—therefore, payment for the cleaning was made in a lump sum of fifty rupees for the two jeeps to just one of the boys each time. As the boys empty their buckets, scraps of dissolved pigeon shit and powdery city dust they have scrubbed off taxis trickle into the dry, earthy foundations of the building site; they spread like extended fingers into the ground and slowly disappear. Even before it is has become a structure in its own right, this emerging building has already absorbed gallons of Mumbai's dhooli cascading out of Ali and Hamza's car-washing buckets.

The routine of cleaning is remarkably choreographed between the boys as they wash Mumbai's environmental accumulations off the taxis and then send the dhooli into the depths of Mumbai's earth. Ali slathers the metal parts of each kaalipeeli, and Hamza follows to wipe the glass. By 10:30 a.m. they have inched through the montage of parked cars to get to Hafiz's and Karim's taxis. They are on time and on schedule and plan to keep cleaning as they usually do until noon, when they have to leave to attend their own afternoon schooling or taalim at the mosque. However, today, Ali and Hamza were alerted by laborers on the building construction site that for the next month, the water supply would be turned off in the late morning to accommodate the digging and plumbing needs of the building. On hearing this news, the boys begin to move faster and one of them runs home to get two more buckets to fill for reserve water. In addition to Hafiz's and Karim's cars, they still have four more cars to wash.

The temporalities of car washing and the removal of the city's dhooli are singularly tied to these arbitrary shifts, stops, and starts in the water supply. The water supply is directed and stopped from places and by people that these boys will never see (Björkman 2015). However, that they have so little control over the main resource of their work is taken gently in stride. Car washers like Ali and Hamza are always adjusting their work to these shifts in water supply and adjust their own tempos of work accordingly. They have also learned to use less water by first doing a thorough dusting of the cars before they wet them so that loose dhooli dissolves back into the air rather than into the declining water levels of their soapy buckets.

Hafiz and Karim hurriedly fold their newspapers, slide off the hoods of their taxis, gather up prayer mats from their cars, and move toward a sheltered area under the last of the tall trees on the construction site behind them. In anticipation of the water stoppage, construction laborers are also standing around the tap, filling water bottles and other small containers for drinking water to keep them going through the imminent heat of the afternoon. These workers are far from home, cut off from the jaalu of settled living that the chillia enjoy. They are usually migrant workers, who sleep in the open under tarps close to construction sites with little access to regular water supplies or the protection of trees or cars. If the drivers and car washers use this water for cleaning themselves and their cars, the construction workers imbibe it as drinking water to keep their bodies running. In this way, water, how it is used, and the labor practices it enables in Mumbai signal the multiple vulnerabilities and possibilities of urban work (Anand 2017; Björkman 2020). While these different constraints on the water supply and on how the water is used at the naka signal different relations to work, the water itself has a significant tactile place in this ecology of practices. While Ali and Hamza use the water for washing and play as they await their filling buckets, the construction workers find tactile relief in its coolness as they stand around drinking it and splashing their hands and faces with it, taking pleasure in the sensation of cold relief on bodies that have been lifting and drilling for hours in the beating sun.

Hafiz and Karim lean over the same tap where Ali and Hamza fill their buckets and where the construction workers scramble for drinking water and relief from the heat. Both men wash their feet, hands, and faces with the cool water—cleaning and cooling their bodies for the devotion that will follow. The same water supply that washes their cars also cleanses and cools their bodies for the auspicious occasion of their namaaz (prayers). The loud-speaker at the mosque several blocks away begins to crackle. We hear the *maulvi* (priest) clear his throat before he drops his voice to begin his undulating chant that calls the neighborhood to prayer. While the roads are rife with honking, the naka is characterized by these undulating chants. Chillia drivers move in and out of roads and nakas as much as they do between the sounds of horns and prayer. These distinct sounds formalize place for drivers as sound distinguishes the places of rest and reverence from those of movement and mobility.

As the drops of cleansing water on their bodies evaporate rapidly into the humidity of the morning, almost in unison Hafiz and Karim hurl their thick prayer mats open and away from the construction and under the shade of the last two rain trees left on the construction site. They sit down side by side on their mats on the most even part of the uneven surface they can find and close their eyes in prayer. As is customary in Muslim prayer, they bend their heads all the way to the ground several times as they quietly—and audible only to each other—murmur verses from the Koran. The dust from their unpaved surroundings blows onto their mats and onto their faces as their beards gently brush against the ground their foreheads share with their parked cars. The surface of driving has been transformed into a surface of worship, and the wheels of the taxis and the praying foreheads of the taximen are imprinted with the same dhooli. It is an intimate moment of shared silence that I have seen them perform many times in the same spot over many years. This is a silence shared only between them. The rest of us, myself, Ali, and Hamza, cover our ears as we jump out of the way of a honking, bellowing cement truck backing itself into the construction site while the manager yells expletives at the truck driver to be careful. This meditative and shared silence, practiced through daily namaaz, amid the noisy onslaught of the city has become a way for drivers like Karim and Hafiz to live through the sensory and environmental assaults of the city. Their work, their claims to kinship, their piety, and their capacity to enjoy a shared silence all coalesce in this jetsam space of debris, noise, dust, dhooli, receding water supply, and prayer at the naka.

TOPOGRAPHIES, ECOLOGIES, AND SOCIALITIES
OF PARKING/NO PARKING

It was an early August afternoon in 2010 (fig. 2.03). The *azaan* reverberated from a loudspeaker on the roof of the *badi-masjid* (big mosque): *Allah hu*

Akbar (God is great). The din of bargaining vegetable vendors in the bus-tling market around the mosque, horns from passing auto-rickshaws, and the screeching of chickens on the slaughter block at the butcher shop were drowned out for a few short minutes. Two months of a heavy monsoon had peeled through the fragile surfaces of almost all the roads in the market out-side Pathanwadi. The road, on which there was once a designated taxi stand, now resembled a broken trail. Unlike the naka on the other side of Pathanwadi where the building is emerging, which had never been a paved road at all, this paved road was fast becoming an unpaved naka of floating concrete. Drivers had moved their cars out of the pool of dissolved concrete to a less mangy strip of road outside a middle-class, Bohra housing society on the road to Pathanwadi.[12] A petition filed by the housing society the previous year had brought a prominent "No Parking" sign to this part of the road.

I soon learned that this warning of "No Parking" had several semiotic lives on this naka, most of which deviated from what one might think of at first glance as "No Parking." First, because the residents of the housing society had so many cars themselves, there was always an overflow of cars of both residents and their visitors from the compound of the building onto the naka and into the "No Parking" zone. Then, it was common for chillia taxi drivers displaced from the taxi stand due to the floating con-crete to park in this zone too. Therefore, this wide array of cars, fancier new ones that belonged to the residents in the middle-class building and the older kaalipeelis, stood side by side, sharing space on the naka and cooperating in a space otherwise marked by class hierarchy. Whenever the police came by to ask taxi drivers to move their cars, the president of the housing society, Jawad bhai, would intervene on their behalf, arguing that until the municipality had fixed the roads and given the taxi stand back to the drivers, the society was in agreement that chillia drivers be allowed to park there.

It was common to see Jawad sitting on a stool reading newspapers with the taxi drivers between 2:00 and 4:00 p.m., when the police patrol usually took place. Jawad owned a luggage and suitcase sales business in a small shopping center in the neighboring suburb of Kandivili. He had spent most of his youth and middle age first as apprentice to his father and uncles at the store and then as owner and proprietor with his brothers and cousin. He understood hereditary businesses well; now that his son and son-in-law had taken over, he had gone into what he called "semiretirement." His wife had passed away of a sudden heart attack two years before I met him, which

FIG. 2.3. Pathanwadi police patrol

seemed to have left Jawad more than a little adrift and lonely. He was honest with me and with the chillia men around him about how he was still in *pida*, in pain, over his wife's death and that being outside and close to the naka and the life of the bazaar gave him pleasure, or as he said, "Dil lag jaata hai [My heart is happy]." He enjoyed being able to chatter with Bilal and Habib in Gujarati and to be a part of the lively activity, particularly the arguments that unfolded at the naka over parking. The altercations with others who tried to park there and the discussions with police and taxi drivers were Jawad's relief from his lonely one-bedroom flat and his incessantly running television. To interrupt some of this loneliness, every Saturday afternoon Jawad visited his daughter and his grandchildren who lived in another suburb, Khar, and spent the night there. He had a standing ride with Bilal for this trip. For two years, Bilal (or his son) had been driving Jawad to Khar, for which Jawad paid for a roundtrip even though he spent the night and only took the one-way ride. He recognized that Bilal would have a difficult time finding a return trip between suburbs; Bilal initially declined the extra money, though after a few trips began to accept it and pass what he considered unearned money on to the mosque as his contribution to *zakat* (charity).

Many battles that unfolded around Jawad were related to his defense of the road outside his apartment building. On several occasions, truck drivers tried to park here, too, but Jawad would threaten them by declaring that he would call the police immediately. I often saw him wagging his finger at an errant truck driver as he gestured at the sign "Are you blind? Can't you see that there is a No Parking sign here?"

On occasion a truck driver would shout back angrily, "But taxis are here. Why? Why are you interfering? Is this your father's property [Tumhare baap ka road hai kya]?"

Jawad usually held his ground, "Yes, whether it's my father's property or not, the society has declared that it can be used as taxi stand but not as a truck stand. Full stop, bhai. Stop the *tension* over this."

These heated interchanges between Jawad and drivers of various other vehicles were very common. Almost daily after 2:00 p.m. the altercations and finger wagging took place at the naka as various people tried to decipher the possible meanings of "No Parking." The police usually complied with Jawad's understanding of who had rights to park here. Therefore, both spoken and unspoken negotiations had solidified into the right of taxi drivers to park there every day. The close and shared living between working-class drivers and middle-class residents, whose housing society controls access to the road, and the dependence of the latter on taxis for rides to markets and workplaces, resulted in solidification of this space as a de facto taxi stand.

This unofficial topography of parking, present for some to dwell in but not for others, was a result of a social and spatial alliance between different Muslim communities built across class. It was certainly rooted in a shared language (Gujarati) and a common attendance at the *badi-masjid* (big mosque) for Ramzaan (Ramadan) prayers by Jawad and many of the chillia drivers. But it was also rooted in the practiced and sometimes intentionally produced ambivalence between the surfaces of naka and road. Unknowingly, and quite by accident, Jawad and the Bohra housing society had entangled themselves and their cars with the fate of the chillia kaalipeeli drivers through their shared dwelling in the shifting politic and topographies of "no parking" at the naka.

ROAD ECOLOGIES AND RELIGIOUS RHYTHMS

While the slippages between nakas and roads in Pathanwadi are produced through the ecologies of practice characterized by and produced through the coalescence of debris, politics, environmental accumulations, and chillia piety, driving work in Mumbai also routinely encounters the reshaping of the road landscape by public, collective, religious gatherings. Therefore, it is not just environmental, seasonal, and natural ecologies that shape the sensorial domains of driving; and it is not just infrastructural domains that determine the topographies of driving. Instead, crowds, the noise from temples and mosques, and the spillage out onto spaces of driving produce the milieu in which driving and the road are practiced and produced.

In September 2016, during the Hindu Ganapati festival, I drove around large parts of central Mumbai with Bilal's son Hamid. Hamid had found that he was able to pick up a number of late afternoon and evening customers from the new office parks in the area who wanted to spend their evenings at the Ganapati festivities. As we come off the flyover at Dadar onto the SV Road, which is one of the main arteries connecting various parts of the city, we see several Ganapati *pandals* (raised pavilions) built along the sides of the road. As we drop off Hamid's evening worshippers, we see hordes of others being dropped off along the roads. Under the watchful eyes of the Ganapatis, the crowds and lines of worshippers waiting in line stream onto the road and snake around the corners. By around 6:30 p.m., barricades appear as vertical lines to cordon off the lines of worshippers from the traffic. The road has shrunk to half its size; it has gone from being a road to being half a road and half a temple complex. By 7:00 p.m., the barricades are moved from vertical lines to horizontal ones to stop the traffic altogether. While two-wheelers manage to squeeze by the barricades, cars and taxis are redirected to a side street. The SV Road is now fully a temple complex, while the side street, the gully, and naka have become the road. Most worshippers arrive in taxis. Hundreds of kaalipeeli taxis stop outside the barricades to let passengers off and then chug away onto the naka.

Hamid tells me that those who organize the Ganapati *pandals* are connected to political parties. This allows them to get permission to have police present and to move barricades around as they please so that worshippers can enter and exit the *pandal* areas easily. The *pandal* committee, even if unintentionally, changes the directions of traffic and shapes detours around the newly placed barricades. Therefore, those in charge of religious events effectively reimagine and then materially affect when a naka becomes a road for the movement of traffic and when a major artery becomes a place of moored, religious worship. Those in charge of particularly prominent and large *pandals*, like the *Lalbaug cha raja* (King of Lalbaug) in lower Parel, have the authority to bypass the police altogether and are allowed to erect their own barricades. These affect where and at what times traffic might pass around the areas through the night for the month of the Ganapati festival. In this way, collective and public religious festivals shape the forms that a road might take, and drivers mold their practices around these shifting domains of the road. Hamid knows that when he enters these areas he must have an exit plan. This means he needs prior knowledge of the side streets and escape routes to avoid being caught in the crowds, harassed by the police, or showered with flowers that stick in the engine of the car or with *gulal* (powdered color) that settles as stubborn pink stains on the seat covers and is an irritation in his throat. While Hamid enjoys watching the festivities and the crowds, as a Muslim man, he is afraid of being stuck in a Hindu religious mob if he mistakenly drives over someone's foot in the crowd or accidently bumps into a barricade.

By 10:30 p.m. the main road, which has now surfaced as a temple complex, has lost all the sounds of honking and wheels, which have been replaced by the clamor of bells, excited shouting and talking, and singing blasted through loudspeakers. The paved road is strewn with flowers, crumbs from the thousands of kilos of sweet offerings to the gods, and trampled-on plastic water bottles. The surface has been transformed from the cold hardness of engineered tar and bitumen, to one of flying, drying petals, and congealed sugar. By 5:00 a.m. the city's sweepers arrive to sweep up as much as they can of this debris, to scrub the stickiness of religious offerings off the pavement, and to remove the barricades; this makes SV Road a space for cars and taxis again. By 8:30 Hamid comes back with passengers making their way back to work in the offices around the area. Hamid is unsure how many of the barricades might have blown back onto the road, or what the previous evening festivities might have done to the surfaces of the road. He reorients himself from the noisy, flower-strewn, temple complex to the morning terrain and rhythms as he shuttles people between work spaces. However, he always anticipates something of the previous evening's debris left in the crevices of concrete as he listens for the squelch of his wheels flattening a discarded bottle, or feels the tangle of the discarded flower garland catch his axle.

STRIKES, EMPTY ROADS

Today is the fifteenth day of Ramzaan, but it is also the twelfth day of the taxi strike, during which most chillia drivers have kept off the roads. They have chosen to stay close to the naka today. As all the taxis are off the road, the naka is a space of dense parking and congestion of stationary cars. This close packing meant that no one can get in or out of their taxis without touching or banging someone else's car. I walk all over the city to see taxis parked in nooks and crannies of every small naka and street. Many are parked in petrol pumps and around building and construction sites. Drivers who have close relations with the employees and managers of particular petrol pumps or with contractors at constructions sites, as Karim and Hafiz do, work out informal rights to park their cars on their property when not in use. These places of rest and off the road are also often referred to as "sitting on a naka." The congestion of the roads has found its way into the naka, but without noise or honking or movement. This is a congestion of resting cars and of stillness.

On typical days, taxi drivers sit on and in their taxis all over the city, at taxi stands, under trees, outside hotels, stations, and airports, giving their stationary cars a sense of life and potential for movement. During a taxi strike, however, the cars are parked, locked, and vacant, bringing an ominous silence to the city. The roads, the places of movement, stretch for several kilometers as empty lines of concrete. A taxi strike like the one today, returns the roads to some of their linearity; the lower density of the traffic makes the traffic lanes more visible, and the surfaces shift to accommodate other forms of transport. Buses, auto-rickshaws, two-wheelers, private cars, and bicyclists romp around the roads with abandon. Given that several labor unions now represent both auto-rickshaw and taxi drivers, increasingly transport strikes are being organized for both forms of transport together. While in some parts of the city these transporters are in competition, the entrance of Ola and Uber, which provide introductory cheap fares, almost as low as an auto-rickshaw ride to attract new customers, has brought some solidarity among these transporters. When full transport strikes are called, and both rickshaws and taxis are off the roads, the city is emptied, and it becomes clear how much these transporters contribute to Mumbai's mobility.

On this twelfth day of the strike, the roads are unusually silent, but the naka is buzzing with activity and conversation. While taxis are off the roads and the city is emptied, there are other kinds of frenetic movement going on. This is the movement of information, discussions on WhatsApp groups about where to go for protests, and updates on the status of the latest union negotiations. These circuits of information and people are important in organizing such collective work stoppages. The dispersed citywide circuits

of information accumulate and become most visible at the level of neighborhoods where drivers and those involved with the auxiliary jobs that support the taxi trade live. Lately, this ability to create a shortage by taking
taxis of the road for several days has been an effective form of bargaining
in a city where consumers routinely complain about the undersupply of
taxis at rush hour or during heavy rains. Chillia drivers are protesting the
most recent mandate that kaalipeelis more than fifteen years old be retired.
The ability to create a shortage by taking taxis off the road for several days
has a long history in the city going back to the early 1920s (Rao 1972; Staff
1960b). Most chillia drivers in Pathanwadi know this history well. These histories have circulated and percolated as family narratives and through kin
networks of the taxi trade for generations. Several chillia drivers sit on the
hoods of their cars at the "No Parking" taxi stand that has been so labori-
ously conjured into legitimacy through the negotiations between Jawad
and the police.

This afternoon is the culmination of another round of speculation over the
fate of Padminis. Due to confusion over what might instigate the police to
fine taxi drivers, and in protest against the transport authority's unfair
treatment of joona taximen, Pathanwadi's drivers have stopped driving. The
practice of taking taxis off the roads is historically known as "flag-ups."[13]
This has long been a strategy for drivers to demand fare increases, protest
rises in fuel prices, or demand clearer rules for issue of taxi permits (Rao
1972; Staff 1960a, 1960b). While so far the mandate had specified that
twenty-year-old taxis must be retired, the news has traveled within a few
hours through the various circuits of the city's taxi industry that the age
limit has been lowered to fifteen years. These circuits are made up of a vast
and dispersed infrastructure of people (Simone 2004): taxi drivers across
the city, leaders of the taxi unions, garage owners and car mechanics, workers at the gas pumps where taxis are fueled with CNG (compressed natural
gas), and smugglers of spare parts who supply parts to Padmini taxis. Some
nodes within these circuits are mobile themselves while others animate
movement of people, cars, and information (Sheller and Urry 2006; Urry
2007).

As drivers discuss what they should do next, Habib, who has driven a
taxi for over forty years, shakes his head sadly but says nothing. Instead,
Habib slips off his resting place on the taxi and raises the hood of his car.
As if seeking comfort in the familiar, tactile connections he has had with
his car for three decades, Habib begins to tinker with the engine (Franz
2005). This tinkering seems to take him out of the uncertain political

future into the world of mechanical pleasure that he can shape. Bilal looks at Habib's tinkering fingers, and smiles wryly as he points to Habib's old taxi:

> By getting rid of older kaalipeelis, they want to make Mumbai like Singapore; but if you want to make Mumbai like Singapore, you need to start with the roads. Look at these stones all around us. How can we become Singapore when we live in this *kachra* [dirt]? We have to develop our city according to our own local conditions, not according to the conditions of a city in some other country. We live in *kachra*; by that I don't mean we are dirty, but we live in stones and dirt. We have to make *Bambai* out of this only, not out of something else. Don't come and tell me to learn to eat with a knife and fork to make me become modern. I just need a plate. Let me do my dhandha, drive my car, and live my life, and I will find my own plate, I don't need a knife and fork.

CONCLUSION

"We have to make *Bambai* out of this [stones and dirt]" is a powerful illustration that Hafiz, Karim, and Bilal have come to develop an astute understanding of how and where they dwell and what kinds of lives and futures they can make there. As they encounter the social, political, and environmental accumulations that emerge and grow around them, they develop and sustain practices that allow them to find ways of dwelling and even flourishing in these environments. Driving work develops as an ecology of practices where the senses and sensations are vital. The sensory ecologies of practice that surround driving work produce the environments and infrastructures that driving takes place in, and conversely, these environments materialize, are woven, enmeshed in, and shift around the work of driving. The ecologies that drivers encounter in the form of dust, debris, nakas, roads, and surfaces are less about fixed matter and more about the *materialization* of social, political, and ecological possibilities. These *make* cities but they also *make* lives. These shifting ecologies emerge as sites (or interfaces) for public intervention, the expression of kinship and sociality, labor mobilizations, social and environmental amalgamations, and contrasted, if not conflictive imaginaries. The taxi dhandha is a form of dwelling not just at the road level, but also at the street level, naka level, and mud and sludge levels of the city. These are where Indian automobility lives its most sensuous and sensory life.[14]

3 JOONA

Time and the Off-Modern

IT IS COMMON TO ENCOUNTER OLD, DUSTY, PADMINI TAXIS PARKED along the sides of roads or left discarded in the compounds of the regional transport offices all over Mumbai. While hereditary taxi drivers are enmeshed in deep social and economic ties, it is impossible to separate this from the material objects like the Padmini that tie them together. The Premier Padmini car is a significant object in the shifting structures of the taxi trade, and it is at the center of most current debates over shifts in the taxi industry. It is a car that has been cast off as a thing of the past, and yet it doesn't quite die. Rather, as an object of the taxi trade's past, it continues to animate struggles over its present and future.[1]

As I encountered Padminis both as working cars and as obsolete ruins, I began to recognize the contradictory temporal realms that they occupy. Though considered "ruins," Padminis persist across the urban landscape and set the terms of the debate over who and what belongs on the roads of the changing city. The Padmini, along with those who drive it, and even those like Rahim, in chapter 1, who have discarded it for something else, are central to how, Mumbai's *off-modernity*, unfolds. I draw the concept of the "off-modern" from the design theorist Svetlana Boym (2001, 2017).[2] For Boym, the term off-modern signifies a historic and temporal recognition of the porous nature of historical time. In material terms, the off-modern is a sensibility that recognizes how material objects of earlier modernities have the power to drive both the present and the future. The off-modern reflects the realities of the twenty-first-century experience in most parts of the world; and arguably, the Padmini and the claims of those who drive it, operate in this realm. Further, the off-modern confuses a clear sense of temporal direction by forcing us to explore sideways and into back alleys to take a detour from the deterministic narrative of history (Boym 2001, xvi–xvii). Ethnography, media archives, and literary texts reveal deeper politics of time and the biography of automobile objects (Kopytoff 1986) and subjects in Mumbai's taxi trade. The off-modern is a useful way to understand the twenty-first-century experience of Indian automobility because it accounts for automobile objects and people that are both *of the city*, as in "being part of," and *off*, which marks their distance from it (Boym 2017). The Padmini kaalipeeli taxi and those who drive it operate this way—they are of the city but also "off-modern" and distant from how the city's future is being conceived by many others.

I observed the dusty, discarded taxis that had once heralded postcolonial India's new automobile industry, alongside those that still ply the streets and are denigrated for being obsolete, dirty, and out of time. I listened to the debates over what cars and what kinds of drivers belong in the city's future. I listened to the claims taxi drivers make over their rights to the road as *joona* (original) drivers and as technical experts on India's first, joona automobiles. It became clear to me that the taxi industry was important to how different ideas about Mumbai's (off-) modern future were being played out through conflicting temporal claims.

The laboring and material value of transport and the automobile in Indian cities have been significantly shaped through temporal claims and collisions. These temporal collisions are what anthropologist Laura Bear (2014) calls the heterochrony of claims over modern time. Debates over obsolescence, mandates to purchase new cars, and a politics of time that privilege visions of newness reside here. However, the abstraction of capitalist time conflicts with concrete experiences of time, that in turn produce divergent, yet intertwined value claims (Bear 2014, 7). For taxi drivers, this value is produced through the embodied and multisensory experiences of time where the collective work of repair, urban knowledge, and technical expertise are most important—the off-modern realm of what it means to be joona, original, and "*of* the city."

JOONA TAXIMEN

On a muggy June afternoon in 2015, the office of the Mumbai Taximen's Union in Central Mumbai is buzzing with chatter and activity. A high, laminated counter looms like a ragged mountain over the room. Inkpads, stained with countless thumbs that have pushed into them, sit forlornly on the counter. Behind the counter are precarious pyramids of binders, each jammed with sheaves of yellowing paper that give off a faint moldy odor. This odor circulates around the room, well-aided by the ceiling fan that runs at full speed all the time. Somewhere from beneath and behind this mass of paper a telephone shrieks. No one seems interested in answering it. A long line of worried taxi drivers snakes out of the room and down the corridor of the crumbling, musty building.

This long line of disquietude is the daylight manifestation of the dark and sleepless night after an important government announcement the previous evening. The transport authority had announced they would reveal a new date for how long old kaalipeeli taxicabs of the Premier Padmini model could keep plying the roads. The practice of announcing another impending announcement is a common strategy of the transport authority. Dates, deadlines, and debates over these announcements loom large in the public discourse and percolate as one of the main topics of discussion at taxi stands and taxi union offices. I had observed this contention over dates of taxi retirement, the shifting deadlines, and the perennially imminent threat of retirement and demolition since 2011. Many of the announcements are simply announcements that there will be a more definitive announcement in the future. Often the definitive announcement itself does not materialize. This chain of notices that something is to be expected causes plenty of chatter and upheaval. Drivers learn nothing concrete from each notice, but they have become habituated to the constant sense of an imminent announcement. Padmini drivers have lived with this heightened sense of imminent demise for over a decade. For chillia drivers, the sense of imminence assimilates as anger, hope, hopelessness, creativity, and reconciliation as they continue to work and earn their livelihoods.

By 2010 plans to modernize the taxi industry were linked to ongoing conversations and concerns among transport planners and middle-class citizens about the pollution produced by older kaalipeeli taxis and the misbehavior and recalcitrance of the men who drove them.[3] The consensus seemed to be that to progress as a modern city, old cars would have to be retired. Further, their drivers would need to change their behavior and comportment by cleaning up themselves and their cars, putting on uniforms, learning English, and, most importantly, changing their practice of refusal of rides.[4] The date at which a Padmini was to be retired had already shifted from twenty-five years to fifteen and then from ten to twenty. This afternoon, the time was rumored to be lowered again to fifteen years. Each announcement of a new date for retirement and, in many cases, demolition of the Padmini by transport authorities was met with significant tumult that reverberated in various places connected to the work of the taxi trade.

Car manufacturers, transport authorities, and planners alike were baffled over driver protests. They regularly scratched their heads over why drivers were so closely attached to old cars and outdated, obsolete technology.

They could not understand why drivers don't comply when offered incentives to purchase new cars with air-conditioning and advanced suspensions that would shield their bodies from the sweltering heat, the backbreaking bumps and potholes, and the unpredictable disintegration of tar that characterize the experience of driving in Mumbai. In others words, they could not understand why drivers did not jump at the opportunity to protect themselves from the sensory onslaughts that are associated with driving an older car in Mumbai. They expressed this bafflement in several ways. Sometimes it was moral denigration of drivers' incapacity to move with the times. At others, it was specific disdain for the resistance of "technologically backward" people to understand urban and technological progress. At still others, it was scorn for drivers' *cruel optimism* (Berlant 2011) for a life and livelihood that many in Mumbai feel is better abandoned in the name of progress. These mandates over retirement of cars marked obsolete transport objects. They also sought to manage a sector of urban labor that was placed outside global visions of modern automobility.

However, despite what seemed misguided and baffling to these groups, even as opportunities for auto financing expanded and many new automobile brands were easily available on the Indian market, protests by drivers against these calendrical dates continued to become more intense. The protests unfolded in anxious lines at union offices; they erupted in scuffles and police stops outside offices of transport bureaucrats, and on the bustling roads of Mumbai; they settled as mantle of both nostalgia (Boym 2001) and anger in households of self-employed, kaalipeeli taxi drivers who watched the mobile artifacts central to their livelihoods marked as anachronistic. Often, threats of taxi strikes succeeded in slowing down and deflecting transport authorities' decisions, which kept the delayed, twenty-five-year retirement date that the union had fought for in place. At other times, authorities held firm on retirement but deferred a decision on dates, which left drivers in a state of permanent uncertainty over when their cars might suddenly be marked as anachronistic and obsolete, and when their livelihoods might abruptly end.

At yet other times, dates for retirement were set and drivers were encouraged to look for alternative ways to join the future. They could do this by giving up their taxi permits to corporate fleet companies who leased them cars, or else plunge into the credit economy to purchase new cars to stay in the taxi trade. More recently, if drivers purchased new cars they could also attach themselves to what in India are known as *taxi aggregators* like Uber or its Indian equivalent, Ola. Finally, those unwilling to do either because they did not want to give up control over their own time by working for someone else in the case of fleets, or in the case of Ola and Uber, for what drivers called "a foreign computer," were marked as irrelevant, obsolete, backward men, with no place at all in a modern city. This volatile landscape where calendrical dates shifted regularly kept drivers in a permanent "hold in time." More poignantly, these drivers also experienced their associated structures of hereditary, self-employed labor, and the sensory lives they have created around the city placed at both spatial and temporal distance *outside, out of time,* and *unfit,* in the modern city. As Frantz Fanon has reiterated in the case of the African continent, the negation of time, the positing of some notions of time as out of joint, and the assumption that particular subjects are incapable of expressing dispositions toward a future has long legacies in the colonial and postcolonial world (1965; Fanon [1963] 1965; Mbembe 2015). Not surprisingly, the debate over time and futurity and of who belongs there continues to inflect how the terms of off-modernity are negotiated in the taxi trade.

I am waiting at the union office with the chillia driver Habib. Habib awaits his turn resignedly, despite his anger toward union leaders who he feels have been ineffectual in recent negotiations with transport authorities. He complains loudly to the man behind the counter at the union office:

> My car has a *new* body, a *new* engine, a new CNG gas tank. So how old is my car anyway? Because it is a joona [old] model [Premier Padmini] I get pulled over all the time. If there is a scratch, or the car is too dirty, I have to pay a fine. If it stalls in the heavy rain, then they say it is has outlived its use. In Bombay, who does not stall in the rains? If I stop my taxi on the side of the road and open the bonnet to fix something, police will come up and fine me saying, "Your taxi must be too old because you have to keep fixing it." The government decides when the taxi is not good enough to drive. It is dirt because it is joona even if it runs well.
>
> There is no place in *Bambai* for anything joona [old] and since I am old and do not speak English, there is no place for me either. However, if we are all gone, Mumbai will also not remain like it was and people like me, old taxi drivers with old cars, will have no future in this city.

The bewildered man behind the counter speaks in a daze, uncertain whether he is speaking to himself, to us all, or to bustling Mumbai outside as he says:

Today, the taximan has to be constantly worried about what is joona and what is modern. The government does not want this kind of taxi business; they want Ola-Uber because that it is modern and run from America. What is old will be *killed* by the government, by the public. The death of the kaalipeeli and the self-employed driver is the death of Bombay's *shaan* [pride]. The old kaalipeeli has to be retired, and demolished at the RTO [Regional Transport Office] and the old taximan, he must also die. Even if he joins Ola-Uber, the joona taximan who has driven a taxi for hundreds of years is dead.

Habib interjects angrily, "The joona taximan may be dying but he is not dead."

There is good reason to pay attention to what Habib calls *joona* as much as to his invocation of the dying, rather than the dead, joona taximan. *Joona* has etymological roots in Sanskrit and Hindi and is a common term in the local language of Marathi (Molesworth 1857).[5] In Marathi, *joona* is an adjective for something ancient or old, long-standing, or long in use—not recent or modern (Molesworth 1857, 186). Given that Mumbai is home to diverse linguistic groups, the term *joona* circulates among speakers of different languages, and has both pejorative and empowering connotations depending on who is speaking. As Habib applies it, joona refers in celebratory ways to the taxi, the man who drives it, and the structure of self-employed labor that has undergirded Mumbai's taxi trade for over a century. It can denote urban artifacts and practices that are "original" and hence historically significant and agentive, but also those that are dirty, out of date, time, and place. In fact, state authorities use the term to devalue kaalipeelis and their drivers. By rendering kaalipeelis joona, they are also rendering them obsolete and anachronistic. Over the course of my research, I heard different versions of the following lament from transport authorities, investors in taxi fleets, and car manufacturers: "If we want a modern city, we cannot have these *joona, dirty, old*, rickety cars on the road. New cars have GPS. Passengers are willing to pay, why is [the driver] not willing to drive [the new cars]?" These distinctions between old and new cars reflect a tension between those who conceive of the city through ideas of "modern" capital and calendrical time, where obsolescence discourse dominates, and those who see it through joona, the other, off-modern experience of time.

Thus, joona is a temporal, moral, and nostalgic claim. For joona drivers it is also a claim to careful and creative knowledge that they have developed through decades of sensory proximity to their cars and the city. Though, as Habib's invocation suggests, the nostalgic claims of joona might be less for something that is lost than it is a refusal to be categorized as out of place and out of time. This refusal works in many ways. Taximen like Habib refuse being written out of this future and out of time. They refuse the state's material devaluation of an artifact of transport; and they refuse its declaration that both the extant structure of labor and the aging bodies of the men who drive are obsolete and out of step with a modern future. Disability studies scholar Alison Kafer (2013) argues that discursive notions of a *future* are used against bodies that do not fit normative or dominant visions, and that unfit bodies can participate in futures only if they are cured of whatever ails them—including, in the case of the drivers, aging.

However, if governments and capital devalue age using charges of obsolescence, age and aging are important spheres of value and dignity in joona claims. For chillia, a joona driver of an older kaalipeeli is an "original" driver, a pioneer in the taxi trade, and joona is therefore a mark of pride, social status, and embeddedness in Bombay's urban history—a claim of authenticity (Björkman 2020). However, transport authorities and others use it to denote something that has lost its value. Joona is therefore an articulation of contradictory temporal and value claims to the city as much as it is an articulation of an off-modern urban subjectivity. Joona lies in this tangle between who can claim to be *of* the city and who must resist being dismissed as obsolete, out of time and place.

Anachronism, obsolescence, and joona operate as competing understandings of value in the taxi trade. The value of laboring urban objects (cars that labor as taxis) and the value of the laboring lives of urban subjects (taxi drivers) are entangled not only with each other but also with other domains of producing value. These are articulated through contradictory experiences of time—the synchronized time of urban obsolescence that posits singular, periodized conceptions of time, progress, and modernization on the one hand, and the alternative, socially produced time of joona that emerges through proximate and sensory practices of labor, biography, repair, and care, on the other.

Joona, as drivers here suggest, is a moral and dignifying claim to the city's past and to originary and creative aspects of urban work. However, it is also a claim to the city's present and future—a temporal, but nonlinear, off-modern, articulation of time. The public acceptance of old taxis as anachronistic has allowed transport authorities to fixate on the determinate lifespan number—fifteen, twenty, or twenty-five years. This approach also devalues those who drive old taxis and the structures of labor that underlie the kaalipeeli trade. It marks them as people unwilling or unable to join the new, technologically driven economy. Media and public discourse join the debates by arguing that kaalipeelis are unaligned with technologies associated with modern life; they have no central call centers for booking taxis, no capacity to order taxis via online services, old, unreliable and easily fixed meters, no air-conditioning, and no GPS or GPRS.

The average life of an automobile in advanced countries is between five and seven years. However, in India, the average life of a car is closer to twenty years. Unlike in the West, in India the cost of maintaining an old car is low due to the vast range of informal mechanical expertise and possibilities for repurposing of spare parts. For example, engines of the Padmini can easily be made to comply with worldwide pollution norms by making changes to the carburetor or the ignition. Therefore, while the question of mandated retirement dates gets posed as an environmental or technological question, it really is a social and political one. The chronic deferral of decision-making on retirement has important political effects. No doubt, these confusions cause immense frustrations, but they also enable taxi drivers, mechanics, and unions to deploy alternative claims of value based on alternative conceptions of time. It also produces the capacities for refusal, if not outright resistance, to the obsolescence discourse of the authorities.

While it is more difficult to find challenges and refusals of joona drivers to policing in the historical archive, my ethnographic evidence suggests that attitudes toward police and those who govern the roads are not unambiguously fearful or respectful. For example, one afternoon, I am in a kaalipeeli taxi with Jalal, a chillia driver who has been in the trade since he was in his late twenties. Now in his early sixties, Jalal makes claims to the road as a joona driver. On this afternoon, we have dropped off a passenger at the Bharat Petroleum Corporation (BPCL) headquarters in the Ballard Estate area of South Mumbai. BPCL was one of the first distributors of CNG fuel. The company is both derided and praised for its connections to the taxi industry. They are derided because drivers say they do not provide enough filling stations for CNG, which leads to long, snaking queues at the pumps during the busiest times of the day; and praised because they *do* provide CNG and have helped lower the costs of being on the road. This afternoon, Jalal is in his mood of derision as he looks disdainfully at the building where his fare alights: "I am a very joona driver so I have seen what this company has done for many years. They are in the government's pocket; CNG is not profitable for them so they don't provide enough of it. What do they care if drivers are sitting on the road waiting for CNG for two hours?" I nod my head in agreement with Jalal. He continues, almost under his breath, "Yes, it does not seem that anyone cares."

We turn left onto a blind corner toward Horniman Circle, a historic area in South Mumbai. Jalal stops briefly at a roundabout; as he moves forward to lift the gear on the steering wheel into first, there is a loud thumping on his car. When I look behind me, I see two heavyset traffic policemen moving around at the back window. One bangs on the car, an indication that the driver needs to stop and pull over; the other gesticulates wildly to point Jalal to a corner of the road shaded by a lush, thick tree—a joona banyan tree. Jalal groans in frustration, mutters softly under his breath, but obeys. One of the policemen appears at his window: "Show me your license," he demands gruffly in Marathi without ceremony. Jalal reaches into the pocket of his pajama and draws out a small, folded envelope. He riffles through a collection of folded papers out of which he plucks his driver's license. He thrusts his long arms out of the window to show the license but does not let it go. The policeman ignores my presence entirely. This is common to most of these interactions between drivers and police. The interaction between practices of surveillance and its refusal at these traffic stops is only between traffic police and those they govern. Most passengers caught in these situations assume that drivers know more than they do about how to handle police. In cases where passengers do get involved, I have observed that they overwhelmingly side with drivers. In my case, while my instinct was to jump out, defend Jalal, and yell at the police, I had learned that this strategy would only harm him and extend the interaction that he was trying to cut short. So I keep quiet and surf the internet on my phone like most other passengers would.

The policeman tries to pry the license out Jalal's hands. "Give me your license," he says raising his voice. Jalal responds politely and firmly, "You said show me the license, I won't give it to you. I am a joona driver, I know my rights." The police officer breaks into a taunting grin. "Okay, give me your registration papers. Yes, yes, you are joona, and your car is also joona, did you know that? You will get a *challan* [ticket] for this joona car." Jalal immediately pulls a ragged piece of paper out of the same envelope. "Joona, yes, but still valid until 2018," he says politely but with a wicked gleam in his eye. The policeman hurriedly gives the paper a look. As Jalal starts to fold the paper and license back into the envelope, the other policeman circles the car. He then appears at Jalal's window and says, "This is a joona car, but your papers are in order. But did you know you took an illegal turn? I am giving you a challan for that." It is not uncommon in these interactions with police for one alleged offense to be challenged by the driver only to become another.

Jalal begins get out of his car to negotiate with the policemen, perhaps even offer them a bit of money as a bribe, but before he is able to put shoes onto his bare feet, one of the policemen hastily scribbles something onto his pad of challans and thrusts it onto Jalal's seat through the open window. "Come to the station and pay your fine," he said hurriedly. Then, in a miraculous act of speed, the policemen got onto two motorcycles and sped away. There was no request for a bribe, no negotiation, just a piece of paper that signaled a sense of authority for a violation that was murky at best. As Jalal gets back into the car, I ask him concernedly about what he is going to have to do. He breaks into his characteristically toothy grin and says defiantly, "What will I do? I will tell you what I will do, and I am shouting out loud about what I will do. I will throw this challan into the gutter [English term], just like I have thrown all my challans into the gutter. This challan is *nalla* [fake], only given to scare me. But I am joona here, and that is one thing about being a joona driver; joona drivers have a lot these nalla challans and we can tell the nalla from the real; mostly they are all nalla, so where do they go? In the gutter."

"Won't you be caught if you don't pay off your challan?" I ask. Jalal reassures me, "Any other driver would become scared by this nalla challan and would go to the police station and pay some money. But joona drivers, no, we know fake from real. So we take the challan and keep driving until we find a gutter." Incidents like these are common on Mumbai's roads. They are important markers of how drivers deploy joona claims to challenge the immediate authority of the police. They also illustrate how drivers refuse characterizations of obsolescence that are rooted in the judgments of sight that motivate police to pull them over.

Notably, debates over obsolescence and decay have a deeper history. For example, British colonial governments regularly deployed temporal discourses of obsolescence and decay in their colonies. Allusions to decay, particularly to intersections between decay and aging of objects and people connected to urban transport, are stark in classical literary texts from the British colonial period and news media in colonial Bombay. These literary and media texts exemplify trajectories that discussions of transport obsolescence took in colonial cities.[6] They also tie the British colonial governments' management of urban obsolescence as a politics of time that privileges vision to the claims of joona, the off-modern, multisensory experience of time in the contemporary period.

DIRT AND DECAY AS STRATEGIES
OF BRITISH COLONIAL DISCIPLINE

Charles Dickens's first published fiction, *Sketches by Boz*, provides an early literary glimpse into the hackney in mid-nineteenth-century London. Dickens writes specifically about how hackney coaches went from being vehicles of genteel and "private" use to a "degraded" place in the public life of the city at the taxi stand. Here are some excerpts from the text:

> Why should hackney coaches be clean? Our ancestors found them dirty and left them so. Why should we, with a feverish wish to "keep moving," desire to roll along at the rate of six miles an hour, while they were content to rumble over the stones at four? (Dickens 1894, 76)

> [B]eside a cab's lacking that gravity of deportment which so peculiarly distinguishes a hackney coach, let it never be forgotten that a cab is a thing of yesterday and that he was never anything better. (Dickens 1894, 78–79)

Dickens's insistence that "hackney coaches, properly so called, belong solely to the metropolis" (75) highlights connections between early wheeled mobility and urban life. These connections were re-created, if reshaped, in colonial cities like Bombay. References to the fall of taxis from gentility to decay were common in literary fiction on Britain, its colonies, and postcolonies from the late nineteenth century onward. Another example is V.S. Naipaul's celebrated novel *A Bend in the River* (1979), set in an unnamed country in twentieth-century postcolonial Africa. Naipaul describes how colonial norms of "disinfection" of public service vehicles like taxis emerged when other realities of decay became ungovernable.

> Nobody wanted to move that rubbish. But the taxis stank of disinfectant; the officials of our health department were fierce about taxis. And for this reason. In the colonial days public vehicles had by law to be disinfected once a year by the health department. The disinfectors were entitled to a personal fee. That custom has been remembered. Any number of people wanted to be disinfectors; and now taxis and trucks weren't disinfected just once a year; they were disinfected whenever they were caught.
> (Naipaul 1979, 87)

In late nineteenth-century Bombay, bullock carts were used for goods, and horse buggies or hackney carriages for passenger conveyance. The latter went through material modifications to preserve distance between bodies of British passengers and native drivers. Buggies built for two riders (one of whom was the driver) were early modes of taxi conveyance. Passengers sat next to drivers, creating discomfitures of class. Later, carriages were modified to put drivers on a perch in front of the two passengers. This allowed two passengers to travel more comfortably. The *Times of India* reports that this stabilized the discomfitures of class and person: "It was a distinct advantage to each of them [passengers] that he did not have to sit cheek by jowl with a *jehu* whose person and wardrobe alike had but the most superficial acquaintance with soap and water" ("Hackney Carriages" 1897).

While Europeans practiced segregation from natives in urban interactions, modes of transport were sites where practices of segregation were forcibly broken down. The expressed disgust over native bodies and contamination in colonial urban environments was important to how the British colonial state dealt with urban problems (McFarlane 2008). Bodies and behavior of drivers were discursively marked outside the *modern*. Soon European notions of hygiene and cleanliness, and discourses of dirt and decay, were also applied to carriages. Buggies were labeled as unhygienic and "Ladies were reluctant to receive visits from cavaliers who swaggered up to their bungalows in such unsavory vehicles" ("Hackney Carriages" 1897).

Horse-drawn Victorias, or *gharries*, appeared in Bombay in the 1880s (Dwivedi and Mehrotra 1995). Victorias were hailed as modern artifacts of transport that would supersede the outdated and dirty buggy. They were initially greeted with fanfare, as they arrived to replace its "despised predecessor" ("Hackney Carriages" 1897). However, enthusiasm over Victorias as positive successors to buggies quickly waned as talks of dirt and decay reemerged: "How often do we step into even a tolerably well-appointed Victoria? To anyone fresh from the luxuries of London, the untidy and probably ragged cushions, the worn and soiled upholstering, the roughness of the springs, and the general air of neglect pervading the lamps, trappings, and other paraphernalia, there is borne an impression that human nature in the East must be remarkably long suffering" ("Hackney Carriages" 1897).

Indian horses were not spared either: "Emaciated, half-starved, and quite unable to do the work that is required of them. . . . It is by no means an unknown experience for a horse to drop dead when urged to draw a very ordinary road up Malabar or Cumballa Hill and be unable to proceed until the charioteer has descended from his box and gone through some mysterious maneuvers with his equine friend's legs, endeavoring apparently to force each in turn into the horse's body" ("Hackney Carriages" 1897). The sad state of horses intertwined with the "lack" surrounding the behavior of men who drove carriages or buggies. It was common to link antiquated, obsolete vehicles with an antiquated, less "civilized" comportment of drivers.

Even in the late nineteenth and early twentieth centuries, police constables stopped hackney drivers and fined them by claiming that horses and carriages were badly looked after, too old or diseased, and unfit for the roads. Further, murkiness between bribes and "fines" taken during police patrol, which persists for drivers today, has historical precedent: "Places might be named within a few hundred miles of Bombay castle, where the inquiring policeman will submit to receiving an insult of four to eight *annas* to let the offender go" ("Hackney Carriages" 1897). Several press accounts I came across attributed the low standards of Victorias and the bad health of the horses to the fact that Indian passengers (unlike English ones) bargain with *gharrywallahs*. Giving them less than the fixed, legal fare reportedly lowered their earnings and capacity to maintain Victorias according to London standards.

The narrative that distinctions between Indian and British customer practices were so great resulted in a division of Victorias into two classes—superior vehicles charging a premium fare and second-class carriages with lower fares. Carriages charging lower fares were slower, with lower requirements for upkeep and upgrade. This fare structure was based on the assumption that second-class carriages would be used only by Indians whose desire and needs for speed or technological advancement lagged behind those of Europeans. This created a classing of vehicles operating as though in different *times*, as much as they traversed different spaces at different speeds. Division of public conveyance into "classes" produced new practices of licensing and regulation. Despite attempts to standardize taxis to mirror practices in Western cities like Paris and London, the debate over "classes" of public conveyance continued to reappear. Relatedly, differentiation of "natives" from the British continued not simply as a spatial problem but also as a temporal one.

In this context, we see that discursive and governing practices were undergirded by assumptions of defect, backwardness, and lag in this early period of wheeled passenger mobility in colonial Bombay. In the age of motorization, this assumption was recast rather than removed.

MOTORIZATION OF BOMBAY'S TAXI TRADE

While motorization appeared in colonial Bombay between 1908 and 1909, drivers of horse-drawn *gharries* continued to ply their trade until almost a decade later. This meant that old and new technologies continued to exist side by side. The first motorized taxis came to Bombay through Paris-based, Belgian syndicate Baron Baeyens. The history of export of motorized taxicabs out of France and into other parts of Europe, and connections between European capitalism and automobility, have been studied extensively by transport historians (Mom 2003). However, this historiography ignores that non-European regions were importing automobile technology at the same time. Similarly, while the impacts of automobiles on European and Anglo-American societies are widely heralded, transport historians only limitedly acknowledge the impact of the early automobile in other places.

Indeed, the automobile had significant, if divergent, impacts and trajectories outside the West. The French began exporting cars as taxis to the East at the same time they were exporting them to the West, and motorized taxis came to South Asia at around the time they began plying the streets of London and other European cities. People grumbled that it was a French, rather than a British (or Indian) enterprise that brought motorized taxis to a British colonial city. Printed reports of the arrival of motorized taxicabs focused on quality of cars, behavior of drivers, and capacity of meters to set fares accurately. The four-cylinder cars were similar to those already on the roads in London and Paris. In London, the General Motor Cab Company had similar vehicles to those in Bombay. Therefore, the arrival of motorized taxis was a symbol of progress that put Bombay on par and *in time* with modern and cosmopolitan Western cities ("Taxicab in Bombay" 1909). There was also the promise that cars would be put in the charge of a "thoroughly reliable driver" ("Taxicab in Bombay" 1909). The drivers of these motor cars were to receive strict training under "experts" and undergo a practical exam by the police commissioner's Motor Vehicle Inspection Department. It was only after this test that they could be granted certificates and a motorist's license for a public motor vehicle. There was also the guarantee that cars would be well-maintained and that a "European" engineer would always be in charge at the garage ("Taxicab in Bombay" 1909).

Maintenance at this stage was a specialized form of surveillance, practiced by hired mechanics but under the supervision of a powerful authority.

Motorization also brought new laws and regulations. The Motor Vehicles Act of 1914 was the first of such regulations. The Motor Vehicles Act gave wide powers to the police commissioner to set rates of carriage and certify licenses. The commissioner of police and his delegates had sole powers over fares, deciding on the viability of different classes of taxis and on the procedures for inspections. The Public Conveyance Act of 1920 extended these powers to the police commissioner (and his delegates), making his office singularly responsible for denying licenses. While the Motor Vehicles Act regulated motor vehicles more broadly, taxis became key targets of this legislation. The Motor Vehicles Act set the standards for the conditions of car maintenance, road behaviors, and conduct of the drivers. The focus on behavior, conduct, and upgrade of cars persisted in subsequent amendments to the act; the most recent amendment was in 2019 where road safety took center stage.

The Motor Vehicles Act put a heavier burden of motor taxes on taxis than on private cars. The justification was that taxi drivers use roads and spend more time on them than private owners do. This is the common logic of what economists call *externalities* (Callon and Rabeharisoa 2003) of automobile ownership. It is based on the logic that the true cost of a car should include paying for the infrastructure of roads and their regulation, for the costs of medical bills for those harmed by the car, and for the cleaning up of the environment polluted not just by use of the car but also during its manufacture. However, for professional drivers, the externalities collapse onto the owners of the cars themselves as extra costs—while everyone bears the brunt of Mumbai's infrastructural chaos, policing, and pollution, taxi drivers bear it even more. Moreover, taxi drivers had to pay taxes in advance and annually—which none of them had the means to do given the unique daily rather than monthly or annual temporalities of accumulation of money in the trade. Therefore, the taxi trade has long been a form of modern automobility that lived alongside other, joona spheres of value accumulation.

OBSOLESCENCE AND THE MODERN, POSTCOLONIAL CITY

India gained independence from the British in 1947. By the 1950s, permit-granting powers were transferred from the police commissioner to the Regional Transport Authority. Therefore, regulatory and policing bodies were materially separated, but their functions and powers remained inter-twined. By 1947 the city government introduced the "driver-owner-scheme." To rid the taxi trade of financiers and black-market purchases of permits by racketeers, elected representatives encouraged taxi drivers to form cooperative societies. Cooperatives procured permits for members who were owner-drivers rather than financiers ("Taxi Drivers Co-Ops" 1959). New regulatory frameworks and credit and cooperative societies were set up to help drivers get out of the clutches of predatory speculators, enabling drivers to enter an age of individual technological ownership. It also allowed them to develop technological intimacies with their cars through mechan-ical upgrades and maintenance. Cooperative ownership of taxis became a hallmark of early postcolonial India. During this period, Premier Automo-biles began mass production of cars in India. The Premier Padmini, their flagship model, was based on a 1950s Fiat design. The Premier Padmini was marketed as India's first "luxury" car. This model and nomenclature became the symbol of a nationalist, "indigenous" car. Taxi credit societies and coop-eratives were encouraged to provide low-interest loans to drivers to sup-port mass production of the Padmini. Drivers in my research came of age during this time. By the 1970s, kaalipeeli, Padmini taxis were everywhere.

Premier Automobiles and the Indian government were keen to buttress the domestic automobile market. To this end, they created regulatory con-texts and financial incentives for taxi drivers to purchase Padminis. As a result, by the 1970s, the Padmini became the only taxi on the roads in Bom-bay. These were manufactured until Premier's manufacturing plant closed in 2000. When production of Padminis ceased, the challenge of procuring spare parts gave rise to several new enterprises in taxi-driving communi-ties. Mechanics would buy smuggled parts from Japanese cars sold in Bombay's *chor-bazaar* (thieves market) and refurbish them to fit Padminis. This refurbishment and upgrade has continued. The knowledge of how to upgrade and fix the car and to creatively incorporate technologies from dif-ferent times and places into the Padmini became important to how joona drivers came to see themselves as technological experts who could counter charges of obsolescence.

For example, Habib's cousin Rahim speculates sadly on his own car that was recently called in for a demolition because it no longer complied with age regulations. Pointing to his nephew, who runs a mechanic shop in the neighborhood, Rahim says, "We have put in a new engine, a new taillight, new brakes, and a new CNG tank. Everything is new, but they have decided it is too old, only because it looks old. Tell me really, what was the real age of this car? Is it joona or is it not?" Rahim raises a critical question here about age and aging that clearly aligns with Boym's notion of the "off-modern." It is an artifact that represents multiple past and present modernities that make it fit for the future. From the indigenously produced and distributed car to the conversion of taximeters in the 1960s to the metric system and decimal coinage, to upgrading of engines and fuel capacity from petrol to diesel, to CNG, the kaalipeeli as both joona and technologically tinkered has become symbolic of what is temporally unfinished, unsettled, and possible in postcolonial India. It is a remarkable example of how, as time goes by, an object of technology is reworked into the local system. This is what engineer John Powell refers to as a condition of "maintenance by constant repair" (Powell 1995, 12). The openness of the Padmini to constant repair is arguably why, despite over a decade of efforts to bring the taxi trade in line with a standardized, rationalized vision, the tinkering with dates, and the tinkering with cars and regulations continues to animate Mumbai's transport politics.

REGULATORY PRACTICES IN CONTEMPORARY MUMBAI

Until the early 1990s, the Indian economy was protected from foreign investment. By 1991, the central government formalized a policy of economic liberalization. Broadly, liberalization instigated monetary and industrial reforms aimed at jumpstarting growth through attracting foreign investment and opening up consumer markets. An early marker of liberalization was the encouragement of Indian companies to set up partnerships with international car manufacturers to create more options for Indian car buyers. Since the taxi market held the promise of bulk sales, it was a particularly important segment for car manufacturers. At the same time, as India tapped into broader conversations on air pollution and emissions in the wake of the Rio Earth Summit, taxis became central to conversations on pollution. Until then, officials at the Regional Transport Office clandestinely passed diesel engines even when they did not comply with emissions tests. The Transport Authority and police are infamous for allowing regulatory compliance to slide in return for bribes. Discourses of obsolescence serve both bodies well since obsolescence is deployed to move along this economy of everyday bribery (Anjaria 2011; Gupta 1995).

Ambiguities over what makes a taxi old means that authorities and police can pull drivers over and slap them with a charge that something on the taxi does not comply with age. Drivers, on the other hand, acknowledge that the car is noncompliant but that they themselves are joona and therefore have right to drive a joona car and have the right to be a joona driver on the road. During my rides with chillia drivers, joona drivers like Habib and Nawaz, who pick up regular passengers in the same general areas, have amiable and familiar relationships with the traffic police officers on their beat. For these men, a traffic stop solidifies the relationship between driver and officer through a small bribe and assurances that there will be no further action for several months. Or as we saw in the case of Jalal's declaration that the fake traffic challan belonged in the gutter, it is a way of renegotiating relations of knowledge between drivers and police. Additionally, Regional Transport Offices around the city rapidly became centers for petty intermediaries or *dalals* (brokers) who helped drivers navigate murky grids of permitting and licensing structures of the state for a price. Taxi drivers see them as necessary and more reliable evils than state officials to help them move paper and politics around. These *dalals* would fix dates on forms that extended the life span of cars beyond mandated calendrical dates.[7]

By the early 1990s, as narratives of pollution became prominent, kaali-peelis were cast as highly polluting. By the mid-1990s, the state minister for transport instated "pollution control drives." These were checks conducted through the Regional Transport Office to identify and fine vehicles that did not comply with Pollution Under Control (PUC) guidelines (Naik 1995). While the late 1990s and the early 2000s saw creation of new government cells for monitoring of pollution, this period also saw the rise of middle-class citizen groups and environmental lobbyists (Baviskar and Ray 2011) who got involved in antipollution campaigns. Several citizens formed watch-dog groups called "flying squads," reminiscent of practices of disinfection that Naipaul notes in postcolonial Africa. However, here, middle-class citizens rather than bureaucrats took the place of the formal state (Anjaria 2009). These squads partnered with police to identify and impound vehicles that "looked" like they were polluting (Devidayal 2002). These were usually cars that appeared *out of time*, usually models of cars that were associated historically with India's preliberalization (pre–1991) period. Since car ownership in India was still the privilege of the wealthy and well-connected, or else of government agencies, it was difficult to charge these groups with noncompliance. Therefore, older cars, driven by government officials and on official duty fell outside the government's surveillance, but taxis did not. As a result, it was usually taxis that were most subject to heavy citizen policing. Disinfection as the modality of governance of public service vehicles in the colonial period found new expressions in these twentieth-century environmental debates over pollution.

In response to pressure from environmental action groups, the Transport Authority decreed that taxis convert to the less polluting and cheaper fuel of the future, compressed natural gas (CNG). Negotiations between the Regional Transport Authority and the Taximen's Union led to a resolution that drivers would install CNG tanks through a phased approach. Since the cost of CNG is lower than petrol or diesel, drivers agreed to the expense and effort of conversion. However, conversion kits were in short supply and it took almost ten years for all drivers to receive conversion kits. During this time, taxis operated within different technological/energy domains. Some were able to fit their taxis with CNG conversion kits. Others were pulled over by police and subjected to fines unless they were able to provide evidence that they had applied for a conversion kit. Finally, by the early 2000s, all taxis in Mumbai were running on CNG.

CNG demands increased rapidly as other public transport vehicles such as buses were also demanding CNG. Because these were run by government-affiliated agencies such as the BEST (Brihanmumbai Electric Supply and Transport), these vehicles reportedly got priority over the owner-operated taxis. The limited numbers of delivery stations were unable to keep up with all the demand. The landscape of the city continues to be marked by long waiting times at CNG refueling stations. Long lines of cars extend out of the CNG delivery centers and onto the road of moving traffic. These lines where taxis are at rest make a naka out of the road for certain times of the day. During these waits for CNG, drivers sleep or eat their packed lunches in their cars. Some get out of their cars and walk around talking and socializing. Others get out and walk into the delivery center to sit in its shade. Drivers often make decisions about the rides they will accept and those they will turn down based on how close the destination is to a CNG filling station. This has added to complaints from impatient passengers over commute times and difficulties of finding a taxi, adding to what union leaders call the "public relations" problem of the city's taxi trade. The move to CNG in particular, highlights important temporal contradictions. On one hand, moving toward this more advanced and efficient fuel brought drivers in line with energy futures. However, on the other, it also caused tremendous inefficiencies and delays.

Nawaz, a chillia driver with whom I worked closely, agitatedly explained it to me:

And just because the car is joona we do not have the *right of refusal*. Just the other day, I refused to take a passenger to where he wanted to go. It was 4:30 p.m. I knew that I would have to stand in line at the CNG station to fill gas and then go in another direction to give my car back to the other driver for the evening shift. In Mumbai's traffic who knows how long all that can take. It could take one and a half hours or it could take three hours. If I had taken that passenger, I would have been stuck in the city forever. But he was so angry and said he would complain about me. He shouted at me saying, "What more can I expect from a joona taxi driver like you." Ola-Uber drivers have the right to just refuse or take a ride on their app and the passenger never knows who has refused and who has not. For us, because we are in the public and not on an app, refusal means we are no good and need to go away.

Nawaz's reflection on connections between moral discourses over age and labor refusal is significant. In the volatile debates over the problems of Mumbai's taxi trade, the matters of age of the car and the refusals of drivers are two of the most prominent. It is what the media reports most often, what passengers complain about most often, and what drivers experience as the primary sources of opposition, first to Padminis and later to all kaalipeeli taxis. These problems are tied to each other in public discourse. They also seem to reflect the marriage of ideas about urban progress with those of labor consent. Refusals of the past and refusals of labor are therefore inversely related, and both are tied to different articulations and practices of time.

AMID THE RUINS: DECAY

In the intense heat of another Mumbai summer, I spent several afternoons at the large grounds of the Regional Transport Offices (RTO) in Mumbai. While the RTO is a place where the business of transport takes place, such as procurement of driving licenses, transport permits, driving tests, approval certificates for cars, trucks, and buses—the business of the life of mobility—it has also become a place of abandonment for obsolete vehicles. From the abandoned kaalipeelis and the cars of fleet companies that entered the industry surrounded by both hope and refusal but that now lie abandoned along with Padminis, one can read, almost in the archaeological sense, the obsolescence of different iterations of the taxi industry over the last decade. Boym (2017) reminds us that ruins are central to thinking with an off-modern sensibility. While ruins may be interpreted as "col-lapse," they are far more important as remainders and reminders. I made regular tours of the ruins of discarded taxis over many years. This allowed me to see the temporal ruptures of the trade in stark material terms. The vari-ous cars that were once used as taxis and then discarded here illustrated both the past that *could have been* and the future that *never took place.*

The abandoned ruins of taxis at the RTO are surrounded by a rich vari-ety of other scraps of waste and abandonment. One particular car from Tab-cab, one of the fleets that were supposed to lead the way as Mumbai's Singapore model, bares the entrails of its mangled, rusted engine. Under its crumpled bonnet are layers of both human-made and natural waste. Dried leaves and pigeon shit share the insides of the car with plastic cups, bags, and even an old pair of worn pants that look like someone walked all over them in boots covered in cement and paint. These are remains of another kind of labor, perhaps. A jumble of old paper, discarded documents from various divisions of the RTO, orange peels, and other dried-up food have accumulated under the bonnet and inside the car. One of the RTO offi-cials comes out of his office, still chewing the last morsel of his lunch, and walks up to this car with an open bottle of water. He takes a large sip of water, rinses his mouth vigorously, and spits the water into the open bon-net of the car. He then washes his hands into the car, tosses the bottle care-lessly behind him and goes back inside without a second glance. The bottle lodges gracefully into the crevices of the car's torn fender. Adjoining these ruins of Tabcab, now a struggling fleet taxi company, stand two abandoned kaalipeelis. One is a Padmini and the other a van made by the company Maruti, another model of car that has been discontinued. Crouching inside the Maruti van, a young man, who tells me he is a recycler, is scraping around and under the car looking for anything of "value," he can find. He is desperately sure that he can find something here that can give life to some-thing else, or something that can make him a bit of money to feed his fam-ily. This ruined, abandoned kaalipeeli has a sticker on its side window that cheerfully declares, Chalo Haji Ali (Let's go to Haji Ali), poignantly remi-niscent of an earlier and more hopeful time when the taxi probably plied to this famous Mumbai attraction, the shrine of the Sufi saint Haji Ali, which is one of the most-visited tourist spots in Mumbai.

A few feet away, a young man scrolls through his phone as he lounges in the backseat of the other Padmini kaalipeeli to escape the searing afternoon heat as he waits for a friend to finish his driving test. These abandoned cars, rendered obsolete by several instantiations of the taxi industry, cease to be what they were meant to be and have become something else entirely—a garbage receptacle, a washing sink, a source of raw material, a waiting room—enablers of other kinds of laboring even as they are abandoned, dying, joona, and still. What is also intriguing is that these joona cars sit in ruins on official property where the licensing and permitting of new taxis, and testing of the health and compliance of these new cars, proceeds frenetically from early in the morning to late every evening. What was, what is, and what could be all exist in this space together.

TIME, SPEED, AND GOVERNANCE

In the midst of the turmoil over phasing out old taxis, confusions over age, the discordant ages of different parts of the taxi, and the varied understandings of time, the question of road safety crept into the discussions through another temporal debate—the matter of speed. What it means to be *out of order* and obsolete became intertwined intriguingly with the problem of the *disorder* of speeding. While speed in other contexts is tied to technological modernity (Virilio 1986), in the case of Indian roads, speed became synonymous with backwardness and disorder. The debates over the problem of speed were intertwined with a new piece of technology known as the "speed governor."[8] In 2015 the central government passed a law that commercial vehicles like buses and trucks be fitted with speed governors to solve what was ascertained as the main problem on India's roads—speeding. By 2017 the requirement for speed governors was extended to cover taxis. The mandate required all buses, trucks, and taxis in India to purchase this device in order to pass annual inspection. The speed governor is intended to limit the speed of trucks and school buses to forty kilometers per hour, tempos (light commercial vehicles) to sixty kilometers per hour, and taxis to eighty kilometers per hour. These limits are based on curious (mis)understandings of how vehicles move in India. When I mentioned this to one the leaders of the taxi union, he angrily recounted the rather vexed story of speed governors.

The rumor circulating among drivers (and possibly initially floated by the taxi union, as this is where I heard it first) is that someone affiliated with a small technology-manufacturing firm in Kerala started a foundation known as the Suraksha Foundation (Safety Foundation). This foundation was tasked with collecting data on India's roads. The main finding was that the biggest danger on India's roads was speeding. The foundation filed an order in the high court of Bangalore to make a new device called a speed governor that was to be mandatory for all commercial vehicles. The only company manufacturing these was to get all the contracts for supply. When the mandate was passed by the Karnataka High Court, the manufacturing firm filed a case with the Indian Supreme Court. The Supreme Court reportedly went along with the mandate, and by 2017, taxis all over India were required to have speed governors. Mr. Q, the leader of the Mumbai Taximen's Union declared, "This foundation only exists for purposes of helping the company sell speed governors that cost each of us three thousand rupees. The courts just said yes without thinking. If you think about it, if a lorry has to drive with goods from Mumbai to Delhi at forty kilometers per hour, how will you ever get there? And which taxi in Mumbai can run at eighty miles per hour anyway? And so many of our taxis will have to be retired soon, so who wants to spend three thousand rupees to put the device in when the car will be scrapped in two years? But the drivers are trapped because they have to show they have the speed governor if they want to pass their inspections every year."

The shortage of speed governors on the market mirrored the shortages of the CNG conversion kits a few decades earlier. The taxi union filed a petition with the Mumbai High Court asking for an extension for Mumbai taxi drivers. This extension remains in effect. Drivers complain about how this is just another way for technology firms to make money rather than a serious mandate to target road safety. The views of drivers of Padminis, and other older cars in particular, are well represented by the chillia driver Hamid's astute observation when he says, "Speed governors are just another way for the police and the government to target and gain money from joona cars and joona drivers. You tell me this, can my joona kaalipeeli ever go at eighty miles per hour? But I still have to have a speed governor, and if I don't, then I pay a fine. This is the state of our roads. The cars that move the slowest are the ones that are fined the most for speed. What kind of world is this?"

Driver debates over speed governors revolve around its irrelevance in the tangle of Mumbai's traffic, where neither speed nor indeed distance are modalities of measurement at all. Taxi drivers experience their journeys in terms of the "times" it takes to get to their destinations, which has little to do with either distance or speed. The snarls of traffic, the daily contest over who gets to move on what roads and where, define the experiences of driving in Mumbai far more than speed does. The disjuncture between experiences of a motoring life based on time and that based on distance and speed have become particularly evident in the lives of those who drive for the platform-based Uber and Ola. Ola and Uber in India have incentive structures that reward drivers who drive the longest distances and accept the most rides over a certain period of time. However, traveling distances in Mumbai takes exceedingly long periods of time; if a driver accepts a ride that helps him travel a long distance, the time it takes him to do so prevents him from taking on additional rides. If he takes on several shorter rides to save him time, he loses his incentives for distance. This illustrates how the incentive plans are inherently set up to compete with each other. No driver in Mumbai can gain both incentives even if he sets out do so, because he has little power over the "externalities" (Callon 1998) outside his control.

While speed is, of course, closely related to time, speed itself has little currency or meaning of its own in the taxi trade—the only currency is time. Therefore, a device targeted at governing speed in a place where everyone knows that speed limits are built into the surfaces of the roads themselves is anachronistic and out of place. As Rahim said again and again, "If they want road safety and better driving then do something about the roads. Look at the state of the roads." Indeed while complaints over the "state" of the road is often also a critique of the state itself (Verrips and Meyer 2001), the matter of speed governors brings the temporal questions of age, time, and speed into relief. It is a curious bureaucratic move that subverts the assumed relationships between progress and speed (Virilio 1986). It is based on the assumption that speed is a mark of disorder and backwardness that must be reined in—literally "governed"—by a technological device.

While the high court stay over speed governors was still in effect, I observed the process through which taxis are given a pass or fail evaluation based on their speed. In May 2018, I went to the Regional Transport Office in Tardeo with Hamid, the oldest son of Bilal, whose family I spent a great deal of time with in Pathanwadi (see chapter 4). Hamid needed his license renewed. As we drive to the RTO, I ask him about the speed governor. He smiles and says, "Don't worry, today the speed governor will come out of hiding." Hamid catches my bewilderment as my eyes dart around the car looking for the speed governor. Hamid reaches forward into the passenger-side glove compartment and pulls out a small, gray contraption with several thick wires hanging out of it. It looks to me more like a portable blood-pressure checker than a menacing governor of driver behavior.

As I start to inspect the machine, Hamid goes on to explain, "I just keep the speed governor in my glove compartment and take it out if I need to get the car inspected. Who actually needs a speed governor for speed? If I drive my taxi too fast, even if I can on these roads, do I need a speed governor to tell me this? Am I mad that I would let my entire body be battered from driving fast? I can govern my own speed. This is just for passing the car. So we all just adjust for the passing test and then move on." Adjustments to the material realities of the car are indeed common practices to adjust to the needs of the bureaucracies (Miller 2001; Verrips and Meyer 2001). Newer cars are now expected to have built-in signaling systems, inseparable from the car itself, that alert drivers to speed. However, older cars like Hamid's treat the governor as an appendage, outside and external to the car—a political artifact to help inspections, rather than a technological one. This allows drivers to make easy adjustments that either cut off or temporarily suture the appendage to the innards of the car. Hamid is a skilled mechanic and knowledgeable about the interactions at the RTO that might result in a speed inspection. The periodic attachment and cutting off of the speed governor has become a routine technological as well as political-economic adjustment to his car.

When we arrive at the RTO, Hamid parks his car and walks toward the licensing office while I wait outside in the shade of an outdoor gazebo-like structure. It is open on all sides with a desk piled high with papers. Right in front of this structure is a long roadway with a sign that says "Driving Test Track." A long line of taxis waits at the start of this track. A sullen and serious-looking RTO official with an old clipboard gets into the first taxi in line. He directs the driver into the passenger seat and settles into the driver's seat. Almost immediately, I hear him turn the key roughly in the ignition. The car groans, chugs, and then suddenly lurches forward onto the track. The official slams harder and harder on the gas to make the car go as fast as it can but sadly, the result is louder and louder groans rather than faster and faster speeds. Hamid comes out and stands next to me and chuckles, "They are testing the speed governor, trying to make the car go fast, up to eighty kilometers an hour, but this old Maruti van will die before it gets there." As the groaning car lurches back the other way, a pedestrian steps onto the roadway. The official honks loudly and bellows at him to get out of the way, all the while desperately trying to speed up the weary car that responds with nothing but a sad whimper. He gives up and gets out of the car. He signs vigorously on the paper of his clipboard and gives it to the driver. "Pass," he says, and moves on to the next car that behaves in much the same way. The tester is fast losing faith in his own test.

CONCLUSION

As I observed at the RTO inspection, officials try hard to coerce uncooperative cars to speed up. The groaning and heaving of cars who refused speed became a mundane and rather cynical routine of testing at the RTO. Miraculously, by late 2018, the debates over speed took a strange turn. India's transport minister, Mr. Nitin Gadkari, himself began to express contradictory statements when he declared that he was going to take steps to abolish any limits to speed. He declared that since India was progressing and that the building of new roads and multilane highways were at the heart of Indian progress, it made no sense to *limit* speeds. Instead, Gadkari urged Indians to embrace their capacities to speed into the future. Drivers and their unions, despite their own antagonism to these governors and some relief that they may not have to bother with these, accused India's central government of indecision. So far, the government has made no definitive statement on policy. This presented drivers with yet another hold as they waited for a decision on whether they should bother with speed governors at all—and they continue to wait.

The contradictory discussions over the place of speed is only the most recent signal of the temporal and discursive collisions—the off-modern dynamics—of the taxi trade. Different domains of value are articulated through contradictory experiences of time. On the one hand is the synchronized time of urban obsolescence that operates largely through the privilege of vision, and posits singular, periodized conceptions of time, progress, and modernization. On the other is the multisensory, socially produced time of joona that emerges through sensory practices of labor, biography, repair, and care. The tensions between obsolescence and joona, and between speed and progress, lie at the heart of the broader temporal and moral debates over transport systems. Joona, like obsolescence, is also a temporal, moral, and value-making domain. It is applied to both objects like Padminis and subjects (older, aging drivers) of urban life. Joona is a way of claiming a deep temporal connection to the city at the same time that it signals the capacity of urban subjects to maneuver and navigate Mumbai as experts and agents of a different kind of off-modern future.

4 JAALU

Autobiographies and Automobilities

CHILLIA DRIVERS REPEATEDLY REFER TO HOW THEIR EXPERIENCE of work and life itself unfolds as a *mixture*, a web, or what they call a *jaalu*.[1] Chillia understand jaalu as a complex, shared, and collective arrangement between the genders, the generations, and both lateral and vertical kinship relations between parents, children, siblings, and fictive kin. While men are the ones who drive, women in Pathanwadi do piecework, what they call *maal* (commodity) work. Further, in this pious Muslim community, women are also important religious teachers. Households that are central nodes of maal work and veteran driving, are also those with active religious teachers; the standing of particular families depends on this mixture of men's driving work and women's maal work and religious piety. This is how automobilities and autobiographies intertwine, because kin and women are an integral part of the automobile lives of male drivers.

I use the metaphor of the jaalu as spoken about by chillia to show how people become enmeshed, mixed, and woven into places of work and life. The experience of living this way illustrates how gendered and sensory labor practices shape the relationship between men's taxi driving and women's domestic work. For chillia these connections draw from four key characteristics of the jaalu. First, it refers to intertwined work and life; second, it relies on and materializes in contexts of kin and is gendered; third, it is an openness to complete dependence on others. Lastly, it has fundamentally sensory aspects—people feel and sense its obligations in ways that has material impacts on their lives. Here I touch on each of these aspects and conclude by suggesting that both the visible work of driving and the more hidden practices of maal work and religious education have been key to the flourishing of chillia communities in Mumbai.

JAALU AS OBLIGATION

Jalal's taxi lets out a muffled and raspy cough as it moves into its usual parking spot on the road leading into Pathanwadi. Jalal takes his calloused foot off the clutch and slides it quickly but gently onto the blistered, worn-out brake pedal. His calluses mirror the places where his feet meet the softness of the crumbling rubber and the sharpness of the metal that emerge like small needles from somewhere inside the pedals. The calluses on his feet reflect the callousness of the Mumbai roads that force his feet to move from pedal to pedal, from needle to needle, thousands of times a day. Like other drivers here, Jalal drives without his shoes. This barefoot driving allows drivers to give in to the surfaces of the road and to be able to adjust more deftly to the sudden changes in the road surface or to stop suddenly and maneuver without warning. Jalal keeps his shoes tucked one on top of the other under the front seat as he motors through the city. He puts them on when he has to get out to walk somewhere along his routes and when he gets home. Unlike most of us who encounter the roads of the city through the accoutrements on our feet, Jalal's feet and his shoes know the surfaces of the city differently; his shoes know Pathanwadi and the way to the mosque and the bazaars, and the stairways to the union and licensing offices; but his feet know the roads and the nakas of the city.

Jalal's feet move in concert with his hands. As the taxi gasps slowly into parking position, he quickly moves his left hand to pull at the handbrake as though he knows that the cough emanating from deep within the motor might move the car a few extra inches into the tin fence in front of him, even after the keys are out of the ignition. The road is paved, but the paved surface has broken and cracked open into speckles of ditches and dust. This is neither naka nor road. As Jalal comes to a halt, a puff of dry dust flies up into his exhaust pipe. The car slides to a halt, the dust settles. Both Jalal and the car let out a soft sigh of relief. Jalal does not get out of the taxi. Instead, he opens both front doors, lifts the heavy loads of both legs onto the front seat and then stretches his body outward. He then sits up, reaches under the seat for his shoes, and emerges from the taxi and into the bazaar outside: "While driving around *Bambai* each day, it feels like someone has taken a hammer [*hathaura*] and hammered my body so that each bone is paining. It is the road, it is the traffic, it is the public, it is the noise; the noise of the horns that never stops that is also like a hammer, a hammer on my brain that also feels like it is hammer on my body; really everything on the roads feels like a hammer. But when I come home my body and my soul are relieved."

He sits in his car for a few minutes, almost as though he is shifting from one form of dwelling—that of the road—to another, that of what he calls the jaalu, a place of relief, silence, and soft surfaces.

When I ask him what the biggest source of relief is, he says almost instinctively, "My own *time*."

I ask, "What does that mean?"

He pulls on his old shoes as he says,

See, part of this is that when I come home I feel like I have come back to my own time; I can go to the masjid, and the only noise here is the voice of the *azaan*; nothing is like a hammer here; it is soft and comforting like a *malmal* [soft cotton] cloth. I can control my time here. You might think that there are so many people in my house so on the roads I feel free; but I am not free there, I am only free here. On the road I am on the time of the road, the traffic, and the public. But I am doing the work that my family and my community have done for so many years. The car is my family's so it is also a part of me. So I can carry on my family business; but more than that, this khandani dhandha also gives me control over when I want to stop driving and come home to rest. When I rest, someone else will take this car and hammer his body. So we all know the pain of this *hathaura*. It is a shared car, but it is also a shared pain. This is all our khandani dhandha. It is pain on the body, but it makes us free by putting us in a jaalu, by obligating us to the dhandha.

The taxi dhandha and maal work depend on articulations of kinship and operate through relations of social and gendered hierarchy. These kin relations are also relationships that people actively cultivate with other things, both material and spiritual/theological. Most importantly, both driving and maal work fundamentally depend on the principle of distribution of collective financial risk. Chillia see the distribution of social and economic risk as consonant with their Islamic piety. Sometimes, the weight of fulfilling these obligations of living in the jaalu is too heavy to bear, both socially and economically. Yet this is still the preferred way to live for most chillia. In fact, it is the inability to fulfill obligations that is the heavier weight. For those who fail to fulfill their duties of dekh-bhal, it feels like the weight of economic and social betrayal; it also creates a lonely burden of not being able to make claims to being a *real* chillia. Chillia know well that if their relatedness were to be fundamentally disrupted, it would disrupt their capacity for both economic success and social cohesion. Therefore, the relations of gendered hierarchy and obligation do not diminish or fetter the attainment of full personhood, but rather constitute and enable it.[2]

Obligations in Pathanwadi unfold as sensory practices and experiences. When Jalal says that he shares the hammer of the city with others, he also marks how kinship is about shared pain accrued from the surfaces of the city and shared experiences of these surfaces. This jaalu and the care and dekh-bhal that it produces encompasses those who work and experience things together in this place. However, expectations of care and obligation also circulate out into the city. For example, when tensions between the kaalipeeli taxi trade and the fleet and app-based taxi industries were particularly intense, kaalipeeli drivers and their unions claimed that these services were bound to fail because they misunderstood the role of taxi drivers in a city. They claimed that taxi drivers were not simply transporters but that they had other, moral duties to citizens of Mumbai; and that in return, citizens invest kaalipeeli drivers with their trust, their *bharosa*. In this way citizens of the city also move in and out of the jaalu because of these mutual obligations.

Obligations were understood as duties of care and dekh-bhal of other people along the road. For instance, Jalal often said, "I work for the public. If I have someone in my taxi that falls ill while he is in my taxi or someone on the road has an accident . . . I will immediately rush them to the hospital. Who will do that in the Meru or Ola-Uber?[3] They do not *care* and do not want to get involved. It has become difficult to get involved in accidents these days—even if you are only the one who stopped to save someone's life, you get implicated. But I don't care about the fear of being implicated, all I care about is saving that person's life. What happens when the person regains consciousness? Even if they blame me for the crime, that is okay; at least I saved their life." Many kaalipeeli drivers talked about these commitments, not just toward specific passengers but to citizens of the city more broadly. This commitment to saving lives is not simply discursive. Concrete evidence suggests that taxis are a commonly used form of transport for the critically ill and injured poor and working classes in a city that has a severe shortage of ambulances (Roy et al. 2010).[4] In this sense, Jalal invokes a sense of connection with others in the taxi trade and all those who are vulnerable in the city. These experiences of the city as both proximate in terms of close kin, and distant in terms of citizenry/public, together produce life as jaalu.

CARS, KIN, ENTANGLEMENTS, DEPENDENCE, PAIN

It is a cool and sunny December morning in 2016. Drivers have taken their cars off the road to protest another government announcement about retirement of old cars. Habib raises the hood of his Padmini. Habib and his maternal first cousin, Nafees, who owns a small mechanic shop close by, both reach into the car with dirty towels to wipe off what looks like a combination of oil, rust, and the leftovers of the morning's dew. Habib's two nephews, his sister's sons, are sprawled inside his car with their feet perched on each of the front window frames. Their bodies automatically fold into positions so unfamiliar outside the car but so instinctive in the seat of the Padmini. They know so well the angles of this car and the welts in the front seat where some seat springs slowly dissolved into Mumbai's roads and others erupted like razors into the green velvet fabric. Sprawled in this familiar way, they half doze off, entirely undisturbed by the thumps and shakes that Habib and Nafees periodically unleash, as they wipe and scrape under the bonnet.

Both these younger men were scheduled to drive the car for half-day shifts today while Habib was to help his sister Najma with preparations for the upcoming engagement of her youngest daughter. The family of the groom, related to Habib's wife's sister, was arriving from Palanpur later that afternoon. As a maternal uncle, Habib, along with the older brothers of the bride, was obligated to provide a meal to the family of the groom chosen for his niece. However, Habib had suffered from crippling pain caused by kidney stones for several days. He had been unable to sit for long periods in the car or on the roads. He had chills that made his body shiver uncontrollably; his constant need to urinate made him fear being caught in the snarls of traffic without a bathroom nearby. These are men who have an intimate, almost familial relationship to bodily pain. They live with it, and accept that it is an integral part of their work. Habib's case of kidney stones and Jalal's experience of the road as a hammer on his body are just two examples.

The world over, taxi drivers, truck drivers, and others who drive for a living have high incidences of renal and genitourinary diseases. These diseases are so frequent among professional drivers relative to the general population that diseases linked to what is called "infrequent voiding" of the bladder are medically referred to as *taxi cab syndrome* (Mass et al. 2014). The recognition of how bodies and work are intertwined, and how labor transforms the laboring body, is critical and has been noted in studies of the laboring bodies of factory workers and industrial labor (Baron and Boris 2007; Harvey 2000). Drivers have their work imprinted on their bodies in a different sense. Jalal's calloused and blistered feet are imprints of the breakdowns of his car on the bumps of the road. Perched on the open driver's window all day, his right arm is sun-scorched and intensely darkened by the city's sun. And then there is Habib with the snarls of pain, stones in his kidney like the stones and debris strewn all over the city's roads and nakas. Those like Habib who have been driving for decades have literally accumulated the snarls of urban traffic as deposits into organs of their body. The jams of traffic that have slowed down Habib's car are manifested as stones and deposits that jam Habib's bladder. These deposits are implanted onto his body slowly and unavoidably, much like the smile and the curve of his mouth that he shares with his sister Najma or the dark gray eyes he shares with his oldest son, Mir. They have become part of who Habib is and shape how he fulfills his kin obligations.

On prodding from their mother, Najma, the brothers of the bride had agreed to drive their uncle's car and to give half the earned cash to Habib and keep the other half for their own obligations to their sister. It was a creative and collective way for monetary obligations to flow in the direction of conventional kin obligations. It allowed each of the men with such obligations to use the same car to raise money to fulfill their obligations toward their female kin. However, since the cars are off the road due to another uncertain announcement over age and retirement, Habib is particularly distraught. He is distraught not so much over the loss of income as for the loss of face as a brother. Habib's sister Najma is less worried about the direct financial impact of this potential loss of money, which she said she could always borrow from the mosque or her own sister who lives elsewhere in Pathanwadi. What worries her more is the prospect of dishonor for her sons and her brother in front of others from their village. For her brother, she is particularly concerned that he will be taken down in front of his wife's relatives. "This *uttari* [humiliation] will follow them out of Mumbai and into Palanpur.[5] And if he ever wants to get a loan from people in Palanpur for a new car or something, they will not trust that he can pay them back," she said worriedly.

The practice of raising money and obtaining no-interest loans from other Momins in Palanpur is a common strategy to avoid the prohibited *riba*, or interest. Chillia consider riba as wrongful appropriation and exploitative. Since riba occurs largely through debts, the one who provides a loan is asked to give additional time to the debtor in times of financial difficulty without charging interest. Lending without riba is a *qard hasan*, or an "admirable loan." This kind of loan is equal to a charitable activity (McAuliffe 2002). For chillia, on one hand, these admirable loans are taken from kin in Palanpur to avoid riba. However, these loans also weave village and city into obligatory relation. While Palanpur is talked about discursively in nostalgic terms, this nostalgia operates quite fundamentally as an economic resource. Marriage alliances were particularly important for Palanpuri Momins in the taxi and mechanics trade to sustain connections to the village. In material terms these connections were talked about as cultural and social ties with a native place. However, they were also significant in economic terms since capital from the village supported work in the city and those with shared connections to the village secured possibilities for work in Mumbai.

Calculations over how to raise money and how to maintain relations is a key part of the taxi trade. The cars and the men who drive them, and the women who make and maintain relations that make this work possible, are implicated in this "microcosm of relations" (Strathern 1988, 321). This microcosm of relations is articulated through practices of motoring and mechanics by which men are understood as social and economic subjects, as persons, and as mobile urban workers. However, men cannot do this independently of their relationships with women (Bamford 2004; Bonnemère 2018), or independently of their cars. Further, making and maintaining these relations is hard work and gendered labor of its own, where practices of care are deployed in different ways by both men and women; this care is directed at both cars and people as dekh-bhal.[6] Najma worries about her brother's capacity to keep both an operable car to make a living and flourishing kin relations to address the two forms of dekh-bhal. Further, both cars and kinship relations have to anticipate breakage and breakdown. For cars this presents as mechanical and political breakdown, and in the case of kinship, as social humiliation. For Najma, looking out for her brother's interests is as much about forestalling humiliation and breakdown of relationships as it is about nurturing and producing them.

Habib's body clearly suffered various kinds of pain this afternoon. The first was the excruciating swells that pulsed from the depths of his body, through his back and into his groin before it subsided into nothing only to swell up again. The other was the weighty and unrelenting anguish of shame, anger, and helplessness at being unable to drive that day. He tried to find comfort in the best way he knew, by channeling agitation over his failure to one form of kin toward fixing another—his car. He resignedly but lovingly scraped crow droppings from the bottom of his engine. Other chillia drivers congregated around Habib's car. Bashir, Habib's neighbor, announced to everyone there, "See now the Kaalipeeli is like a *souten* [a mistress] for the government. At one time we were desirable but just like a man who has tired of his wife and wants another, younger, fresher, newer one, the government is tired of the kaalipeeli." Habib looked down into the engine of his taxi, and said quietly, "I hope the government realizes that what they do to my taxi, they do to me, because really, my wife is the government's *souten*, because she is the original lover, joona like me." These slippages between gendered obligations to kin and the discarding and neglect of loyalty by the state are fundamental to how social and economic life is lived as a jaalu and how men and women act in both social and economic spheres.

How, then, is this jaalu made and what does it feel like to live in it?

PALANPUR-MUMBAI: WOMEN, LOCALITY-BASED KINSHIP, AND KIN-WORK

Chillia claim relatedness in Pathanwadi through a shared relationship to the Palanpur region of Gujarat. Anthropologist Helen Lambert (2000) calls this relatedness "locality-based" kinship, while others use the term "village kin" (Marriot 1976; Vatuk 1969) to denote those who have migrated from the same village but might not be strictly related by blood. Many taxi-driving families in Pathanwadi are from the village of Badargarh. However, those who come from other villages but who are also from the greater Palanpur region are incorporated as village kin and provided opportunities in the taxi and mechanics trade through claiming the caste identity of chillia. If people are of the same generation, they are referred to using kin terms like cousin, brother, and sister. If they are of a younger generation, chillia refer to them as nieces or nephews, even if their parents continue to live in Palanpur and are not directly known to the Mumbai chillia. Often this village kinship established with a younger generation of Palanpuris in Mumbai is deployed to generate Islamic, financial loans from their parents in Palanpur, making village kin reliable even if they do not migrate into Mumbai. Further, while neither biology nor blood are determinative in establishing who is village kin, kin terms incorporate both biological and locality-based kin.

Locality-based relatedness helps men's work in the taxi trade in various ways. While women do not participate directly in the driving work, locality-based kinship also arranges the labors of chillia women. Even if women's work is practiced in domestic spaces, their work is inseparable from men's social obligations. Locality-based kinship incorporates women into the same economic and kin relationships that support the endurance of the taxi trade. Since chillia usually marry other chillia from the same village, for chillia women in Mumbai, the presence of other chillia women from

Badargarh tempers the alienation that women feel when they move from natal to conjugal homes. It also provides women opportunities to join and participate in a new urban world of work, leadership in religious education, and expansion of economic and social interdependence that was not possible for them in Badargarh. Over the years, for many if not most older women in Pathanwadi, their natal village had moved with them into the conjugal city. Several have brothers, sisters, and first cousins in Mumbai with whom they continue to have close, supportive, and loving relationships. Younger women marrying into chillia families in Mumbai are happy they don't have to move away from their parents, siblings, and neighbors, and ties with natal families remain strong throughout the lives of chillia women. Most continue to participate after marriage in economic labor and kin-work with other women from natal and conjugal families as well as with women they claim as village kin. Men are collectively engaged in the jaalu of obligations through driving. Women are part of the jaalu through their role in social reproduction and through collective participation in the paid work of Koran and religious education, tailoring, and the piecework of maal. While religious classes and tailoring bring in social and economic capital from local sources, the work of maal is conducted locally but engages with feminine economies of buying and selling of fashion trinkets outside Pathanwadi and in the rest of Mumbai.

MAAL: THE GENDERED WORK OF MAKING
OBJECTS AND MAKING LIVES

Maal literally means *commodity*. Throughout my fieldwork, a manufacturer of plastic and velvet hairclips and headbands delivered bags of clips and hairbands along with packets of beads and sequins to a vegetable shop in Pathanwadi's market. Women pick up bags and drop off completed work at the shop once or twice a week. This labor of transforming dull things into fashionable commodities that other women want to buy and wear is undertaken by groups of chillia women. These collectives who work together consolidate relationships between particular households and usually reflect the configurations of households who also share cars and driving. Those who work together are often, though not exclusively, from the same household. Therefore, it would be more appropriate to call these "relational work collectives" rather than strictly "household-level" economies. Most collectives I was a part of reflected a combination of women who lived in the household in which the work was conducted and those who lived elsewhere in the community.

Men in the taxi trade conform to what is accepted as a pious way of laboring by participating in equity-based rather than debt-based finance (Rudnyckyj 2018). This is reflected in joint ownership and driving of a shared taxi in order to share risk and to assume joint investments rather than individual, monetary loans. Even if one party in this partnership contributes more money toward the car, others do not have financial debts of loans to this person, even though they accumulate other nonmonetary debt and obligations to this contributor.[7] The maal work of women similarly operates according to principles of joint investments and distribution of risk. Individual women are not singularly responsible for the work done. Many women told me that this shared responsibility provided freedom over how to structure their other domestic and kin duties, knowing that others would fill the gaps when they could not. Just being part of the collective meant that one had rights to the earnings no matter how much of the work one individually completed. The earnings from this work are shared equally across all the women in each collective. Women often had arguments with each other over things such as the bad behavior of someone's children, or about how to dress modestly. However, in the nine years I observed and participated in this work, I never heard anyone, even in private or in frustration or anger, directly accuse someone else of not contributing enough to the work or of getting more than they deserved of the earnings. In many cases, where one household unit had more members in the collective, this one family may have received more than others in this distribution, but no one family accumulated too much of the remuneration. This does not mean that women are always happy with what they got or that the money earned from women's work was inconsequential; in fact, women's earnings were integral to household maintenance. When men's earnings from the taxi trade fluctuate, earnings from maal work help to tide families over during uncertainties. Throughout the last decade, when the taxi industry has been uncertain and men have often been on strike, earnings from maal work provided important sustenance.

Often economic links between women in the collective followed and thickened already existing links that men had made through the taxi trade; in others they actively expanded the jaalu by producing new and ever-expanding economic and social obligations between and through families who were not strictly related by either blood or marriage. Further, periodic cracks in the groups of particular women who collaborated on this piece-work were often indicators of the fissures in the relationships of men in the taxi dhandha and vice versa.

Examples from the two households that I moved between highlight the dynamics of economic and social cooperation around maal work. These were the households of taxi drivers Bilal and his oldest son, Hamid, and their wives, Noori and Ayesha.

BILAL AND NOORI

Bilal's father and grandfather had been taxi drivers who lived in the Central Mumbai neighborhood of Byculla before they moved to Pathanwadi in 1970. Bilal married his wife, Noori, in 1972 and they have lived in the same house in Pathanwadi ever since. Noori was born in Palanpur, but since her father and brothers were also taxi drivers in Mumbai, she had lived in Mumbai most of her life. Her parents had passed away, but her oldest brother, Usman, still lived in Pathanwadi and drove a taxi. From the first day I met him, in 2010, Bilal was frustrated with the state of the taxi trade and told me that his body was too tired to be sitting in Mumbai's traffic. He was waiting for both his sons to join the trade; though for various reasons, neither was able to, at least not then. By 2017, things had changed and both sons were driving taxis, though through different kinds of relational arrangements.

Noori and Bilal have five children, two sons, Hamid and Farid, and three daughters, Benazir, Amira, and Bisma. When I began my research, their younger son, Farid, was attending a madrassa (religious school) close to Ahmedabad. I was initially told that their older son, Hamid, was trying hard to get into the taxi trade. However, because of the government clampdown on permits, Hamid was unable to procure a permit. He gave up and took a job as a driver for a real estate developer. At around the same time, Hamid moved out of his family home to live in a rental home owned by his parents just around the corner. This separation of households seemed significant to me at the time. For Bilal, Hamid's choice of career felt like an economic abandonment of the khandani dhandha, even if this was temporary. It also marked a broader social and emotional estrangement between Hamid and his natal family. This abandonment and estrangement was never talked about explicitly, nor was there overt hostility between Hamid and his father. Rather there was a profound and lingering sense of deep disappointment in all their interactions, which Hamid admitted caused him more pain than overt hostility might have. Hamid and Bilal both recognized that they remained enmeshed even if their immediate social interactions were heart-breakingly awkward and unfulfilling. Both men performed their social obligations as always, but with hurt and disappointment. This hurt and disappointment was well known in the community because both men spoke of it to others.

When I later moved to spending more time with Hamid's family, I saw that this sense of betrayal and disappointment had affected Hamid's access to the jaalu that his father and brother were embedded in. He was still part of the jaalu, but was unable to find his way into the complex relationships of paternal love and obligation that his brother had access to. If driving was a hammer on the body for most drivers, for Hamid, not being able to drive as he should have in the hereditary line of labor meant that the hammer also pounded at his heart. He spoke honestly of his broken heart in front of his wife, children, and me. However, I never heard him say anything to his father, and both men and their families carried on with their daily duties of dekh-bhal even if they felt the pain of abandonment and betrayal. Being in the jaalu can be burdensome, though being cast outside it is much harder.

When I first met the family in 2010, Noori and Bilal had their three daughters living with them; however, two of Hamid's four daughters, who were young at the time, would scamper over from their house to spend time with their aunts, Benazir and Bisma, who doted on them. I spent time in both Bilal's and Hamid's households and saw regular and close interaction between Hamid and his sisters and between his sisters and his daughters. I rarely saw any visiting between the parents and Hamid or between the two brothers. The close and warm relationship between Hamid and his sisters seemed to smooth over the economic and social tensions between the households. While the anthropological literature on kinship emphasizes the ties between parents and children, what anthropologist Janet Carsten (1997, 2004) calls *siblingship* or relations between siblings is given less attention. In Pathanwadi, thickening of siblingship was vital to relatedness and was often the basis through which both men and women could *act* in their relations with others (Bonnemère 2018; Strathern 1988).

As is customary for chillia girls, Noori and Bilal's daughters went to a school where the language of instruction was Gujarati, until grade eight. After this, they stopped school to conform to purdah norms. These norms limit girls' access to public spaces as they approach puberty. However, they continued to participate in the women's *taalim*, Koranic religious education in the neighborhood led by senior women especially learned in theology.

This woman-led religious education is important to the circuits of social and economic obligation and expertise that are woven through life in Pathanwadi and the taxi trade.

Noori is a religious teacher and she regularly hosts crowded gatherings of women who come from across the neighborhood to listen to her speak, read from, and interpret verses of the Koran. Noori is a tall and soft-spoken woman. At the last religious *taalim* she hosted, and that I attended in 2018, she sat tall and upright on a low stool while the ceiling fan hanging from the aluminum roof of her home scattered tepid air. As always, her head is covered with a long, maroon-red dupatta that hides her silvery hair and sweeps like a pool of deep roses down over her shoulders and chest. When she is doing the maal work, Noori allows this dupatta to fall and flow off her shoulders with ease. However, in the presence of the Koran, held decisively in her long, slim hands, and with the crush of women huddled on the floor in front of her, her deep rose dupatta clings devotedly to her head and body.

I sit on the floor with at least forty-five women and their young children. There is no more space on the floor for anyone to sit, yet more and more women jam in. Each of us balls our bodies into smaller and smaller pieces to accommodate the growing crush. Soon we are all sitting with our hands closed tightly around our knees, with our shoulders folded inward. Our bodies touch and I feel the warm breath of the women all around me on my hair, my back, and my folded shoulders. I smell the faint mixture of cooked food and perfume from the sea of black burkas (outerwear worn by Muslim women) all around me. No one seems to mind the crush or the close touch of knees and elbows or the proximate breath of others. Noori's voice lilts up and down as she finishes one verse and begins another. Each time she turns a page, she looks up and smiles delicately, and the women line both palms together, raise them to their foreheads, and respond by murmuring *amin* (amen; God keep us).

I do not know the teachings of the Koran, and everything I learned came from these sessions with Noori and others. The reading of each Koranic verse is followed by a rough translation into Gujarati. Sometimes she speaks of obligations to God, and at others she speaks of women's obligations to controlling the modesty of their bodies. As the sermon progresses, Noori's voice becomes louder and louder as though she is exhorting her audience to understand something deeply. Most women have their eyes closed as they immerse themselves deeper and deeper into the world that Noori takes them into. Their young children have either dozed off in their laps or walked outside to play with stones on the unpaved road outside. As Noori's voice rises to a crescendo everyone opens their eyes and raises arms toward the roof in devotion and agreement. Noori stops and closes her eyes. Her long, graceful torso rocks back and forth gently. The room is silent for a split second, and then suddenly the approximately sixty women and children who had rolled and crouched themselves into the tiny room begin to unfold into the world. The rustle of fifty burkas settling back onto upright bodies and fifty niqabs (veils) flipping back over faces fills the room. One or two mothers gently try to rouse their sleeping children. No one else speaks. Some women turn to Noori and murmur "Allah hafiz" (May God protect you) as they float out of her door. Noori stays seated and quiet, watching everyone gather and rustle out of the house and back into the city. Once everyone is gone, Noori's daughters briskly rearrange the house to get it ready for the next order of the day, which is the maal work and preparation of lunch. Noori's house regularly shifts in this way between the rhythms of prayer, commodity work, and domestic work.

Noori's oldest daughter, Bisma, wants to follow her mother in becoming a religious teacher. Bisma was married to a taxi driver but was divorced when I met her. Her husband had beaten her and been unable to consummate the marriage. When things became unbearable, at the urging of her older brother, Hamid, and her father, Bisma requested a *khul* (extrajudicial divorce) (Sonneveld and Stiles 2019). The painful negotiations over Bisma's *khul* were a performance of obligatory cooperation between father and son who put aside their disappointment with each other in the interest of their daughter and sister, respectively. *Khul* is an Islamic divorce procedure initiated by women and through which women can request their husbands to set them "free" from the marriage. Sometimes *khul* allows women to request ongoing financial maintenance (Sonneveld and Stiles 2019; Vatuk 2019). After being set free, Bisma returned to her parent's home and has lived there ever since. Her return was welcomed by her parents and her siblings and the relationship between Bisma and her family is affectionate and loving. Bisma is responsible for running the household. She is famous as an excellent cook and the best chai maker in Pathanwadi. When I began my research, Noori and Bilal's middle daughter, Amira, was recently married to a man who still lived in Palanpur. However, as per what was customary in this community, she remained in her natal home during the first year of marriage. This is customary practice in many South Asian communities. For chillia families whose daughters were married to men who remained in Palanpur, this also served as a waiting period of sorts until men accessed networks of employment in Mumbai. Until these men prove to be pious Momins, and become chillia, which can only be claimed by migrants into Bombay, men with wives in the city have to wait to consummate their marriages.

For young, newlywed chillia like Amira, the anticipation of male employment opportunities and conjugal fulfillment went hand in hand. Usually Palanpuri men moved to Mumbai to access economic networks through their wives' families. When chillia men from Mumbai married women from Palanpur, the women moved to the city after the first year. Despite financial, social, and cultural ties to Palanpur and frequent nostalgia for the village, chillia men and women across generations displayed a deep affinity for the city and a strong desire to move to stay there. In Amira's case, her husband had obligations to his family's agricultural land in Badargarh and she was destined to go to her in-laws' home the following year. Amira did not look forward to leaving Mumbai. She was particularly sad about leaving her sisters and mother behind. She declared, "My heart is attached to the city," and she was unsure how she would adjust to "village life," and to being away from the industrious and collective work of maal that she did with her sisters and mother.

The sisters had a close, loving, and informal relationship with each other and with their mother. This comfort was particularly evident when they worked together on the piecework. Fortuitously for Amira, and much to her delight, in 2014, after living in Palanpur for two years, her husband found a job with a Momin-owned diamond business in Mumbai and the couple moved into a small one-room house close to Pathanwadi. While he was at work, Amira spent all her time at her mother's house and rejoined the household's maal work. Around the same time, her husband's sister married a chillia mechanic from Pathanwadi and moved to the city. She also frequently joined the maal work at Noori's house. In this way, the maal work continues to weave new forms of economic and social relatedness. These do not strictly conform to demarcations between households. Rather, they are intentional and dynamic calculations made by different women as to the economic collective that is most beneficial to their social and economic well-being in the city.

Benazir is the youngest of Bilal and Noori's daughters and was unmarried when I met her. In 2017 she was married to a chillia man from Mumbai who works as a receptionist at a small interior design company in the Andheri area of Mumbai. He has long hours, so Benazir, like her older sister Amira did, until she had children, spent most of her days in her mother's house working with the rest of the family. These networks of marriage, work, and sociality that stretch between Palanpur and Mumbai show that the taxi trade and the associated maal work undergird comings and goings in Pathanwadi. However, they are also part of a broader ensemble of economic, social, and geographical practices that support chillia life. While women make calculated choices about how to arrange their maal collectives, men also can move in and out of several work arrangements before finally settling into the hereditary profession in Mumbai.

For example, in 2014, Noori and Bilal's younger son, Farid, finished his education at a madrassa, got married, and moved back into the house with his new wife, Malika. Malika identifies as Momin but not as "chillia," since her family has nothing to do with the taxi trade. Her father runs a carpentry shop and she was raised in a middle-class Momin housing society nearby. She was educated at an English-language school and was keen that her husband try his hand at white-collar employment. On her urging, he enrolled for a diploma in graphic design. While Malika gets along well with her husband's family, their relationship is lumbered by a quiet tension between her desire for white-collar, class mobility and the obligations that Farid has to his family's dhandha.

Overtly, Farid's family, especially his mother, encouraged his study of graphic design. However, before he finished his course, Bilal announced that he was ready to retire and would like to pass on his permit to Farid. While Bilal's Padmini had three more years before it had to be retired, Bilal had been pulled over multiple times by police who inquired about papers and proof of age of his car. He decided that he would take a loan from a relative in Palanpur to buy a new car. He passed on this new car and his permit to Farid, though he continued to drive the car two mornings a week. This simple act of passing on the permit and the car changed the course of Farid's career and he has become the next generation of drivers in the family. Farid dropped out of his design course and began driving with his father. By 2017, Farid and Malika had a young child, with another on the way. Bilal stopped driving entirely and let Farid take over responsibility of supporting the growing household with his taxi driving. However, because Bilal has financial connections to help others purchase new cars and is famous for his magic touch with machines, he is still summoned to taxi stands as financial adviser and mechanic.

The year 2017 also marked the immediate aftermath of India's November 2016 demonetization where large amounts of cash were taken out of circulation. Dhandhas, like the chillia kaalipeeli trade that depend entirely on cash, were severely affected. Farid spent a lot of his time waiting around for rides that never came. The pressure of dekh-bhal of the growing family was weighing heavily on him. He often talked disappointedly about how he wished his older brother, Hamid, would help out. I knew, however, that Hamid was also stuck in the same cycle. Hamid would wait at the taxi stand until lunchtime. Then he would drive into the city with no fare and try to make a bit of money driving around the city. Sometimes he would find a paying ride back, but most days he came back empty. The brothers rarely talked to each other but they were both mired in a state policy that had severe effects on their capacities to act for themselves and for their families. Finally, when business was very bad, Farid pleaded with his wife to join his sisters and mother with the piecework so that they could produce greater weights of maal together. Malika, whose natal family had protected her from the need to work for money, reconciled herself to the needs of her conjugal family and grudgingly joined the family's maal work.

HAMID AND AYESHA

Hamid and Ayesha live with their four daughters in a house owned by his mother's family a few doors down from his parents. Hamid pays his parents a modest rent. While Hamid's wife, Ayesha, tells me that he moved out because he was making enough money to support himself, over the years I have known Bilal and Hamid, I sensed more to this decision. Hamid was not initially interested in taxi driving, which had caused tension in the family. He worked in a chillia-owned restaurant for several years before he was noticed by a property developer who took him under his wing. He worked for this developer for six years as both his assistant and his driver. However, after being overlooked for promotion, he left the property company. On his father's continued urging, he decided to move into the family trade of taxi driving. However, by now, his father and younger brother were sharing the car and the taxi permit. Because of the clampdown on taxi permits, Hamid could not get a permit of his own. That his father would privilege his younger over his older son caused Hamid a great deal of pain. As a later entrant into the trade, Hamid lacked the collective, financial support that most chillia drivers of his generation had. Despite this, Hamid saw few other options available to him and was able to lease a taxi to help him until he could buy his own.

While Hamid is always ready for work at the taxi stand dutifully each morning, I notice a sadness and sense of longing from him as though he wants be somewhere else but that he is increasingly losing a sense of where to go or how to do anything else. Ayesha senses this sadness in her husband and says that she prays every day for something good to come his way, but that it never does. Hamid is in his late forties and most drivers of his generation already have stable relationships of car ownership or leasing. Hamid struggles outside the jaalu that his brother and father live in. His former job taught him to read and write in English and gave him considerable experience with accounting and finance. Yet even though Hamid thinks he might be able to get a different job, the pressure to maintain social stability with kin overrides his own aspirations for social mobility.

When he decided to join the trade, his brother was already driving his father's taxi and Hamid did not have the money to buy his own car. His sister, Bisma, intervened to help him lease a car from her then husband at an affordable rate. When Bisma's ex-husband flew into uncontrollable rages he would threaten to raise Hamid's leasing fees if she disobeyed him. Bisma tried hard to stay with her husband, not simply for the sake of her marriage but also, she said, for the sake of her brother's capacity to keep working. She knew that he already felt abandoned by his father and did not want him to feel let down by her too. Hamid and Bisma are very close. When Hamid heard that Bisma was being beaten by her husband, he quickly urged his father to help Bisma initiate the divorce and requests for maintenance. Bisma's father-in-law and her father had jointly leased a taxi in the early 1980s before each of them bought their own. They had migrated to Bombay together and had distributed financial risks through this joint leasing for years. However, the breakdown in their children's marital relationship demanded a different kind of spreading of social risk. In the interest of keeping their thick relations cordial, her father-in-law urged his son to agree to offer Bisma some maintenance, which he agreed to. I understood that this support still comes to Bisma, though it has become more erratic since her ex-husband remarried. However, what comes in supports not just Bisma's needs but also Bilal and Noori's household.

Bisma's divorce had a big impact on Hamid's taxi lease. When Bisma divorced and moved back into her parent's home, Hamid's relationship (and finances) with his leaser had to be renegotiated. Unable to bear the awkwardness of paying a man who had mistreated his sister, Hamid gave up this car and looked for other options. Hamid did not want to take a loan to buy his own car. Since most men his age were already in established leasing relationships or collective ownership arrangements, Hamid was lost about what to do. It took him time to find a reasonable car lease, during which time he relied on income that Ayesha and his daughters brought in with their maal work. For a brief period, when his father had a slipped disc and was laid up in bed for months, Hamid shared his father's car with his brother. This allowed him to tap into the family's resources for a short period of time and to move in and out of the jaalu that was already permanently functioning for his father and brother.

Around this time, Hamid's oldest daughter, Salima, got engaged to a chillia man who owned a mechanic shop and a taxi. During the talks about the engagement, Hamid negotiated a reasonable rental for the car, and this is the taxi that he now drives. Chillia commonly commit their adolescent children to marital alliances several years before a marriage takes place. This incorporates people into *imminent* articulations of kinship but *immediate* expectations of obligation. While Salima is betrothed and to be married years into the future, the entanglements—what feminist theorist Karen Barad (2007) calls the *relations of obligation*—materialized between the families much earlier.

Hamid and Ayesha proudly declare that their daughters—Salima, Meena, Nafisa, and Khadija—would be "engineers" if they could be. Ayesha and Hamid's pride in the intelligence and dexterity of their daughters is accompanied by the acceptance that none of their girls could ever actually aspire to a formal profession like engineering. At the same time, they acknowledge that the kind of "engineering" acumen that the girls apply to all their work is not recognized as skilled expertise or generative of value in the more conventional sense. Nevertheless, the proud parents think of their daughters as being as close to engineers as anyone in their circumstances could be and the work is clearly valuable to the family's income and to the respectability of the household.

Salima, Meena, Nafisa, and Khadija are eighteen, sixteen, fifteen, and thirteen, respectively. While the men around them tinker with cars, these girls use their hands and bodies to make other things. Meena is an exquisite sketch artist. She spends hours on her father's cell phone watching drawing lessons on YouTube. Her fingers are perennially stained with black lead from her sketch pencil until she washes them before her namaaz (prayers). Salima, Meena, and Nafisa are all remarkably skilled on the sewing machine and spend their days cutting, designing, and stitching clothes for their family and their neighbors. Salima can stitch a kurta-pajama set in one afternoon. She stitches the white kurta-pajamas that her father and uncle wear to drive their taxis. This is the piece of clothing that is the proud mark of chillia ownership of their means of work. It marks that they are owners rather than employees in the taxi trade. Salima is left-handed and this means that fabrics float through her hands and through the machine at a different angle than for anyone else. According to her mother, while her left-handedness was initially a cause of distress in the family, it gives her sewing a special touch. "You can always tell which clothes were stitched by Salima. She has an *ulta haath* [opposite hand], but a beautiful touch." This dexterity and precision allow Salima and her sisters to work extremely fast on the gluing and designing that is required by the intense and intricate labors of the hand—maal work.

HANDS, TOUCH, AND RELATEDNESS

Bilal's daughter Benazir and I drag two, large, heavy plastic bags down the path from the Pathanwadi market. We are returning from the vegetable shop where Benazir and others pick up their biweekly delivery of dreary, black hairclips and headbands and the packages of sparkling sequins that will be so carefully glued onto them to bring them to life. Twice a week, women walk to this vegetable shop to pick up these clips and to drop off their completed work. The shopkeeper weighs what they return on his vegetable weighing scale. He writes down the weight of the bag and a name on two separate slips, one of which he gives to the woman who brings the bag and one which he presumably gives to the client who will pay for the work. On Benazir's slip I never saw him write anything else other than "7 kgs," with the name of her father "Bilal bhai." At the end of every week, usually on a Friday, as this is when most families cook an elaborate meal, women shop for vegetables and pick up cash payments for completed work. Who delivers the lifeless clips and bands to the vegetable vendor, and who picks up those that are adorned with life and glitter, no one really knows. All that matters is that the cash payments are regular and that the work gets done.

As we dislodge one bag from a jagged edge of the road, the bellow of the early monsoon thunder relieves itself in the first downpour of the year. I hear squeals of both excitement and mild aggravation from everywhere. The excitement comes from young children who emerge buzzing from their homes and the local school to watch the downpour and to catch the raindrops on their outstretched tongues. The aggravation comes from women who dart out of their houses to collect the clothes hung out to dry, or to move the barrels where they store water for the household cooking and chores out of the muddy trickles of rain sliding off their roofs. It also comes from men scrambling out from under the body of a taxi at the mechanic shop as they scoop up the plastic cans of various other liquids and oils to protect them from mixing with the rain.

The romance of the monsoons is legendary in India. It brings cool relief to sweltering summers, and it brings hope and fertility to land and agriculture. But monsoons have an ambivalent place for the urban poor and bring obstacles that other seasons do not. For taxi drivers in Mumbai, monsoon is the most difficult season of all. It floods the roads, and it bores new ditches into the road that cause endless jams and stalls. For Padminis that require fixing and pushing while on the roads, driving in the pouring rain is onerous. The one advantage is that the demand for taxis goes up in the rains since commuters don't want to wait outdoors at bus stops or walk long distances. Though one of the key complaints from kaalipeeli drivers is that while services like Ola and Uber can surge their prices during periods of high demand such as during heavy rains, kaalipeeli drivers cannot.

As the early drizzle turns rapidly into a downpour, Benazir and I run for shelter under the asbestos roof of the nearby *kirana* shop (general supplies store). The chillia shopkeeper, Asif bhai, who is also a major landlord in Pathanwadi, greets Benazir and she greets him back as *chacha* (paternal uncle). Asif moves a stool toward us, indicating to us to put our bags there rather than on the wet ground. "Maal che beta [Is it maal, my child]?" he asks. Benazir nods. Bisma has been standing at the stove in their house stirring fried onions into the dal for lunch. Glimpsing our struggle through the kitchen window, she quickly turns off the gas, throws her dupatta over her head, and shuffles behind the door for an umbrella. She climbs gingerly over the high threshold that marks the entrance to their house and that protects the family from the rush of water in the downpours. Under the shared shelter of her small umbrella the three of us bring the maal home. The work will begin after lunch.

Lunch, as all meals are in households here, is laid out in the middle of a large mat on the floor. The large, communal bowl of dal is placed at the center of the mat as are the box piled high with chapattis and a plate of sliced tomatoes and onions. There are no individual plates or utensils. Instead, everyone takes their place on the mat, picks up a chapatti that they break in their hands and then dip into the communal bowl. Everyone carefully keeps an eye on what others are eating before they go back for themselves to make sure that everyone gets enough and that no one person eats more than others. Occasionally, someone will pick up a slice of tomato or onion from the shared plate. Chillia eat as they live and work, collectively.

Bilal, Noori, all three of their daughters, their daughter-in-law, Malika, and I all sit down to lunch. Malika must customarily observe purdah in the presence of her father-in-law. While she sits cradling her eighteen-month-old daughter in her lap, she holds her dupatta over her face with both hands and does not begin eating until Bilal has finished and retired to the back room for his afternoon nap. Living together in such small and close quarters requires much of this unspoken work and delicate choreographies of gender and generation that respect the hierarchies of relatedness.

After lunch is cleared, the afternoon routine begins—working with the maal. The front room that minutes earlier was the eating area is transformed into a workshop. Everyone knows what to do and has a part to play in this transformation. No one needs to say anything or to give or take instructions. My offers to contribute are accepted politely by everyone. However, even after many attempts, the fact that I am someone who comes and goes in this space means that I am unable to properly learn the embodied judgments required for the work to begin. Despite all the embodied and sensory work that the women do to set up this workshop, placing tables at the right height, kneading the glue to soften it, and checking the glue sticks for their strength, there is nothing instinctual here even if it might look like it. Physiologist Jacob von Uexküll (1957) cautions that when we assume that routine, feminized practices are instinctual, we erase intentional subjects and miss the cognition and knowledge that go into routine work. As media and disability studies scholar Jonathan Sterne (2003) reminds us, when techniques are mastered to become expertise, they begin to look like second nature and ordinary dispositions of the body. The work the women do here indicates a deep sensory knowledge, technique, and skill acquired over time and cultivated carefully. While it is collective work it is also work in which each one plays a part.

Benazir brings out a small, low table and places it in the same place inches away from the window every day. She adjusts it ever so slightly to make just enough space on all sides for four people to sit around the table. She surveys the space to ensure enough surface area for four small pieces of cardboard with six sets of hairclips clipped on. Malika and Benazir open a bag and empty out a huge pile of hairclips. Several small, plastic pouches with sequins also slide out. Benazir looks at the pile of clips, runs her hands over them, and then empties three pouches of sequins onto a small steel plate on the table. She did not count, but the quick caress of the hands tell her exactly how many sequins will be needed for the pile of clips they will work on today. Malika's eighteen-month-old daughter, Saira, toddles around the table. Socialized as I am in the "baby-proofing" social milieu that is American parenting, when I first saw this happen, I gulped in trepidation for what Saira might do to all these glittery things. My initial feeling was that I could make myself useful by watching the baby, the only other person there who might be as ill-attuned to all of this as I was. However, against all my assumptions of what young children do around shiny things, Saira touches nothing. Instead, she walks around the table, jabbering away, and into the back room where she lies down with her grandfather and promptly falls asleep.

Bisma goes to a shelf under the stove and extracts a small cloth bag, which contains boxes of matchsticks and tubes of some unusual-looking, homemade glue. These are the ordinary but vital tools of this work. The matchsticks gently touch the mouths of the glue tubes to catch the smallest amounts of its stickiness. These matchsticks move with each woman's hands to pick up sequins from the wooden block. The sequins are dabbed onto the clips in different shapes and designs until they cleave permanently onto the plastic or faux-velvet-lined clips. As the flurry of the setup settles down, Noori goes to the front door to call out to Naseem and Halima, the daughters of Altaf and Muna, who live in the house just opposite them. Altaf owns two taxis, which he leases out, and a car lubricant business, where he spends most of his time. Both Noori and Bilal refer to Altaf as their brother, though it was not clear to me whether this meant that he is related by blood, shared work, village, or the relatedness his daughters have to the maal work next door. Most likely, all of these forms of relatedness play a part in how he has come to be called brother.

As though they knew that it was time, even before Noori opens the door, Naseem and Halima come bounding out carrying their own table. They walk in, greet everyone, place their table next to the other one and sit down to begin work. While Naseem and Halima have their own table, they work with the same tools as everyone else and with the same bag of clips and sequins. Benazir, Malika, and Bisma all work at one table while Naseem and Halima work at the other. Noori moves back and forth between the tables.

The clips are bare, blank slates and each of the women chooses to create the designs she wants with the sequins. Just as each shared taxi in Pathanwadi moves differently at the hands of different drivers, each of these commodities emerges differently from the hands of each of these women and might appeal to different tastes of the women who will buy them. Benazir and Halima's designs are perfectly geometrical. They place the sequins in lines and along the edges of each clip and make triangles at the top and bottom of each clip. Noori's clips look like strings of light that crisscross the length and breadth of the clips. "Wedding lights so that each day whoever wears this feels as happy as her wedding day," she says. Malika makes small, careful, floral designs. Bisma is the *mehndi* (henna) artist in the family, so her designs are intricate and incorporate flowers and geometric designs. Naseem likes plenty of glitter; she uses up the largest number of the sequins as she paints them all over the clips. Among the women, there are bursts of chatter followed by short cycles of complete silence. All through the chatter and the silence, the women's hands keep moving, sticking, gluing, and tossing finished maal into a bag.

While the labor here is conducted by the entire body, relatedness is produced through the shared work of the hands and by what they touch. Life experience all originates in touch through the mother's touch of the child (Manning 2006). However, at the same time, actual biological or blood relations are less important than the ways in which activities of touch mark and make kin (Manning 2006, xi). The physical touch of the hands among this group of women is crucial to maal work, just as it is to the driving, maintenance, and repair of cars. The women bend over carefully as they work. Their hands seek, search, and appreciate what they touch. Through their hands, and the passing, examining, and handling of the clips, sequins, bags, and glue, the dispersed pieces of maal work become discrete objects that can be sold. The women enjoy this handling as they run their fingers over the different textures of the beads and the sequins and the velvet and plastic clips that these will adorn. There is a sense of comfortable intimacy both with the objects that they work with and with each other. I noticed that much like for their fathers and brothers, who are tinkering with cars on this same afternoon, the women's hands and touch are vital to this maal work. The movement of their hands looks natural and habituated.

However, there is nothing *natural* about the work that these hands can do. Even after years of training and watching I was unable to do much with the maal. Noori was patient with me in her teaching, though in the end, she kindly advised me that I did not have the *aadat* (habit) or the *haath* (touch). I meekly and somewhat embarrassingly took on the duty of cleaning and sweeping the debris rather than creating the maal. The perfection and beauty of each finished commodity that emerges out of maal work is closely tied to how carefully the hands follow the vision that each woman has for her clips. As their hands move, each of the women speak of this vision, and let the others know what they are planning to do. Once in a while Noori and Bisma, as the oldest women in the group, try to nudge the younger ones to save some of the glitter for others or to follow more structured designs. The ease with which Bisma and Noori are able to make their clips look as they had already envisioned them to be indicates that training and expertise are both at play here. This expertise allows the hands to judge subtle differences in texture and form and trains the hands to work with other senses of sight and imagination.

Barad (2012) argues that intimacies are rooted in touch, and that attention to touch is vital to fully understanding how people relate to each other. Touch also marks a sense of reciprocity (Leder and Krucoff 2008). While touch is fundamental to how men create technological intimacies with their cars, chillia women who work together cement relatedness and reciprocity as the gentle actions of touch meet the industrious work of the hands. Women sit close to each other; they hold hands, lay their legs over one another, and help each other stick and glue things. Hands, touch, hairclips, relatedness— all come together here as the women make things that will make money.

At the end of the day, the clips are thrown into the same bag. On payment day, some cut of the money is given to Altaf's household to compensate for Naseem and Halima's work. These are households that are entangled through this work, which has produced and consolidated relations between them. While Benazir is married and moved out of her parent's house into her own house with her husband about two years ago, she continues to come every day to work on the maal with the rest of the collective in her mother's house. She says, "In my house I am alone and there is no work, but here there is work to do with your hands and there are people here so dil bhi lag jaata hai [my heart is also happy]. My heart and my hands are happy this way."

AYESHA AND HAMID

It always struck me that, while Noori's older daughter-in-law, Ayesha, and her daughters did exactly the same work in their house, their jaalu intertwined in other directions when it came to maal work. Theirs is a web spun away from the relations of "blood" to incorporate a range of other women. Ayesha and Hamid's house is always full of people and chatter. Their next-door neighbor, a woman also named Ayesha, spends almost all her time sitting in Hamid and Ayesha's house where she chats with Hamid's wife, Ayesha, and helps her with the cooking. "We are *same name* sisters, actually, no not just sisters, we are twin sisters!" they say

jokingly. Then on a more serious note, Ayesha says, "Actually, we are relatives from the village. There also we were *aas-paas wale* [close by]." This
articulates claims to relatedness as "village kin," while the reference to
aas-paas wale is a claim of closeness and familiarity. Like men who claim
adjacency in the village to cement relations in the driving trade, *aas-paas*,
invoked as both spatial and social closeness, is how these women experience relatedness. It also signals that urban and rural relatedness are intertwined for them. *Aas-paas* might denote someone who lives close by in
spatial terms, but it also denotes someone who is close or near in social or
cultural terms. In Mumbai, these women are literally what we would call
neighbors living next door to each other, though in Palanpur they were
brought up in different villages. Hamid's wife, Ayesha, comes from
Badargarh, while her neighbor, Ayesha, is from Kharodiya. These villages are a few kilometers apart but these women had never met until
they moved to Mumbai. In Mumbai, the women experience a sense of
relatedness through spatial and social closeness. In Palanpur, the proximity of their village and shared cultural history rather than their own material proximity makes them feel this way.

Ayesha, the neighbor, has two grown sons who both drive taxis, and a
five-year-old daughter named Sana. Sana is much loved by Hamid and Ayesha's daughters and they treat her as though she were their youngest sister.
Sana more or less lives in their house during the day and often sleeps there
at night. Hamid is rarely home during the day when he is usually out on the
roads driving. On occasion, he comes home for lunch if he happens to be
close by. This usually means he has not found fares into the city. Ayesha and
Hamid communicate a lot via their cell phones, through which he keeps her
regularly informed about his whereabouts and whether she should expect
him home for a meal. When he returns in the evenings, Hamid usually
spends about an hour in the house talking to his wife, playing the game
Ludo with his daughters, or watching television. On occasion, his sisters
Bisma and Benazir will stop in to talk and to play with their nieces. Around
six o'clock he goes to the mosque for prayers, where he lingers for several
hours, talking to other chillia drivers exchanging stories about their day.

Hamid is a large and physically imposing figure. However, he is soft-spoken and restrained. Hamid and his daughters share an affectionate relationship, though he asks them for forgiveness for letting them down by not
bringing in enough money. In order to compensate for this betrayal, in 2014,
Hamid bought his daughters a television, something they had been agitat-
ing for. Chillia in Pathanwadi do not have televisions in their homes because

they feel television is a bad influence on younger people. Hamid's was the only household that had a television. While the family enjoyed this television, three years later, in 2017, Hamid told me that his father has been urging him to get rid of his television since he now has four adolescent girls in the house and that he should try his best to protect them from its bad influences. The tensions over the television provide an interesting insight into how even though the households were separate, and father and son did not interact routinely, they remained closely tied as *moral men*. Hamid struggled over what to do, particularly because he did not want to disappoint his father more than he already had. When I went back in 2018, the television was gone.

If Hamid is soft-spoken and reserved, his wife and daughters are rambunctious, energetic, and talkative. Hamid floats in and out of the house silently and with little ceremony, while his daughters bounce in and out from school, *taalim*, or the market spiritedly and noisily. One might often run into the sisters at the market where they hold hands as they excitedly browse the silky brocade fabrics at the fabric shop rather than the vegetables that they were supposed to buy. On days when maal has to be picked up at the vegetable shop, all four girls go together, accompanied by the daughter of a neighbor. They are able to bring three bags home between the five of them. On their slip of paper, the vegetable vendor writes "11 kg" and Salima's name. Even in 2018, when Salima got married and left for her husband's house in Palanpur, her sisters still brought the maal home with the slip of paper with her name on it. This paper acknowledged her continued participation in the household's economic reproduction and has anticipated what I now understand will be her imminent return to Pathanwadi with her husband. Just like Benazir in Bilal and Noori's household, who returns each afternoon from her conjugal household to her mother's house to work on the maal, I suspect Salima will do the same.

While in Noori's house the work does not begin until after lunch, the work at Ayesha's house begins much earlier in the day. I suspect that this is because after Hamid's early morning departure, Ayesha's house becomes an entirely female space. This means that the women can bathe in the small bathing area and get dressed in the house at the same time without having to worry about taking turns to leave the house as the men get ready. Also, this is a household where money is tight and there is pressure to get more work done in a day. After the morning's namaaz, while Ayesha and her oldest daughter, Salima, prepare lunch, the other girls pull out a little table, and sit down to work. Ayesha and Salima join soon after, as does Ayesha from next door, and one of Salima's friends, Fatima, who lives around the corner. Fatima is engaged to be married to the cousin of Salima's fiancé and is expected to move to Palanpur around the same time that Salima will. While Fatima will share some of the money from the maal work, she is also cementing a friendship with Salima that will help both of them settle into a new life in the village where they will both soon move as newlyweds.

In Noori's house, the work is done slowly and meticulously, and mostly in silence, partly because Bilal is sleeping in the back room but also because they have less urgency to produce the maal fast. Further, both Noori and Bisma admit that they have to work much slower because their eyesight is deteriorating with age. In Ayesha's house, the energy, dexterity, and exceptionally good, youthful eyesight make the work go fast. Ayesha's house is much smaller than Noori's. The women work in close quarters and all seven women sit close to each other. Their hands and elbows gently graze each other as they dab and glue, and the knees of their folded legs touch each other familiarly as they move back and forth to pick up a new set of clips from the bag. The girls carry on a soft and steady conversation. The five-year-old Sana is asleep on a small, rolled blanket. The two Ayeshas chatter and occasionally burst into loud laughter. Salima playfully taps her mother's knee when things get too loud. Her mother taps her back affectionately and keeps talking. Despite all this talking and laughing, the work gets done extraordinarily fast. Since payment for the maal is based on weight, Ayesha urges the girls to do as much as possible each week to make the bag as heavy as possible. Hamid's financial obligations, and the fact that he does not own his own car and permit, make this household more precarious than Bilal and Farid's. They need to complete three or four bags of maal each week while Noori's collective only has to complete two.

CONCLUSION

> As the spider spins its threads, every subject spins his relations to
> certain characters of the things around him, and weaves them into a
> firm web which carries his existence.
>
> —JAKOB VON UEXKÜLL, "A Stroll through the Worlds of
> Animals and Men"

The spinning of relations and the intertwined work of motoring and maal make up the jaalu in Pathanwadi. Those who are encompassed in the jaalu are those who look after each other, who participate not just in each other's lives but in each other's *being*; they are "mutual person(s)" (Sahlins 2012, 2). Those in the jaalu are also people and things we *touch*, both physically and affectively, who are touched by us, and with whom we can share and exchange our pain, longings, and our work. By paying particular attention to the gendered and sensory dimensions of the jaalu, this chapter has illustrated the important relationship between taxi driving and domestic work. Relatedness of the jaalu is multivalent. It draws on various aspects of kinship and economic ties as well as multiple bodies—the bodies of kin, the bodies of circulation that make this labor possible—and the entanglements of different forms of generating money, savings, credit, and piety. Further, while men's driving is visible, mobile work, the work of maal and religious teaching conducted by women is part of the hidden labors of the city. Both these visible and hidden labors unfold as sensory domains of touch, love, kin obligations, and disappointments between kin. These sensorial and labor practices allow people to become enmeshed, mixed, and woven into work and life—this enmeshment between driving work and maal work is how chillia autobiographies and automobilities intertwine.

5 DEKH-BHAL

Sensory Technologies of Care

SPEAKING OF THE RELATIONS THAT PEOPLE DEVELOP WITH their machines, anthropologist Michael Fisch reminds us that "machines with which we can be in a relationship are machines that can be in a relationship with us. Trustworthy machines do not demand compliance; they are forgiving and ontologically capacious in their capacity to evolve with collective life" (Fisch 2018, xi). In the world of chillia driving, relations of trust between chillia and their cars develop and deepen through ongoing repair and maintenance. A focus on practices and relations of repair and maintenance is rooted in what technology scholar Stephen Jackson (2014, 221) calls "broken world thinking." Jackson argues that "the efficacy of innovation in the world is limited—until extended, sustained, and completed in repair (224).

Here I take up this question of how people come to develop relationships with technological artifacts and how some machines become loved, and *trustworthy* (Fisch 2018), and how their lives are extended and sustained through the lavishing of this repair and care. What kinds of work do people actually do to shape what technology can become (Latour 1996; 2012)? The driving work of Chillia, the worlds they live in, and their (auto)biographies are intimately connected to the material and technological history of Indian automobiles, particularly to the Padmini. The Padmini's hardy survival in the taxi trade through the decades has a lot to do with the lavishing of care and dekh-bhal through collective practices of repair, making it impossible for those in the trade to discard or write off the car as dead or useless, even when everyone else has. By June 2020, the last of the Padminis turned twenty years old and were to be retired as taxis. However, June 2020 was not a typical June for anyone: the month came and went in the midst of the global COVID–19 pandemic. In India, as in many parts of the world, there was a complete lockdown of government and transport business and disruption of any semblance of a "normal" life. As of this writing, I have no definitive evidence that owners of the remaining Padminis have been able to comply with the rules for their complete retirement and demolition. Of course, the COVID-19 pandemic has been a bewildering and unprecedented event; however, this accidental material survival of the Padmini, even when it was to be definitively and legally dead, seems to be the final attestation to the indomitability and flexibility that drivers and mechanics have always claimed for it.

Padminis were never static or closed technologies. Instead, they were in constant need both of care and of the careful work of repair and maintenance—of looking after. Taxi drivers and mechanics never took their Padminis for granted or assumed that they were machines that keep going. They also know that if something goes wrong with the Padmini, its repair cannot be delegated to a detached specialist who simply replaces parts and keeps the basic technological structure of the car unchanged. Instead, the Padmini is a taxi whose repair and structure is closely tied to the configuration of the families that drive it and by the shared and inherited technical senses of the men who repair it. While tinkering (Franz 2005) is a commonly accepted and embodied engagement of men with their cars, the understanding of tinkering as technological practice assumes individuated and aesthetic attunements, rather than collective ones. However, for chillia drivers and mechanics, technological attunements, fixing, and repair are fleshy, sensory, collective, and obligatory ones, much like the obligations for other kinds of care or dekh-bhal.

Chillia drivers care for their cars because they feel responsible for these things; but even more importantly, they care for and feel responsible for the people who depend on these things (Belacasa 2017). Drivers in Pathanwadi refer to the labor of car repair in terms that they apply to other labors of care—dekh-bhal. In other words, care marks the relationships these men have with their technologies, with each other, and with those they call kin. Kinship with cars and others is guided by considerations of who can be engaged to work on this repair, who can be trusted to repair, touch, smell, or listen to a particular car.

Historically, the situated, sensory practices of repair and maintenance were closely connected to the economic and material constraints of early automobilization in India. In early postcolonial India, even in factories, cars were built and assembled from the start as fluid technologies.[1] Automobile technology did not come to India a priori as an easy or inevitable, incoming transfer. In fact, automobiles were actively "provincialized" and revolutionized over a century.[2] In the face of indifferent state support and limited availability of imported technology, Indian technological experts adapted cars and their related technology. Small engineering firms scattered all over

India supported the indigenous auto industry through careful inventiveness in adapting technologies. Drivers and mechanics, by extending care and looking after their cars day after day, have sustained Indian automobility. In this sense, Indian automobile manufacturers, engineers, drivers, and mechanics are themselves the "technological" ones, rather than the automobile itself (Mavhunga 2014). What this suggests is that one can understand far more about India's technological development by following the technological expertise, creativity, and practices of people rather than focusing on the machine itself. Indian cars left themselves open to this creativity. The expansion of driving, legal, and infrastructural systems such as speed limits, road space, and licensing were shaped by the openness of these early cars to repair and maintenance and by those who used automobiles most.

The Premier Padmini was a proud symbol of early postcolonial India's indigenous automobile industry. It also appears as symbolic of freedom, mobility, and romance in the Bollywood movies of the 1970s and 1980s.[3] At different points in India's history, it has been called iconic and dirty, technologically modern and technologically obsolete. It was a symbol of Indian technological progress as well as of its limits; it marked the fluid possibilities of how a car could be adapted, indigenized, and repaired to keep going. The Padmini as technology came to matter for all kinds of reasons in India. All through my fieldwork, I was compelled to ask why this automobile mattered so much here. Why *do* chillia drivers and mechanics love the car so much? What is it that creates the deep sense of attachment between drivers and their cars such that the car is cared for like kin and where dekh-bhal is routinely, lavishly, sensorially, and technologically deployed?

For chillia it was important not just to have technical expertise but also to have grown to trust the car and the people they repair it with. Michael Fisch (2018) uses the term *technicity* to mark the relations that people develop with the machines they live with and come to trust. Technicity is an orientation to machines rooted in the trustworthiness of technology and in the awareness that the technology is a partner in collective and social life. Given that early Indian cars like the Padmini were incomplete, fluid machines, Indian orientations to automobiles are rooted in this technicity that has relied on everyday repair and maintenance. Several veteran drivers told me, "When the Padmini was the only car available, you had to learn how to trust it to make a living out of it." Sensory, technological, and kin-work is only possible because chillia have come to trust their cars and are able to share their lives with them much like kin do.

PADMINI: ICONOGRAPHIC TECHNOLOGY

All over Mumbai there are designated taxi stands. These are designated as parking and waiting spots for kaalipeeli taxis by the Regional Transport Authority. A central struggle of taxi unions has been over preservation of these stands, as road space in the city becomes more and more scarce. Since these stands were designated at a time when Padminis were the only taxis on the road, the signage on all boards in Mumbai has an image of a Padmini on it. Given the heated debates over taking down taxi stands, it is likely that these boards and the images will remain for several years even after the Padmini itself has been completely phased out. The images will be nostalgic images of a taxi that once was; the metallic signposts of the stands themselves will continue as bureaucratic objects, sites of struggle over where a taxi and its driver might rest their laboring bodies. This iconographic memory is deeply intertwined with how taxi drivers have come to see and value their Padminis as endlessly enduring and persistent technologies with a kin-like legacy.

Almost sixty-five years after the Indian company Premier Automobiles and the Italian company Fiat collaborated on a car that would become the Padmini, Feroze is waiting for rides under this iconography at the taxi stand with his Padmini. Feroze leans gently against his Padmini. That his car is now nineteen years old is significant for him, since it has one more year before it reaches the mandated retirement age of twenty. Feroze says resignedly,

> I am preparing myself like I would prepare for my daughter to leave me when she goes to her husband's house. You do the dekh-bhal that you can, but a man always lives under this shadow that his daughter will one day leave her family; at nineteen that is what is natural to expect. Same way, my Padmini will stay in my family for one more year, then she will be gone; that is how it is meant to be. For the car, the government has decided, and I accept that it is meant to be. I fought, but now I can't do anything. You look after her while she is yours, but then you can't stop your nineteen-year-old daughter from going into her new life.

I ask a rather vague question, "What do you mean when you say you do dekh-bhal for the car?"

Feroze leans more decidedly against his car as his resignation to his family's fate turns into a more impassioned pronouncement of the Padmini's place in the world:

In the taxi trade we have never had another car quite like the Padmini. It is the real car of India, the car that worked best for the roads of *Bambai*. It was *Bambai's shaan* [pride]. It was cheap to buy, cheap to maintain, easy to fix. Of course it needs a lot of dekh-bhal on an everyday basis, but we can do everything ourselves.

I press him further. "What exactly do you do when you are doing dekh-bhal of a car?" I ask.

Feroze glances around the stand and points to all the other taxis around us. "I can make it into whatever kind of car I want," he says, "change the engine, put in a CNG engine, make a new exhaust system, or attach a new pipe to the carburetor. Because many different spare parts can be used in the Padmini it always keeps its *value*." Drivers used this term *value* to refer to the Padmini, using the English word, even when otherwise speaking in Gujarati or Hindi.

I ask Feroze, "What do you mean by value?"

Feroze doesn't skip a beat: "When I say value, I mean it keeps its value as a car and it also has value to me as a taximan. It is valuable as a car because it is strong and we all know that anything in it can be fixed. If you offered me a secondhand Toyota that has already been on the roads as a taxi, I would think twice about buying. The new cars lose value after they have been driven on these bad surfaces for some time. To fix the Toyota is expensive; and the body of the Toyota is weak. So it is doubtful that I can give it a second life as a secondhand car. So after five to six years driving as a taxi, the Toyota has to be thrown away."

Feroze pauses, looks at his Padmini beamingly, and then runs his fingers slowly along the inside of the open window. He pats the protruding rubber around the window frame. I sense that this is both out of a need to connect lovingly with the car and of focused attention on getting the unsettled rubber back into place. He looks up and smiles: "But a Padmini, I know it can always be made to work. Our chillia people can repair a Padmini *phataphat* [in a snap]. So it has value as a car and it is easy for us to make it valuable; but now for the government it has no value as a taxi. In fact, if anyone wanted to buy a secondhand or thirdhand car, the Padmini was always the best. No taximan bought a new Padmini; it was always secondhand so it was already fixed many times by someone else before it came to you."

"Have you always bought secondhand cars?" I ask.

"Yes, of course," says Feroze.

Secondhand is cheaper and this makes it more valuable in the taxi dhandha. And when it's secondhand you get to know that one car is different from the other. My Padmini is not the same as my brother's Padmini. There are plenty of other taxis on the roads now but really, if you think taxi trade, you have to think of Padmini. It is a car that we can make into anything we want. Do you know that the Fiat engine is the most valuable engine in the world today? Every car in the world now has a Fiat engine, same as my Padmini. But the government has worked with the company to kill the Padmini and we have watched it happen. The Padmini is dead not because it has no value as a car, or that there is anything wrong with the machinery, but because it has no value for the government or for the public.

Feroze, whose relationship to wheeled mobility and mechanics has spanned India's entire postcolonial period, has an admirably keen under-standing of how the politics of value works. Theorists of automobility and of disposal and decay have argued that an automobile is what anthropologist Michael Thompson (1979) calls a "transient object that risks losing status and value over time."[4] In this sense, cars are distinguished from "durable" objects (Thompson 1979). Old kaalipeelis that are sent to demolition fields run by transport authorities after they have outlived the calendrical time allotted to them are cast as transient objects; they end up in the category of "rubbish," or as obsolete or noncompliant with state and market regulations. However, transient objects can also refuse to be rubbish and may make the journey back to being "durable" (Heatherington 2004). And this refusal is where the repair work of taxis takes place. The work of making technological objects durable takes place through conduits of kin and extended kin, because kin are those you can depend on and trust with the technicity of your trustworthy machines in use.

TECHNOLOGIES IN USE: REPAIR AND
MAINTENANCE AS DEKH-BHAL

Raised bonnets, a congregation of those who know the car well, and diagnoses of the innards of a car (see fig 5.1) are routine sights along Mumbai's urban landscape. In Pathanwadi, in particular, this mechanical sociality and the application of care and careful, collective looking is a significant part of each day. To understand how a car is cared for rather than just how it is made requires close attention to the car as a *technology in use* (Edgerton

FIG. 5.1. Everyday repair

2007). It is in use that relations of trust, affection, and intimate knowledge are fostered. Feroze clearly articulates that there is a great deal of work that goes into keeping a car on the road in working condition, day after day for ten, fifteen or twenty years. This work involves mechanical and sensory labor. Among chillia drivers (but also other drivers), every day the technical work of maintaining and looking after cars is encompassed within other kinds of looking after, the work of dekh-bhal. Dekh-bhal, in the realm of repair, is tied to kin, technological, and mechanical investments. These produce a sense of relatedness and responsibility between people and between people and their cars.

Dekh-bhal of cars in the world of taxi drivers is vital to the work of both driving and repair precisely because it is how lives are made and how claims are made on others. Repair and maintenance work do not leave the clear, documentary evidence that production and innovation work can; evidence of this work has be excavated through the ethnographic observations of the repair work that people actually do. Maintenance, repair, and innovation often merge in material and empirical terms as well as in practice. As historians of technology Andrew Russell and Lee Vinsel (2018) argue, some maintainers can be innovative, and new technologies can play important roles in maintenance regimes. However, maintenance and repair occupy a different place in documented history than innovation and productionist histories. Usually repair and maintenance practices and histories are subordinated to those of production. The production history of Premier Automobiles is documented in government documents, annual reports, and industry pamphlets (Khanolkar [1969] 2007). However, the practices of repair and maintenance and the technical, sensory, and emotional labors (Hochschild 1983) the Padmini has needed have to be excavated from observations, family histories, and (auto)biographies.

The subordination of maintenance in the history of technology signals the social positions of those who do the work of maintenance and repair. For one, even while it requires significant technical and technological expertise, repair and maintenance are usually done by those who are socially subordinate. It also takes place in spatial and social margins; it is the job of marginal people who perform their work outside the formal economy and who resurrect value out of unvaluable things. For car mechanics and drivers, it is also *dirty work* rather than skilled employment; people's bodies and clothes accumulate dirt, grease, slush, mud, and dust in the course of doing this work (Orr 1996). This work also has gendered dimensions because it represents the mundane labor of keeping things going, the kind of labor that is usually done by women. It also explains to some extent why innovation and technologies were extolled and line up with national and global progress, while the daily work of maintenance and repair of these technologies are cast as obsolete, unrecognized, and undervalued (Borg 2007; Russell and Vinsel 2018).

Further, repair work does not produce tangible products like factory work does. What counts most in repair as expertise and training is the capacity to train the body and the senses as instruments that can decipher, respond to, and fix technological problems. Learning to crawl under a car, lean into an engine, or feel a pipe for rust is fundamental to training and nurturing both the body and the senses to make long-term sense of and to repair things that go wrong. Here, feminist theorists Berenice Fisher and Joan Tronto's (1990) definition of care is useful: "In the most general sense, care is a species activity that includes everything we do to maintain, continue, and repair our world so that we may live in it as well as possible. That world includes our bodies, ourselves, our environment, all of which we seek to interweave in a complex, life-sustaining web" (40). The life-sustaining nature of care is always relational, while both the pleasurable and the dirty work involved are collectively practiced (Tronto 2016). Care requires not just nurturing relationships but also the physical and mental work of taking care of, cleaning up after, and maintaining different kinds of bodies (Tronto 2013). The commitment to dekh-bhal that comes up again and again with drivers' and mechanics' orientations to their cars also signals a feminist ethics of care.[5] This is an ethics of care that is less about maternal or medical care and more about technological and mechanical entanglements that produce and sustain collective and related lives.

While care is assumed to be women's work, men also engage in a number of caring activities, but these are not as easily categorized as "caring" per se (Tronto 2013). However, as Feroze's articulation of care as dekh-bhal suggests, the care involved in chillia driving and mechanical work encompasses both women's care work and masculine obligations and practices that are also caring. Feroze thinks of dekh-bhal of his car as a form of looking after family and kin as well, suggesting and interweaving *technological* and *mechanical work* and *kin-work*. It is precisely because the Padmini needs so much adaptation and fixing, so much mundane dekh-bhal and collective work, that it has become an object both of love and loss for Feroze.

Technical experts like Feroze are not car buffs for whom working on cars is an activity of leisure. No doubt, Feroze and others derive considerable enjoyment, pleasure, and comfort in the sensory engagements with their cars. However, Feroze's dekh-bhal is also directed at fulfilling labor and kin obligations rather than purely for leisure. At the same time, it is difficult to disentangle his kin obligations from what Feroze finds pleasurable because he admits that social cohesion built through collective work brings him the most pleasure and pride. However, as both Feroze's resignation and his anger articulate, the pervasive sense that the object of dekh-bhal (the daughter or the car) will be lost or die permeates all the work of care and dekh-bhal. This outcome marks the inherent pathos of the material labors of technological repair and maintenance: they always carry on in a realm of possible breakdown. In this shadow of breakdown, drivers like Feroze are reconciled to the reality that something or someone will eventually be lost no matter how much dekh-bhal is directed at it.

SITUATED WORK: SPATIALITY OF REPAIR AND MAINTENANCE

Repair and maintenance have a thick sociality, but they also have important spatial dimensions. This is technological work conducted outside the spatial confines of factories and laboratories. It takes place in the city, the family unit, the village unit, and the neighborhood. Further, the dirty work of mechanics also brings a bit of the factory into the city and onto the roads. Work is always a situated and contextual practice, and the particular spaces where work is done also shapes the value the work is given (Suchman 1987). In the case of all kaalipeeli drivers, not just chillia, these spatial contexts are vital because situated practices of mechanics and repair also shape how much time and technical expertise driver-mechanics can apply in a given space. For instance, drivers know well that if a taxi breaks down in the middle of a public space and the driver has to conduct visible repair work out in the city, their cars will be marked as old, as joona, and subject to fines and police surveillance. Therefore, this more public repair work is conducted quickly, in an improvised manner, so that drivers can get back on the roads and out of the sight of surveillance as soon as possible.

However, even in these spaces of provisional fixing amid the chaos of the roadsides, there is an astonishing degree of calm cooperation among taxi drivers to help each other escape state surveillance as quickly as possible. For instance, on one occasion I was driving with Feroze when his Padmini grunted and stalled in the middle of one of the busiest intersections in Byculla. Feroze was only mildly annoyed as he got out and waved for the hundreds of honking cars behind us to scrape around him. The rhythmic horizontal wave of one hand is a familiar, well-understood gesture connected intimately to roads and driving in Mumbai. Police use it to direct traffic, passersby use it to help a driver get into a tight parking spot, and drivers stuck in a breakdown use it to clear the field so that they can push their cars off the road. This gesture says, "Get by me" or "Keep moving." As in the case of Feroze's breakdown, it also says, "I cannot move, so move around me."

When other drivers see this gesture from the driver of a stalled car, the ear-splitting honking miraculously dwindles in recognition of the car and driver's immobility, and everyone becomes focused on trying to steer around to avoid knocking over the gesturing driver. Private cars cooperate by steering around a stalled taxi and then keep moving on with their day. However, in all the stalls I have been in with chillia drivers, without exception, at least two or three taxi drivers pull their cars over to the side of the road and run into the traffic to help the driver push his car to safety. Once the car has been moved off the thoroughfare, these other drivers offer help with deciphering the problem and providing quick fixes like jumper cables or water for an overheated engine.

The afternoon that Feroze's car stalls, two taxi drivers leap over to Feroze; they wave sideways toward a corner, indicating a spot they have ascertained as safe. With absolutely no exchange of words, Feroze gets back in his taxi, the two other drivers position themselves to push on either side of the car, and Feroze steers the car into the corner. Then all three men peer into the open bonnet and quickly exchange some opinions on how the cause was likely overheating. The clipped and businesslike exchanges signal that there is a sense of urgency for a quick diagnosis and resolution among the men. The two other drivers urge Feroze to add some water, while their eyes dart around the traffic stop to make sure there are no police around because Feroze's car is in a no-parking zone. "Just add the water for now and go before the *havaldar* [policeman] comes," they say urgently. Feroze does as instructed. The car starts up, the two other men nod, and then use the sideways wave to push Feroze off into the afternoon.

These quick, provisional, diagnostic events occur almost every day along Mumbai's roads and mark a mechanical kinship between drivers across the city even if they are strangers. However, this provisional repair work that skirts the visibility of the police also has a hidden and deeper life. When mechanical work is conducted close to home, it is reflective, shared, social, and focused on diagnosis and problem-solving rather than on speed and urgency. Therefore, most technical work of dekh-bhal is practiced in spaces close to kin, or at nakas that are *off the road* rather than directly on it. This makes mechanical work alternate between intimacy and distance and between speed, and slow, reflective labor. Drivers regularly differentiate the efficacy of their repair work based on where they repaired the car. Whether it was repaired on the road, at the naka, in the gully, or on the flyover (Harris 2018) affects how much or what kind of attention was given and what kind of repair was possible. In this discursive demarcation of the spaces of repair, drivers and mechanics are also producing understandings of what the road, the naka, the gully, or the flyover are, and of the different forms of surveillance or familiarity that might be afforded to their technical expertise in each of these spaces.

Spatially, repair and maintenance belong in some places and not in others. If a driver is seen tinkering with his car in visible places on the roads, the police and the public automatically assume that the car is too old to be on the road. Drivers like Feroze usually perform the longer, more absorbed maintenance and repair—when the car has to be fully opened up to the world like a gaping, open wound—in the familiar nakas close to home in Pathanwadi or at taxi stands tucked away from public thoroughfares. These spaces are away from visible roads or major arteries. Drivers' efforts to erase from sight anything that needs long and laborious fixing is fundamental to the politics of caring for the car.

This is not unlike the broader invisibility of laborious and mundane care work and dekh-bhal in domestic contexts. Much like the labor of maintaining the household unit is relegated to domestic, intimate, or proximate spaces, long and laborious care of older vehicles is also out of sight. It is work that occupies domestic, familial spaces, rather than urban public space. When the car is moving or working it can claim the city's roads, but when it is still, resting, or undergoing dekh-bhal, it makes its claims on the familial and the familiar naka. This analytic and material and topographical tension between naka and road seems to be a more productive way to think about kinship relatedness in Pathanwadi than the well-worn spatial dimensions of public and private. While it is not illegal to repair a car in public, the fact that a car needs to be repaired at all through the embodied labor of care and dekh-bhal, rather than through the more formal technical expertise of a dealer, signals to the police that the car is too old and therefore possibly plying illegally.

Within Pathanwadi, mechanical work is not spatially confined to garages, mostly because almost everyone who is a mechanic is also a driver, who has learned about cars through driving them. But they have also learned about cars through fixing them. Therefore, there are few spatially segregated garages at all. While chillia call themselves mechanics and run mechanics dhandhas, the spaces of mechanical fixing and the spaces of driving, parking, and repair overlap. In this sense, the taxi stands in Pathanwadi and indeed, nakas, streets, and roads both in Pathanwadi and in the city at large, operate as what science and technology scholar Clapperton Mavhunga (2014) calls *transient workspaces*—areas, sites, or spaces where mechanical work gets performed. These workspaces are transient also because bodies are crawling, crouching, and moving around to repair things there.

Thus, motion and mobility for drivers is not just conveyance from one point to another at the steering wheel. It also entails moving the screeching bonnet up and down with tired arms and wrists, tilting or leaning into the engine to smell for burning or heat, crouching close to the tailpipe to listen for vibrations, or crawling into the darkness of the undercarriage to feel for loose parts. For older cars, technological and mechanical work materializes wherever drivers happen to be and follows them as they move. While this work has its own logic that all drivers seem to understand, it is not tethered to immovable places or the temporal rhythms of a regular workday. Rather, it is tied to a wide range of mechanical and technological spaces and routines that materialize through movement and sensory orientations—crouching, tilting, crawling, and listening, smelling, touching.

They also materialize through the shared processes of reflection, collection, narrative, and dwelling and touching (Orr 2006).

REFLECTION AND THE SENSES

Nawaz raises the hood of his Premier Padmini to look at the twisting, greasy innards of the car. He takes several deep breaths and cocks his silvery head back and forth at slightly different angles each time. Then he gently closes his eyes for a split second before patting his pockets looking for something. He also starts to wave me over to take a look. While Nawaz began his process of reflecting and diagnosing by trying to *look* for the problem, he seemed to have decided that he had seen all he needed and something else was called for. Before I can move close enough to see what he is showing me, he pulls a small spanner out of his pocket and begins to extend his fingers out to scrape something and the greasy spanner to tighten something. As his fingers and spanner extend outward toward the machine, Nawaz feels around the surfaces of his car and cedes sight for touch.[6]

Sight is what sensory scholars call the most masculine and "highest" of all senses, as it is most associated with reason, scientific and technological expertise, and progress (Classen 1997). However, in the world of automobile repair and technical expertise, and particularly for those like Nawaz who were considered veterans, sight seemed to operate only as an *activating sense.*[7] It was a sense through which thought began, but it was not the real technological sense in terms of its ability to resolve a technological problem. Just seeing and looking for the problem never solved anything for Nawaz. Instead, this initial looking activated other senses like touch, smell, listening, and tasting to solve the problem. I, the non-expert, was waved over to see something. I realized this was a recognition of my lack of expertise, that even though I could *see* something, I would never actually be able to solve the technological problem because the rest of my senses know nothing of cars.

Through feeling around the car, Nawaz has found something greasy stuck on the engine. He takes out the comb he uses on his long beard and combs the solidified grease off gently. He leans closer to see if he can smell a gasoline or oil leak. He sniffs around the engine. He touches the engine gently and presses down on a dark red pipe that snakes through the rusty, labyrinthine veins leading from the engine to the twice-refurbished carburetor. He looks puzzled. He walks over to the driver's side of the car and leans inside to turn the key that droops morosely from the ignition, tired and broiled from the blazing sun. It takes two turns for the drowsy key to do the job. Nawaz leaves the ignition on and lodges his ear close to the running engine. He has seen, smelled, touched, and listened to make his diagnosis. Now he leans further in to see what he suspects. He seems to smile to himself as though he is taking deep pleasure in the ease and naturalness with which he has been able to confirm his suspicions. People who have mastery over physical work and engage deeply and sensorially with what they do can feel a visceral pleasure and fulfilment in this mastery.[8] Chillia mechanics regularly signaled some of this pleasure through proud smiles, affirmation from others, and deeper and deeper touch of their cars.

Until recently, diagnosis of automotive problems did not rely on computerized, diagnostic technology. Nawaz is a vocal critic of computerized diagnostic technology. When I observed the care with which he reflected and listened to his astonishingly sophisticated technical diagnosis of his car, I realized this critique is not a technical one. Rather it is a sensory critique. It signals his discomfort with the technocratic ideology (Laplantine 2015, 114) that everything must be revealed at first glance without an opportunity for attentiveness, careful work, dekh-bhal, or elaboration over time with others. For Nawaz diagnosis remains an unmediated use of the senses and a thoughtful reflection on what can been seen, heard, felt, touched, and smelled. Solving a technical problem requires a significant degree of this kind of reflective practice (Orr 1996, 2006), and a form of *tacit knowing* (Polanyi 1966). Nawaz touches, listens, and thinks again. While he has some confidence in his expertise, he decides this reflection is best opened out to others at the naka and done collectively.

COLLECTING KNOWLEDGE, GATHERING TOOLS

If maintenance and repair are reflective for chillia, they are also collective and cross-generational. This collective reflection results in a *gathering* of knowledge before the final technical solution is applied. In his attempt at gathering, Nawaz calls out to the teenager Salman. Salman works for his father, Munir, who is a taxi driver but also runs a mechanic business. Salman is paid to fill up the water in the car every morning and conduct routine oil checks on Nawaz's car. Salman has been on this water and oil duty for almost four years, which means that Salman is familiar with the smells and sounds that emanate from under the bonnet and can decipher if something is wrong just by smelling and listening. Salman does not even have to begin with sight at all.

"Salman *beta* [son], what do you think?" Nawaz asks as he spits lightly onto his finger and tries to clean something off his windshield using the long nail that grows like a small, strong branch out of his little finger. Growing one long nail on the little finger is common among taxi drivers all over the city. I have seen this nail used when a wire comes loose and needs to be gently disentangled; or when a door handle is broken, the nail digs into the small opening where the door handle used to be to jiggle it open. Long nails, I learned, are important tools of men's work, not simply of feminized adornment.

"I have to understand a little more, *chacha* [paternal uncle]. Just one minute," Salman responds cheerfully, as he walks over to crouch close to the car. Salman's long gray pants and his faded red shirt are streaked with mud. Salman spends most of his day crouched either near or under cars, and the dusty roads and nakas have made their mark on all his clothes. Because he often pushes cars to get them to start, the crusty mud on the wheels of the car from old journeys is stirred up and imprinted onto his pants; or else the fresh muddy slush from that day's rain is coughed up onto his hands and shirt from the rear end of an exhaust pipe. Salman's work clothes are a map of all of Mumbai's mud, and these muddy crusts and slushes are a map of everywhere that the taxi has been.

It is the city of Mumbai mapped in mud on Salman's pants.

Salman takes off his prayer cap, under which he hides a small damp towel. This towel is an absorptive buffer between the sweat that presses out of his scalp into his thick black hair and his prayer cap that must stay clean and dry even as he labors outside in the broiling sun. This is also the towel that wipes Salman's hands dry after he has washed his face and hands for prayer at the mosque. Now, Salman gently places this versatile towel on the carburetor of Nawaz's car to shield himself against the scorching heat of the metal as he lodges his forehead under the rusty bonnet. He takes several long, deep, and luxurious breaths, exhales, and then moves lower, deeper into the body of the car, sniffing loudly. His eyes dart back and forth into the innards of the car as he slithers deeper and further under the bonnet. Salman's body folds and leans into cars with relaxed ease. His upper body and the cars he works on are so indiscernible that most drivers at the stand speak only to the grease and mud-stained gray pants that encase Salman's long legs.

Salman's youngest sister, Khadija, usually brings him a packed lunch in the early afternoon. Khadija has become used to delivering lunch to her brother's legs. She usually says little, but playfully taps her hands on the soles of his worn out shoes before she drops the metal lunch box near his feet. Once in a while, when he knows she is there, Salman calls out to her from the labyrinth of metal and pipes, asking her for a hairpin or a particular spanner from the box of tools at his feet. Khadija always obliges either by pulling a hairclip gently from her hair and out from under her burka or by passing the more specialized tool of the spanner to her brother before sauntering off toward home. Her father and brother classify their spanners by number; they do not label their tools but simply ask for a spanner by number and assume that Khadija also knows which one to pass on. When I ask Khadija about this numbering system and how she can tell one spanner from another, she laughingly tells me, "When Salman bhai is under the car, I know he will ask for spanner number four; when he is under the bonnet, I know he will use spanner number one. So that's how I know. I see where he is and just give him one based on that!"

"Yes, *chacha*," says Salman from the depths of the Nawaz's car. "Something smells odd. But no matter, for now I will do a little bit of dekh-bhal and adjustment so you can do your dhandha. But later, I can do the bigger work." Without coming up for air, Salman pulls a small piece of plastic tape out of his pocket and twists it around one of the car's electrical wires near the alternator. Salman carries the garage on his body. He is always able to pull out various bits of wire, string, and tubes that are endlessly adaptable to solve some of the most common problems. Satisfied, he slowly snakes out of the car and straightens into the tall lanky young man that he actually is. He uses his longest fingernail to dislodge the stand holding up the bonnet, which comes down with a gentle screech. He turns to Nawaz and adds, "Since you are here, let us also oil the bonnet to stop that noise." As is quite common in this world of everyday repair, one kind of diagnosis has led to another.

The Padmini is a car that relies on gathering these collective forms of expertise and knowledge; but it also gathers tools that can be used for repair. Tools are integral to collection and gathering. Once an everyday item is deployed as an effective tool, it is gathered as part of the future toolbox. Gathering is a collection of knowledge as well as a collection and expansion of what counts as a tool. Drivers and mechanics like Nawaz and Salman must use their bodies, their senses, and the tools that groom their own bodies to (re)make, fix, groom, and repair. The tools of dekh-bhal are rarely the tools that were involved in the technological innovations of manufacture—factories, machines, or science. Rather, the tools of dekh-bhal are often those gathered from the living of everyday life—combs, towels, straws, water pipes, plastic water bottles, newspapers, scissors, plyers, electrical wires, pieces of clothing, overgrown nails, yesterday's newspapers, leftover clips from the maal work of women.

While these material tools are used to fix cars, they are also put to daily use in the maintenance of relations. In this sense, repair and maintenance of the Padmini operates through a feminized structure of social life. It is feminized because it is rooted in extending the life of objects and people that are closest to you. Like women who use tools easily available in the home to repair household items, which they themselves owned and had close working relations to, chillia taximen usually repair only what they own, blurring the lines between technical expert and consumer of the commodity (Borg 2007). Even if they don't own the car in the individual sense, it is "owned" by someone in the chillia community, by kin. This was how Salman repaired Nawaz's car. Salman is already enmeshed in a jaalu with both Nawaz and the car and is obligated to practice dekh-bhal for both. In this sense, dekh-bhal of cars, like other kinds of looking after, is the work of the body because it entails doing things with the body and the senses to solve problems. But dekh-bhal is also emotional and intelligent technological labor. It requires thought, creativity, negotiation, disappointment, and the art of making do. It also requires talking and discursive and narrative work.

NARRATIVE AND DISCOURSES OF REPAIR

If maintenance and repair are collective, reflective, sensory work, they are also narrative and discursive work. As anthropologist Julian Orr (1996) illustrates in his ethnography of Xerox technicians, these discursive strategies are the most unseen of technological work, because they take place at some remove from the technological object itself. When technological objects are collectively rather than individually used, the discursive work of circulating information is particularly vital. In Pathanwadi, because the same car is driven by multiple people, updates on the car's behavior and its mechanical ticks are passed on from one driver to another daily. Mechanics, drivers, and those who have driven the car earlier in the day and have noticed a quirk of a particular car as it moves through the neighborhood, through households, and through taxi stands provide updates on the car or respond to questions about problems. In the process, information and knowledge about the state of the city's surfaces, the roads, and what routes to avoid to protect the car, to save fuel, or to avoid police stops is also passed along. Knowledge of the city and its continually changing surfaces and topographies are intertwined with narrative solutions for how to make the car work in these topographies. This work of sharing narratives and knowledge about the state of the car and state of the city is an ongoing process that takes place day after day after day.

There are several elements to this work. First, a driver has to experience and sense what is going on in the car. Then he collects and refines his own sensory information on what is going on with the car. Then information about the car has to be passed on to other drivers who share the car or to mechanics who can fix problems. Then someone has to remember to fix the problem, and someone has to pay attention to taking care of the problem the next day. For instance, each afternoon when Bilal returns from his driving shift and passes on the car to his son Farid for the rest of the day, the two men sit on the small ledge outside their house for about fifteen minutes talking. Bilal says things like, "The car was prancing and dancing today, I think the air pressure of the tires is too high," or "Keep an ear on the scraping sounds at the back. It sounds like there might be a crack in the muffler. But if you avoid the digging at Mahim junction then the car will not have to climb and the muffler will be okay. I think we can maintain the old muffler for a few more months if we are careful about avoiding the most dug-up roads."

When Farid hears the warning about the muffler by listening to his father's description of what the scrapes had sounded like, he walks over to the car, squats next to it, and runs his slender, right hand cursorily through the undercarriage. He closes his eyes to shut out all senses but his touch and seems to feel something. He then takes his left hand and strokes a particular spot more deliberately. "I feel a small crack in the muffler, Abba," he calls out to Bilal. "But you are right; it is so small that if we avoid the dug-up roads, then we will be okay." The world of repair work relies a great deal on this diagnosis by touch. While Bilal had narrated his sense of the car and the sounds of the scraping, in the end it is Farid's tactile sense of the problematic object that was the final guarantee of what was really wrong with the car. As geographer Yi Fu Tuan argues (1995, 45), touch is the sense least susceptible to deception and hence the one in which we can come to place the most trust. And it is by touching, as Farid has done, that the most trustworthy diagnosis can best be made.

Farid has confirmed the problem through his gathering of tactile information. However, in this exchange his father, Bilal, has also done several other things. He has passed on his technical assessment of the car, along with his assessment of the city's landscape and suggestions of places Farid should avoid so as not to cause more harm to the car. Because of the arterial structure of Mumbai's road landscape, the stipulations for where taxis (kaalipeelis) can ply their services, and the demarcations of suburban areas where taxis compete for rides with auto-rickshaws, most drivers traverse the same arterial routes. This usually involves several trips along the Western or Eastern Express Highways toward the Island City. On any given day, several drivers have already traversed these routes and know what to expect. Mumbai's road landscape is an unsettled one. While smaller roads and nakas can be blocked one day and open another, even the highways and open roads regularly undergo digging, construction, and related detours, which change from day to day. Monsoons and religious festivals impact the roads, routes, and commuting times and require related planning for how much fuel will be needed or an assessment of how much monsoon floodwater the suspension of a particular car can take. Nawaz, Salman, Bilal, and Farid, smell, touch, look, and listen to their cars, deploying all their senses to diagnose what is wrong. Sometimes they decipher how to fix it, at others they pass on their assessments or listen to what others have to say, while at others they make determinations about the urban landscapes to avoid in order to maintain their spare parts for as long as possible. Each of these determinations is made so that the car can continue its labors for the day, the month, or even the years ahead.

TOUCH: HANDS, *HAATH*, AND FEET

As with the centrality of *haath* (hands, touch) in kinship and domestic work, touch is also central to technological work. Technological diagnoses made through reflective, collective, narrative/discursive, and sensory/embodied practices are forms of knowledge that emerge not just from the looking and deciphering practices of technological science but from sensory attention. Touch is important to this attention. Drivers fix and repair their cars using their hands but they also make political and knowledge claims based on this proximity. Or as Habib said, when he was pulled over for having an old car, "I put in a new engine with my own hands. This car is new. I *know* it, even if the police do not."

From the perspective of car manufacturers, passengers, the regulating authorities, and even the unions, the automobile is primarily a commodity, a form of transport, or an object of urban regulation. However, as the Padmini is being phased out because it is now considered technologically anachronistic and aesthetically out of place, the labors of Nawaz, Bilal, Farid, and Salman mark an important technological and political distinction—between the assessment of a technology based exclusively on vision and that rooted in other senses—touch, smell, and sound—regularly deployed in the practices of repair and maintenance. This multisensory world is where the relations of technicity are forged. No doubt, mechanics routinely rely on visual qualities to diagnose problems, such as looking at the color of the spark of a failed ignition. However, this is still embedded in a kinesthetic knowledge that fuses the other senses and that cannot be easily codified or uniformly applied (Borg 1999, 2007). Among veteran drivers and those who drive older cars, I regularly heard how different kinds of driving and mechanics were about different kinds of haath (hands).

As we also saw in the case of women's maal work, the importance of haath as a signal for touch is worth marking for various reasons. For one, touch marks kin (Manning 2006); and touch can qualitatively change a body that touches and is touched. Because touch is associated with early life experiences between mother and child and with the proximate, intimate, and corporeal senses rather than the distant, reasoned ones, touch is also associated with a feminized, sensory world (Manning 2006). However, in the ways that Farid and Nawaz deploy haath to their machines suggests that touch is profoundly exploratory for these men (Tuan 1995, 41). It opens up the possibilities of how to repair their cars well.

Moreover, the technical and technological work of driving and mechanical repair involved touch that was not about hands alone. There was, for example, the touching of hands, feet, noses, fingers, nails to the gears or to the insides of the car. For drivers and mechanics, touch is also about the feet. Repair work often uses the feet to feel for and decipher the health of the breaks, or the clutch, or the worn-out rubber casing on the pedals. For taxi drivers feet are where surfaces of the city are most deeply sensed in the course of driving. Drivers actually say that they drive and feel roads through their feet; preliminary diagnoses about how the car touches the topographies of the city are likewise made through the feet.

Moreover, in the scrapes of traffic and jams, there is also close contact and touching of cars on the road by other cars, what drivers and mechanics call thok (a hit or scrape). The term *thok* is a linguistic hybrid of Hindi and Marathi. It means to beat, kick, or to strike a blow to an object. Thoks are the most common forms of touch between cars and other vehicles and other people on the road. They are the ways that cars meet other wheels on roads and at nakas, and they are the crumpled dents and holes of metal imprinted on the car that signal the wear and tear on the car's body. Most dents from thoks are made by accidental strikes from other vehicles or objects; however, it is not uncommon for pedestrians or riders on two-wheelers trying to get by in a jam to deliberately smack or scratch a taxi with their hands, helmets, or keys to show their frustration in a traffic jam.

These deliberate thoks are given to any cars, but kaalipeelis seem to collect a majority of thoks along the road. This might be because they are recognized as working vehicles, perceived as old and less valued as commodities, and their drivers seen as working-class men who are presumably habituated to the strikes of the road. While I have seen other drivers jump out to fight the person who struck the blow, taxi drivers usually have passengers trying to get somewhere fast so they rarely bother fighting thoks; instead, they accept this form of touch as part of the sensory experience of driving work. The incremental dents made by thoks make the taxi look older and, therefore, are more surveilled by police. But the hardy Padmini, unlike newer cars, can have its thoks hammered out of its body by a skilled mechanic with minimal damage to the car's frame. To encounter a thok is to be touched fully, first by others who injure the car, and then by the mechanic who heals and repairs.

When a driver or mechanic deploys the term *haath*, he is talking about a coagulation of all the senses in a sense of touch that is not about the hands alone; and while haath is the necessary and familiar relationship of touch between drivers, mechanics, and their cars, thok is the inevitable, unavoidable, and unwelcome relationship of touching and contact with other cars that in turn requires its own fix. Often drivers who bring home cars with several thoks are chastised by mechanics for not having the correct haath; and mechanics with the correct haath are best equipped to extend healing forms of repair and dekh-bhal toward a thok. The Mumbai taxi lives in this everyday routine of haath and thoks, of welcome and unwelcome touch, all of which have the capacity to change the technology and the body of the car.

Interestingly, when chillia drivers differentiate themselves from drivers of Ola and Uber, they often root this difference in different capacities for touch and haath. For example, those who drive for Ola and Uber are required to have the latest cars that require computerized, less sensory forms of maintenance and repair. Much of the critique from chillia of this different kind of technological engagement has coalesced around the technology of the smartphone. For chillia drivers, use of smartphones as technologies of ride-hailing, compared to the waving and shouting along the road for the kaalipeeli, is an important distinction. Chillia drivers see the reliance on the smartphone as a signal of the closed, untrustworthy, technological world both of Ola and Uber's cars and their drivers compared to the open, malleable operation of the kaalipeeli where the driver has developed a relationship of technicity over his car and his routes and surfaces.

Most chillia drivers say they that would not want to give up what they see as the familiar *touch* of repair to replace it by the *touch* of the screen. Chillia, like most urban Indians, are well versed in touch screens. Like most urban families, chillia own smart/touch phones and they use them regularly for a wide range of things, phone calls, text messaging, WhatsApp, YouTube, recipes, and clothing and henna designs. However, as far as use of the smartphone in the taxi trade is concerned, for chillia, they see this as a surrender to a form of touch that signals a different kind of labor agency. The touch screen has in fact become akin to an auto part. However, chillia feel that in the work of driving it operates at a technological distance from the driver. The touch of the screen allows the driver to accept a ride, but does not give him control over where he has been asked to go. The touch of repair and mechanics, on the other hand, gives the driver/mechanic control not just over his time and his ride but over the technological artifact itself.

For chillia, these are significant differences among the touch screen, the new, computer-reliant car, and the haath. One is part of an individual, digital technology of touch while the other is an expression of collective agency over maintenance, repair, and care. In a kaalipeeli, you don't simply need to touch, but you need to use your body, your senses—your haath—fully. Thus, while the burgeoning tensions between the different spheres of the taxi trade materialize as tensions between different labor structures and different relations to capital, they also materialize as claims (even if unfounded or misplaced) that others have different and diminished relations to the technologies of touch.

THE CAR AND ITS SOCIAL AND TECHNOLOGICAL PARTS

Chillia claims to mechanical and technical expertise are singularly focused on a close knowledge of parts. At the same time that parts are no longer being produced for the Padmini, there has been a broader proliferation of spare parts manufacturing in India. This spare parts and secondhand economy is a significant, peripheral economy that surrounds both driving and mechanics.[9] The story of India's early automobile industry is one of the jumble of spare parts produced in dispersed places and used for different kinds of machines. These parts were subjected to political and economic restrictions like import duties and licensing, and it necessitated a wide range of technological experts, decision-makers, and mechanical adaptors in the car manufacturing spheres. Even today, engines are produced by one automobile manufacturer for use in another company's car, and parts are regularly swapped between one car brand and another (Athukorala and Veeramani 2019). Therefore, the car was always an assembly of technological bits and pieces the world over. The work of manufacturing and fixing spare parts has also always been dispersed work. This dispersion, creative assembly, and adaption of parts into different cars is a common and encouraged business practice in the production sphere and in car factories. However, for those who actually use cars, this right to adapt and repurpose car parts outside the factory is discouraged and unsupported, even though the work involved is fundamentally technological. The Padmini and other Indian cars used as taxis today are what anthropologists Marianne de Laet and Annemarie Mol (2000) call *fluid* machines. Maintenance and repair of fluid machines does not follow the procedural structures applied to uniform machines, and it requires particular knowledge and attention to the idiosyncrasies of its spare parts.

For chillia drivers, knowledge of the idiosyncrasies of each car depends on their knowledge and trust in the people from whom they procure their spare parts. They prefer to procure parts from other chillia, thereby connecting the expectations of technical and social trust. Most mechanics in Pathanwadi rely on Atif bhai who runs a secondhand spare parts shop in a *chor-bazaar* (thieves market). How much of Atif's machinery actually comes from thieves is hard to tell. He stocks several things manufactured in other countries decades ago that probably don't conform to current regulations in India. This suggests that although he probably procures spare parts from both licit and illicit sources, they are sources that he has *bharosa* (trust) in. Almost half the shop has items for taxis, particularly for the Padmini and the Hyundai Santro. These are both cars whose manufacture has ceased but that continue on the roads as taxis and remained throughout my research as a large market for used parts.

Atif's shop is stuffed full of metallic objects of every shape, size, and age. The metal glints blazingly in the sun. Atif seems to imbibe and reflect this shine as he sits on a stool under a tarp with his prayer beads tightly wrapped around his fleshy wrist. He is a large and loquacious man who laughs almost as intensely as he shines. Stacks of secondhand tires sit under the tarp with him. The heat of the sun and its reflection off the glistening metal make the tires give off an intense, rubbery smell that spreads through the air all the way to the bus stop a half kilometer away. While this warm, rubbery odor surrounding Atif marks him as a man connected to the life of automobiles, his body is not battered by driving work. Atif is chillia, and he claims he is in the taxi dhandha, but he has never driven a taxi. Instead, since he took over his father's spare parts business, he has been connected to the taxi trade by living closely with and imbibing the shines and smells of taxi parts for over thirty years.

While he sells parts to anyone who comes to his shop, when he knows that a driver or mechanic is chillia he immediately lowers his price or else offers them no-interest loans or deferred payments. Atif keeps close track of what he sells, to whom, and for what car. He has a scrappy ledger in which he begins a new, dated page each day where he records details of each sale, the name of the mechanic who is buying the part, the car that the part will go into, and a contact phone number. He also notes the license plate of the car that will be the recipient of the spare part. All this makes Atif a vital source of information about which parts are going to a particular car and when.

Since Atif's customers are mostly kaalipeeli taxi drivers, he keeps a list of names of drivers who are looking to buy or sell their kaalipeelis. He facilitates communication between interested buyers and sellers, helps set and negotiate car prices, and smooths over ruffled feathers when a deal falls through. While the sign on his shop says he is a spare parts dealer, he has also become unintentionally enmeshed in the secondhand car sales business. Those who enter transactions with him agree that Atif intimately *knows* the taxis that are being bought and resold in a way that no one else does. But he also knows the people who are buying and selling. So he is deeply trusted, which rebuts the commonly held assumptions in Western automobile markets that all those in the used car business are automatically suspect. The secondhand car market for taxis almost always operates through transactions between familiar or vouched-for people rather than between complete strangers. A secondhand car can only be trusted if the seller and buyer are trusted. Trust is established if they are able to defend their knowledge of each of the parts of the car fully.

While taxi drivers and mechanics of older cars have developed relationships of trust and technicity (Fisch 2018) toward their own cars, the conversations at Atif's shop suggest they also expect the same technicity from others they transact with. Chillia drivers who purchase secondhand cars from other chillia who have been past customers of Atif's spare parts also rely on Atif for the careful documentary knowledge in his ledger of what is in a particular car and how trustworthy the car and its parts might be. Atif enjoys his authority over this circular knowledge that keeps bringing people back to him. He admits that he loves the banter and deliberations over cars and parts and creative technological fixes that unfold at a constant stream at his shop. He likes to see the familiar faces coming back to him, but he also appreciates that it allows him to secure permanent customers over several generations who exchange both cars and parts.

CONCLUSION: LIFE, *DUM*, SUBSTANCE

In repair work, chillia call on a wide range of practices that make, sustain, and pass on life to cars and cement relations with those around them. Anthropologists of kinship apply the term "substance" to refer to natural, bodily substances such as blood, semen, or milk (Carsten 2004). These are biological and bodily substances that are shared to cement relatedness. In the Indian context it is well-accepted that the substances that bind kin relationships are extensively and creatively malleable (Lambert 2000; Marriot 1976). If, as anthropologist Janet Carsten argues (2000, 2004), the most important property of a substance is that it is transmitted between persons, and through transmission it cements relatedness between those who share it, the Padmini for chillia is a technology of shared substance, parts, and shared senses. These are heighted in the course of repair. Once an old car enters the realm of use and repair in the chillia taxi trade, it becomes a shared object that cements relations and gives life cross-generationally, thereby taking on the characteristics of a substance.

For example, on an early June morning, Habib's car first coughs, then heaves, and then chokes to a stop on a small by-lane of the Pathanwadi market just as he begins his daily driving shift. Even before Habib calls for help, several other drivers getting ready for their own shifts congregate around the back of Habib's taxi. "Come on put some *dum* [power/breath/life] into the push," someone shouts. There is shouting all around: "Yes, yes, dum lagao, bhai [Put some *dum* in it, brother]." It is not unusual for older cars on the roads of Mumbai to need this infusion of *dum*, which comes from the meeting of force from the bodies of drivers and the electrical circuits from the ignition. Four men hitch up their pajamas and position themselves on each side of the taxi to direct *dum* from their own hands into the lifeless machine. Habib stays in the car and alternatively steers or turns the key in the ignition, trying to find that familiar place where the human power from the push meets the mechanical power of the ignition to bring the car back to life.

While collective forces of *dum* often succeed in getting the car to move, today Habib's car is unresponsive. It has no *dum* of its own. The engine chugs softly, but refuses to power up. Habib's nephew Palam senses his uncle's disappointment with these signs of enfeeblement. He leaves the group pushing at the back, moves to the driver-side window and gently places his hand next to Habib's on the steering wheel. Together the men push and steer the lifeless car onto one corner of the road. Once the car is off the main pathway, the men gather around it, discussing the chugs of the engine. "Habib bhai, there is choke; try to remove the choke," says Bilal. Chokes, as both environmental and technological blockages, live in the respiratory worlds of both drivers and cars.

Habib, who sits in the car for a few minutes, thinking by himself, gets out, opens the trunk, and pulls out a bright blue rubber pipe. He attaches one end of this to the innards of the car; he sucks a dark, thick liquid through the pipe, some of which he spits into a corner of the taxi stand but the rest of which he seems to ingest. As Habib doubles over in a swell of coughing, Nafees, another driver takes over the pipe. Not much comes up the curve of the pipe this time. Nafees spits what did float up into the same corner, after which he pulls the pipe gently off Habib's engine and moves to attach it to another taxi owned by his neighbor Rafiq that has its hood up, also with a choke, awaiting its turn. Rafiq puts his mouth to the pipe, spits, and gives Nafees a turn.

For one brief moment as all these men drink from the same pipe, one cannot tell where the boundaries of Habib, Nafees, Rafiq, and their taxis begin or end. Were they one person, two, three or more? Anthropologist Harris Solomon (2016) illustrates how people's bodies have absorptive relationships with their urban environments that can have impacts on their health and personhood. One might ask in the case of drivers and their cars how these absorptions are also relationships that mark those people and things that are kin. As we see from the shared absorptions of Nafees and Habib, the car and all the dekh-bhal directed at it to give it *dum*—life—mark the car itself as a substance that bring these men together as men.

Habib's car is an amalgam of material and metaphorical substances— oil, gas, and coolants—that give it life. These substances appear, spill over, and are sucked out and absorbed by Habib and Nafees as they try to give it other kinds of life. In this giving and taking of life-giving substances in the course of repair and dekh-bhal, the Padmini cements both life and relations. More significantly, as anthropologist Daniel Miller (2001) points out, while cars are seen as a sign of our modern alienation, they are also a means to resist alienation, to build and sustain relations and relatedness and to direct love and care toward. For drivers and mechanics in Pathanwadi, the car operates this way. Maintenance and repair in the chillia taxi trade and the dekh-bhal that it entails illustrates that relations of technicity are inseparable from the maintenance, care, and reproduction of social life. This care is not without burdens. That drivers and mechanics refer to their practices as dekh-bhal suggests that these are rife with burdens and breakdowns that resemble other contexts of care among kin. However, to ask why it is that the Padmini has come to matter so much in the chillia taxi trade is to recognize its technicity, its presence as a life-affirming substance, as *dum*, life, and as kin.

6 POLITICS

Labor Unions and Competing Forms of Knowledge

THROUGHOUT MY FIELDWORK WITH DRIVERS, TALK ABOUT TAXI unions, visits to union offices, requests to the union for help, and outright criticism of union actions were ubiquitous. I regularly found myself at a union office with a driver who wanted to get the latest information about rules and policies, file a complaint about mistreatment from traffic police, deposit objects that passengers had left behind in their taxi to the union's lost-and-found cupboard, or get a license or permit renewed. Union offices were lively places where the political and bureaucratic actions of the taxi trade took place. As I came to know the union leaders and their staff well, I spent a considerable amount of time at union offices and attended meetings between union leaders and state officials.

The sensory worlds of driving, repair, and dekh-bhal exist alongside the political and bureaucratic spheres of union politics. Union politics also depends on relational forms of knowledge production and on transactions between the same people over time; however, here it is competition between the legal, bureaucratic, and institutional aspects of knowledge that shapes relations rather than the sensory knowledge of the drivers' jaalu. Shifting allegiances and tensions exist between the unions, between unions and the state transport bureaucracy, and between drivers and road safety initiatives. The political maneuvers among those who speak on behalf of drivers are important illustrations of competitive labor politics in a city with a history of many rival labor leaders. However, equally importantly, they are also examples of how competing forms of knowledge about the city and about driving work are produced.

While drivers move in and out of these legal, political, and bureaucratic worlds regularly, and know how to navigate them well, these worlds operate distinctly from the sensory worlds of driving and repair work. The distinction between the somatic and bureaucratic worlds of the taxi trade is intentionally reflected in the ethnographic structure and voice of this chapter as it moves from dusty nakas to offices of unions and politicians. These different worlds and their different configurations of knowledge and

regulation are vital to how tensions over driving work and rights to contemporary Mumbai's roads play out. The shift in ethnographic voice in
this chapter draws attention to the competing, yet intertwined domains of
knowledge and sociality between life at the naka and jaalu and that of unions
and union leaders, and between the somatic, care-work of technicity, and
the technocratic work of urban bureaucracy.

MUMBAI'S TAXI UNIONS AND THEIR MULTIPLE POLITICS

When I ask Mr. Q, who heads the Mumbai Taximen's Union, about the
role of various unions in the city, he sits back in his chair and tells me
matter-of-factly, "See, there are about fifteen or sixteen unions in Mumbai
now. But the RTO (Regional Transport Office) only recognizes three—the
Taximen's Unions, the Taxi Association, and the Shiv Sena's Chalak
Malak Sena. The others, if they say they are unions, that is in name only.
Anyone can put up a board and say they are a union. Union has become a
business. These three are the only unions that have any 'documents.' Others have only boards, no registration documents." Despite Mr. Q's opinion on what he considers legitimate unions with proper documents, the
reality is that Mumbai has several unions that hold different degrees of
sway and influence over drivers. This multiplicity has significantly shaped
Mumbai's transport politics.

On the other hand, Mumbai taxi drivers routinely classify unions according to tactics and charisma of their leadership. I was educated on these
differences by Bilal. There is what drivers call the *moochad* (mustached)
union, referring to the largest union, the Mumbai Taximen's Union, led by
a man with a large mustache who they refer to as *moochad* or mustached
man. Another is the *tod-phod* union, the tongue-in-cheek reference to the
Swabhiman (self-respect) Union that breaks and damages (*tod-phod*) things
around the city (led by the son of a prominent politician from the Congress
Party); then there is the Marathi union (led by a nativist political party, the
Maharashtra Navnirman Sena, that fights to reserve taxi permits for local
Marathi speakers only); and there is the "good union," which also represents street hawkers and auto rickshaw drivers and led by the son of a politician from the National Congress Party (or the NCP). Therefore, the unions
all occupy different places for drivers in the labor landscape. Unions capi-
talize on these distinctions in what they know to be a competitive and con-
tinuously expanding field. They spend a great deal of effort trying to build
and attract allegiances with each other and with drivers.

Generally all taxi unions and their leaders show genuine kindness and solidarity with drivers. They make drivers' struggles visible through the media and valiantly fight the battle of refusal of bondage to private companies and investors alongside drivers at taxi strikes. They also take passively oppositional, rather than openly combative, stances against the transport planning authorities. However, many unions also operate as political entities with distinct electoral ambitions. Much of their time is spent in political jockeying among themselves and with officials in the transport sectors of the state and city governments.

In the Global South there are strong alliances between transport unions and state institutions. Often, unions use these alliances to extract money and other resources from transport workers in return for protection (Agbiboa 2018). However, in Mumbai, relations between taxi unions, representatives of the state, and taxi drivers are less consolidated or extractive than they are strategic and dispersed. These players deploy a range of strategies in their interactions with each other. Competing political parties establish unions to help their longer-term electoral ambitions rather than for short-term extractive gains. The various taxi unions alternate between cooperative and obstinate positions vis-à-vis state institutions and each other. When drivers feel that particular unions cooperate too much with state institutions, such as the transport commissioner's office or the police, they move their allegiance to other unions. Therefore, most Mumbai taxi drivers move between unions and seek different things from each one.

Early taxi unions in Bombay were tied to other labor organizations in the city. The first worker's organization in India, the Bombay Mill Hands Association, was established in Bombay in 1890. Through the early twentieth century, several labor unions of textile workers were established in Indian cities.[1] Following labor strikes in Bombay in 1928, labor unions were usurped under the Communist Party. Political parties such as the Congress and other socialist parties entered the labor movement to counter electoral dominance of the Communist Party, making trade union mobilization and electoral party politics indistinct. Therefore, connections between labor unions and electoral politics goes back to the early twentieth century. The affiliation between trade unions and political parties has had an ambivalent effect on labor.

More recently, transport labor politics has been impacted by the entry of other competing transport labor structures such as those represented by Ola and Uber. Taxi drivers, union leaders, mechanics, and even officials in the transport ministry see these as conjoined evil twins and refer to them in ominous, hyphenated terms as Ola-Uber.[2] This is the irony of these big capitalist giants. As the two companies try to compete and differentiate themselves from each other, for those who are actually on the roads, Ola-Uber, represent the same economic entity and the same economic dislocations.

Additionally, politics is shaped by technocratic programs such as driver training programs and road safety campaigns. The latter are collaborations between government agencies, nongovernmental organizations, private corporations, and transnational agencies such as the Ford Foundation, the World Bank, and the IMF. These initiatives targeting driver behavior are also heavily invested in road and other infrastructural projects. Technocrats associated with these projects gain symbolic legitimacy with their own agencies and with corporate sponsors by connecting themselves to labor and transport unions. Drivers are less than enamored by these initiatives. However, drivers are drawn in by the incentives that agencies offer in return for their participation that fulfills training and reporting mandates. Incentives range from honoraria to free food and snacks, to gift certificates for spare parts. Unions and transport associations are not outwardly hostile to such efforts. However, they rarely endorse them explicitly. For the most part, these efforts are either humorously tolerated or else distinctly mocked. Both drivers and unions see these technocrats and their sponsoring organizations as entirely removed from the actual experiences of the road.

What Mr. Q calls the three main unions—the Mumbai Taxi Association, the Taximen's Association, and Shiv Sena's Chalak Malak Sena—have operated since the twentieth century. He correctly observes that taxi unions have become arms of the various political parties over the last decade. These other unions and associations signal the twenty-first-century shifts in the taxi industry. The fleet taxi initiatives spawned a range of new taxi unions and associations. The entry of Ola-Uber spawned several more. Further, both Ola and Uber are also expanding into platform-based auto-rickshaws and other services such as food delivery. This means that disparate groups of mobile labor are continually being encompassed into the political tangle.

Many of these unions and associations have small offices in shop fronts across suburban Mumbai's settlements. These are structured much like branch offices of political parties and, in many cases, function as such. Since auto-rickshaws only have permits to ply in Mumbai's suburbs, these suburban offices are usually where auto-rickshaw drivers go when they need help. The established taxi labor unions and associations remain located in their historical homes in Central Mumbai where only taxis are allowed to ply. Newer unions tied to political parties also attend to other problems of city life such as housing, slum redevelopment, water shortages, and access to *Aadhaar* cards.

Aadhaar is the biometric identification system (the largest biometric ID system in the world) that the Indian government uses to distribute subsidies and benefits to the poor.[3] Leaders of established transport unions are specifically tangled in these knots of old and new labor problems and demands. For example, at the time of my research, the leader of the Mumbai Auto-Rickshaw Drivers Association was also the president of the Mumbai Hawkers Association and the Brihanmumbai Electric Supply and Transport (BEST) Transport Workers Union. He wears many hats as he attends to all these constituencies. While these different roles allow leaders of unions and associations proximity to a range of workers, they also create conflicting loyalties and political positions. Demands made by new organizations are often different from those of the more well-established labor unions.

UNIONS, LABOR, AND CULTURAL MANEUVERS

It is important to recognize that these different demands are undergirded by ethnic, religious, linguistic, and regional differences that map onto political affiliations among transport workers. The struggles among transport workers rarely map easily onto oppositional social actors who identify as workers, employers, or capitalists. What counts as taxi labor is highly differentiated. As for chillia, first it is differentiated according to regional, ethnic, and religious claims. Second, it is differentiated based on varied migration patterns of labor into the city and into the taxi trade. These different patterns of migration are tied to ethnic and linguistic categories but they are not exactly the same thing. While the extent of relatedness to the city is affected by migration patterns, these migration patterns are entangled with other things like access to documents that prove residency in Mumbai. The latter in turn affects access to permits, licenses, and other regulatory documents that put and keep people on the roads. This differential access to documents determines relations between drivers and different unions. Different groups of drivers go to different unions for assistance depending on what kinds of documents they need. The taxi trade is differentiated based on different positions that taxi labor occupies, not just relative to capital, but also to the many labor organizations who claim to speak for them.

For instance, while driving has historically been dominated by particular ethnic groups, so, too, has union leadership. Konkani Mangaloreans who were associated with other labor movements in the city dominated the organization of taxi labor. The Bombay (now Mumbai) Taximen's Union was established in 1962. It was founded by noted labor leader George Fernandes, who brought together labor agitations in the taxi industry with broader labor movements in Bombay's manufacturing and textile industry. Fernandes was a Christian from Mangalore. Almost all the top leadership of this union—the city's biggest, and now led by Mr. Q—continue to be Mangalorean Christians.

Mangaloreans used to, though no longer, drive taxis. However, they still hold a prominent place as political representatives of the taxi trade. While chillia drivers take advantage of the English and Marathi literacy of Mangalorean leaders to help them navigate permits and other paperwork, they don't always trust that Christians can understand the constraints of Muslim drivers. When regulations requiring new cars were first introduced this suspicion intensified. For instance, after a particularly fruitless day at the union's offices, chillia driver Yusuf angrily remarked, "That [union president] is eating out of the same *thali* [plate] as the government, as Meru and all the others.[4] He is not working for us. He mixes his food with theirs and gets lots to eat as a result. I have been part of the union since 1980. What has the union done for me? One day our leader says this, the next day he says that. He is not interested in anything but money."

The most prominent tension between chillia drivers and the union involves the union's agreement with the government demand that all drivers who want to remain in the trade must buy new cars. Chillia suggest that this bargain represents the union's collusion with the state and goes against the interests of observant Muslims who cannot take loans for the purchase of new cars as easily as others can without violating the Islamic rules against riba (interest).[5] As Yusuf says, "Dealing with any kind of interest payment is against our religion. If the government asks for new cars, what they are really doing is pushing Muslims like me out of the trade. Who will hear from us? Who will speak for us? Chillia have to stick together against this injustice or we have to get out of the business."

Yusuf voices an important debate swirling around taxi stands in the chillia community. It is also one that he has raised several times with the taxi unions to try to get them to slow down the changes on religious and cultural grounds. On one hand, it is a debate among pious Muslims over how to make empowering choices for themselves in the project of globalization and how to remain significant, modern, labor actors on their own terms. However, these oppositional claims have broader economic and political stakes. Labor opposition rooted in Islamic religious claims is a strategy that asks that secular transport policy spread the measures of financial and social risk across the community and across the trade. This allows everyone greater capacity to reposition themselves in relation to future economic opportunities and other economic actors. Urban theorist AbdouMaliq Simone (2014) calls these "maneuvers"—actions by people in difficult urban environments across the world to steer economic transactions and politics into opportunities for inclusion in other future but undefined opportunities that are assumed to be better than what is offered in the present. Capacity to steer the discussions in this way and to criticize the union in terms of their cultural betrayals and insensitivities, and their "secular" economic knowledge, is vital to understanding why chillia continue to drive on their own terms.

UNIONS AND THE DEBATES OVER INSCRIPTION AND LEGALITY

Mr. Q's statement about various unions who have no documents, and are hence unions in name only, notably signals an important connection between legitimacy and documentation. If the taxi trade is intricately enmeshed in kinship and relatedness, it is also enmeshed in a wide range of documents. Unions exist in the inscriptionary world that anthropologists Akhil Gupta (2012) and Matthew Hull (2012) discuss in the cases of Indian and Pakistani bureaucratic practices. Some examples are union registration documents, bank loans, car leases, taxi permits, licenses, pollution checks and approvals, police reports, and *Aadhaar* cards; in the case of Ola-Uber, smartphone plans and contractual agreements. However, unions are also embroiled in fights over other forms of documentary evidence along the road and across the city itself. These are inscriptions that mark permissions to the city and rights to the road in material terms such as Parking, No Parking, and Taxi Stand signs. As Mumbai's roads become more congested, and as everyone struggles over smaller and smaller slivers of the road, unions have been singularly focused on preservation of Taxi Stand signs and refutation of No Parking signs. While these are material signs, they are also ways of asking for rights to particular slivers of road space. Unions produce legitimacy by helping drivers procure documentary evidence. In particular, they help drivers learn when the government and others fiddle with this documentary evidence, by getting rid of signs, by putting up what drivers call nalla (bogus, fraud) signs, or by giving nalla permits and licenses to undeserving drivers.[6]

There is a widespread suspicion that the government is an agent of much that is nalla or fake. Unions charge that nalla permits can be bought and sold on an extralegal market, taxi permits can be leased to people without proper procedure, and Taxi Stand signs can be put up or taken down depending on who can pay off transport agents enough. Unions both work and compete with each other to procure documents that are real, not nalla, to fight battles against nalla, and to educate drivers to decipher between nalla and real documents. Drivers, unions, citizens, and political parties, can all participate in this politics of producing and countering nalla.

While unions spend a great deal of time assisting with documents, since 2010 they have also been engaged in mediating the upheavals and uncertainties unleashed by policies of taxi modernization. By 2015 debates over the legality of companies like Uber and violent protests against them were proliferating worldwide. While Uber entered the Indian market with big plans of disruption, they met severe competition from Olacabs that was already offering smartphone-based taxi services in India. In India, Ola-Uber are known as taxi aggregators. The term "aggregator" was delineated by India's Central Government in their 2015–16 budget. It refers to those companies or people who manage transport through a web-based software application (Shah 2015, cited in Basu 2019); this is what is called ride-sharing in many other parts of the world.

The effects of taxi aggregators differ across Indian cities. Cities like Delhi, for example, have never had a system of hailed taxis that ply the streets or wait at nakas for rides as Mumbai does. Mumbai is exceptional in India in this regard. On the other hand, while unique in India, the hailing taxi system in Mumbai is similar to that found in other major cities in the world. Other small taxi aggregators tried to enter the Indian market, but have been unable to sustain their business against Ola-Uber, making Ola and Uber the two most dominant aggregators. Together they hold 95 percent of India's ride-share market, with Ola holding a more dominant share at 56.2 percent (Salve 2019; Surie 2018). Ola and Uber are fierce competitors in the Indian market and work hard to differentiate themselves from each other. However, despite their efforts at branding, and their different trajectories, for almost everyone in the kaalipeeli taxi industry, they are contained within the same symbolic universe as "outsiders" to the taxi industry. Since 2015 almost all strikes, protests, official petitions, and discussions over the future of the taxi trade have focused on how to tame the effects of Ola-Uber and on how to reign them in.

When I began my research, fleet taxis were the enemy, and fleet taxi companies owned by large corporate investors were creating chaos. This gave rise to new political claims and gave birth to new taxi unions. However, by 2015, fleet taxi companies and the kaalipeeli taxi trade had become allies. The largest and most promising fleet taxi companies, Meru and Tabcab, were no longer able to maintain their business structures. Their major investors began to pull out of their commitments. Venture capitalists who had at one point been so excited about these ventures were no longer interested. These companies had purchased several fleets of new cars that they owned and leased to drivers. When Ola-Uber began to take away massive market share, using their flexible, low-investment business strategy, fleets with their heavy investment were no longer in a position to maintain their cars. Their drivers began to appeal to the taxi unions to protect their rights. Their cars fell into disrepair and the same discourse of obsolescence that was applied to kaalipeelis was applied to cars that had once been fleet taxis.

At a meeting between union leaders and fleet taxi drivers, this condition was summed up rather poetically for me: "When they [fleets] first came to compete with kaalipeelis, they were the snake; then they became arrogant and Ola-Uber came in to crush them—the big snake came and ate up the small snake and all their cars are being dumped in the snake's swamp."

While none of these cars dumped in the "snake's swamp" were "old" in the sense of historical time, the competition between these different spheres of labor and capital also rendered fleets newly out of place in the city. The terms of the debate over Mumbai's modern mobility and modernity were once again shifting and impacting driving livelihoods, and unions were an important part of them. However, in this tangle of shifting ideas about who and what has a place in the city, the discussions over how to fold multiple forms of driving work into an off-modern (Boym 2017) future persists. The most potent expression of this persistence is in the investments that unions make in what they called *ghar-wapsi*—or coming home.

GHAR-WAPSI AND THE MAKING OF LEGAL KIN

Sociologist Aditi Surie (2018) argues that what allows the rapid capitalist growth of transport businesses that depend on digital platforms is that their technological innovation and hands-off approach toward their vast, transnational labor force has far outpaced regulatory innovation. Leaders of various taxi unions and taxi associations in Mumbai recognized this conundrum well. Mr. Q and Mr. S, who lead the Mumbai Taximen's Union and the Mumbai Taxi Association, respectively, both lament that when they first began to protest what they called the "legality" of Ola-Uber, they faced a curious dilemma. Extant transport law in Mumbai had absolutely nothing to say about nonpermitted, privately owned vehicles. Therefore, Ola-Uber were not breaking the laws of mobility as much as they were *exceeding* it. Even Mr. K, who was in charge of taxi affairs at the transport commissioner's office in Mumbai, smiled at them helplessly when they came to complain: "See, there is no law being broken so we can't do anything. One suggestion I have is, why don't you propose making a law that prevents this and then we can pursue it. That is the only way." This meant that the first task for taxi union leaders was to bring the law into being before they could claim that Ola-Uber was playing outside of it.

Mr. Q often said, "Don't worry, these Ola-Uber drivers will have a *ghar-wapsi* [coming home]; they will come back home into the taxi world; it has to happen." What he meant in material terms was that Ola-Uber would soon have to work within the confines of the taxi trade by needing permits and taxi licenses. However, in symbolic terms this was an interesting wish to express. The idea of *ghar-wapsi* signals a form of kinship of a different kind— that by being encompassed by the same laws, the various structures of taxi mobility can become *legal kin*.

One place where the different unions and associations coalesced was around the 2016 proposal called the City Taxi Scheme. This laid out the regulations for what union leaders saw as *ghar-wapsi*. At around the same time, the state governments in other urban centers of India, such as Delhi and Bengaluru, were also pushed by transport commissioners and transport unions and associations to develop their own city taxi schemes. Each of these had some common features while taking into account more specific transport structures of each city. The taxi schemes were also shaped by the voices of unions and associations in each city. In Mumbai, the Maharashtra City Taxi Scheme petitioned to bring app-based services into conformity with the Motor Vehicles Act. It laid out several demands: a requirement that app-based drivers need taxi permits, a commercial driver's license, and the public service vehicle badge that is required of all taxi drivers. These documents were to be the markers of legal kinship— *ghar-wapsi*—for labor across the taxi industry. They were to bring all taxi drivers under an umbrella as operators of public service vehicles rather than to separate those who operated via Ola-Uber as private contractors. The requirements for permits and other public documentation was also a clever strategy to slow down the proliferation of app-based taxi cabs, which otherwise required no waiting period and minimum regulatory paperwork from the transport authorities. Union leaders and drivers consistently alleged that the ease with which Ola-Uber increased supply by putting more and more cars on the road, paired with their ability to lure customers with lower fares, coupons, and other incentives whenever they wanted, had significant effects on the business of all other taxis.

Ola-Uber in Mumbai are not entirely unregulated as in other parts of the world or even other parts of India. They operate through a permitting system of tourist permits or what in the taxi trade is simply called a T-permit. T-permits are issued to cars hired for what is known as "point-to-point" travel. This is the travel that caters to tourists or travelers who travel outside the official boundaries of the city. T-permit cars have a red letter T painted onto the body of the car. Tourist permits were never intended to be used for taxis that drive people within the city limits, and cars with a T-permit cannot be flagged down or hailed. Nor are their fares based on taxi meters. Therefore, historically, T-permits signaled a right to the roads outside the city, while a taxi permit and taxi badge permitted a right to the city's roads. The tension between these two distinct modes of being on the road *inside* and *outside* the city mark the current debates.

The use of the T-permit was an easy way for Ola-Uber to enter the Indian market. Their use of smartphones instead of government-inspected meters to determine fares meant that they were not strictly breaking the law. Similarly, because these cabs cannot be hailed or flagged down and have their pickup and destination points prearranged, they can claim that they are in fact "point-to-point" vehicles rather than the intermediate public transport that kaalipeeli taxis are. This is what makes the debate over "legality" so vexed. It is not easy for unions to claim that any law has been broken in present legal terms. This is why *ghar-wapsi* calls for a future law to be put in place on moral and ethical grounds. Both union leaders and government transport officials bemoaned their inability to respond effectively to complaints about Ola-Uber's legality. A key transport official shook his head earnestly when he told me, "Union leaders want me to ban Ola-Uber; I understand their demand and their frustration, but I have told them to first help me make the law that I can then enforce against Ola-Uber. Right now there is no law, so what can I enforce?" Mr. Q of the Taximen's Union told me that this prompting from the transport officials encouraged unions to draft the City Taxi Scheme.

The City Taxi Scheme also includes regulations that all app-based taxis be required to run on CNG fuel like other public service vehicles and that their minimum and maximum fares be brought in line with those of metered taxis. Another important recommendation is aesthetic, that is, that all app-based taxis use the same color to mirror the quick recognition and identification as taxis in the same way that kaalipeelis are marked. While the taxi scheme proposal was drafted in 2016, a few months later, drivers from Ola-Uber challenged the scheme at the Bombay High Court, claiming that the requirements laid out by the scheme put an undue burden on them. Many of them had purchased cars using expensive car lease and loan schemes sold to them via Ola-Uber recruitment centers. They were on the hook for car payments and claimed that the permitting and waiting would put most of them out of business and prevent them from being able to pay off their debts.[7]

TANGLES, CHALLENGES, MEETINGS

This challenge by Ola-Uber drivers significantly slowed down the scheme's approval. Much like the shifting decisions on dates for the retirement of the kaalipeeli cars, the dates for the City Taxi Scheme approval also keeps shifting. In March 2017, both the Taximen's Union and the Taxi Association told their members that a vote and implementation would take place by the end of that month. However, rising opposition and the threat of strikes by Ola-Uber drivers forced a one-month extension for the approval. In early June, the transport commissioner's office called an emergency meeting of the leaders of the major unions. Due to the generosity of several in the transport ministry, I was able to get myself invited to this meeting.

Mr. Q told me that leaders from nine unions across the city had been invited. When I showed surprise that there were so many unions, he smiled knowingly, with more than a little bit of disdain, and said, "Only nine have been invited; there are about sixteen to seventeen unions; unions have become a *business* you know. Everyone has a taxi union."

When I asked if Ola-Uber were invited he responded adamantly, "No, only *stakeholders* in the taxi trade have been invited; Ola-Uber are not stakeholders so they will not be there."

In the weeks leading up to this meeting, there was a great deal of anticipation among all the union leaders. In the union and association offices, the words "June 13 meeting" flew around with great regularity whenever drivers brought in a complaint about how their business was being threatened by Ola-Uber or about how they were being treated by police, or even about the sad state of the roads. They were mollified by the reassurance, "Wait until the June 13 meeting at Mantralaya.[8] We will have answers. The City Taxi Scheme will soon be approved and then we can do everything. Until then, keep doing your dhandha."

The big day arrived and on the morning of June 13, 2017, I wait outside a conference room at the offices of the transport commissioner. Mantralaya is the seat of the state government offices. As we are entering a state government building, all of us need approvals and to be cleared on a list of visitors in advance of the meeting. Leaders of the Taximen's Union and the Bombay Taxi Association, the organizations with the deepest history in the transport trade, are ushered through the gate with no clearance questions. They seem to be known well by the guards and gatekeepers, while others are asked for much more information. Differences in processes of entry into a government building indicate different positions each organization occupies relative to the government bureaucracy. Not unsurprisingly, I, the strangest face of all, receive the most questions. After we make it through guards and questions, we are led up to a clean, air-conditioned office floor.

Leaders of seven transport unions and associations mill around the corridor talking on their mobile phones. They acknowledge each other politely, warmly, and familiarly, but there is little conversation among them. While I had talked to each of these men at great length over the years, this was the first time I see them all together. In their conversations with me, they always displayed a respectful acknowledgement of the work that the others do. When specifically asked about interunion cooperation, all of them always nod and say, "Yes, we are with them [Hum unke saath hain]." However, despite some solidarity, each of these men also works to distinguish themselves and their organizations and claim to be more involved than others in the "urgent" work needed. There is no outward hostility toward the others. Instead, each one claims that while they believe the others have good intentions, these others are limited by experience, knowledge, or distance, from those who really need their help. They wait here today in a familiar and yet distant manner and without much exchange. This ambivalent, distant, familiarity is fairly typical of their interactions. These are men trying to demarcate different realms of political activity not so much to get out of the tangle but to establish some dominance within it.

The transport commissioner is held up at a meeting elsewhere, so his assistant requests we wait outside the conference room until his arrival. She specifically indicates to me to take a seat on a small couch in the corner. Already seated there, and texting vigorously on their mobile phones, are three others whom I have not met before. The first is a man who introduces himself as a representative of the Maharashtra chief minister. The second is a man who works for a Bengaluru-based technology company, Sun Telematics. He informs me that Sun Telematics is partnering with city governments to build smart mobility and transport management systems. The third is a woman working as a consultant with the Maharashtra chief minister's office on what she calls "urban technology issues."

Technology, smart mobility, and transport management—I begin to suspect that this will not be the meeting that union leaders expected. These are all technocratic realms that I do not think union leaders want to talk about. They are focused instead on the immediacy of passing a bureaucratic scheme that had been delayed by these technocratic interruptions.

We make small talk about Mumbai, its traffic, and about pressures of commuting in the city as we wait. At about 10:45 a.m., forty-five minutes after the meeting was set to begin, two men dressed in security-guard uniforms noisily exit the elevator and walk decisively into the conference room. One carries a briefcase, and the other, a stack of files. "*Saab* [sir] is here," a female voice declares from inside one of the many geometrically arranged cubicles facing the elevator. Briefcase and files often precede the entry of government officials and bureaucrats in India. On cue, the second elevator opens and the transport commissioner steps out. His mobile phone is firmly implanted against his right ear. He nods and half smiles at the union leaders in front of him before sailing down the corridor. All those seated with me on the couch bounce up to a standing position. He acknowledges our gestures of respect with a cock of the head before he slips through the door held open for him by his file carrier. As the union representatives begin to put away their own cell phones and walk over in anticipation of being let in, the door clicks shut in their faces. For the first time that morning they begin to talk to each other in hushed anticipation. Suddenly, the door opens wide and we are invited in.

We enter a large, bright room with a wall of windows where the early monsoon sun shines through. In the center is an oblong conference table surrounded by chairs. The transport commissioner is already seated at one end of this table. The chief minister's representative takes a seat right next to him while the rest of us find places around the table. The transport commissioner promptly calls the meeting to order. Apart from three government officials, there are seven transport associations around the table, in addition to the urban planning consultant, the representative from Sun Telematics, and me. The meeting is conducted in a combination of Marathi and Hindi. After introductions, the chief minister's representative begins by saying that we have been invited here because the government wants to respond to the complaints of taxi drivers and has decided to invest in creating an app for taxis and auto-rickshaws. He feels that this would counter the unequal competition from Ola-Uber. The representative from Sun Telematics chimes in, "Ola-Uber have upset the urban ecosystem; would all taxis and auto-rickshaws agree to join a central app-based system customized for Mumbai? Our company can offer to make this."

Apart from the whirr of traffic circling the roundabout on the road outside, there is complete silence.

The chief minister's representative jumps in to paper over the awkwardness and to reassure everyone of the expertise of Sun Telematics. "They have US trained experts, from MIT," he says with his eyes gleaming.

The union leaders glance around the table at each other quizzically. I sense a ripple of quiet exasperation float around the room. I think I hear Mr. Q whisper to himself under his breath by repeating the acronym "MIT."

The sound of everyone shuffling in their chairs, and crossing and recrossing their feet under the table punctuates what comes next. The back and forth that commences illustrates how Mumbai's unions make claims on the state together at the same time that they stake out distinct positions in the landscape of transport labor politics.

Mr. R, who represents the auto-rickshaw union, pushes aside his exasperation and says gently and politely, "We are not opposed to an app-based system. What we are concerned with is that Ola-Uber circumvents the law. They have a *free hand*. So let's us try to implement the City Taxi Scheme instead of focusing on the app right now."

All the union leaders sit straight up in their chairs, encouraged by this suggestion.

The chief minister's representative jumps in impatiently, "The CM (chief minister) wants to focus on the app not on the City Taxi Scheme. So, let's talk about that."

Everyone slouches back into their chairs with a quiet defiance.

Mr. S from the Taxi Association shakes his head: "We have tried an app system. But it failed. It is not that we cannot use apps. We can. Our problem is that our fares are fixed and Ola-Uber can manipulate their fares. They are lower so passengers prefer them. So you have to first implement the City Taxi Scheme to regulate fares and then talk about apps."

I cannot help but notice here how much this *app-talk* frames the discussions on all sides.

The chief minister's representative brandishes his left hand onto the center of the table as he tries to find words to counter this challenge. He begins to say, "Let me tell you one thing—" Before he can finish, Mr. Q, of the Mumbai Taximen's Union, passionately interrupts, supporting what Mr. S has just said. "The City Taxi Scheme has not been implemented. That is most important." Then as if to reshuffle the burden back to the government, he adds, looking at the transport commissioner boldly, straight in the eye, "You also said that we could get online permit applications. That has not happened."

This mode of exchange, fluctuating between deference, defiant silence, and passionate accusation, is common in these meetings; it marks the stops and starts in this world of political and bureaucratic negotiation. It also illustrates the different kinds of expertise and knowledge that leaders can claim, ranging from the technical (app led) to the bureaucratic and policy-led (taxi scheme) domains.

The transport commissioner twiddles nervously with the stack of papers in front of him and turns accusingly to his subordinate, his additional commissioner, Mr. SB. The latter squirms at this accusatory glance from his superior that insinuates that his office has not done what it should to allow new taxi permits. He looks back at Mr. Q pointedly and says, "I want to correct you by saying that the system is now working again so online permits can be applied for." Mr. Q is not interested in this correction and turns the conversation around again: "All that is important is that the City Taxi Scheme needs to be implemented. Definitely do an app, we are ready to join an app, but first implement the City Taxi Scheme. Why one app? Get ten apps. Kaalipeelis will join. But why is Ola-Uber being given protection by not implementing the City Taxi Scheme?"

The transport commissioner looks at the chief minister's representative and says, in agreement with the union leader, "Yes, it is true, the City Taxi Scheme will bring all the aggregators under the same minimum and maximum tariff. That would solve that problem. Since our permits were frozen in 1997 at 62,000 now there are only 50,000 taxis on the road. That is a problem. We need more people going into the taxi business. And by not looking into the City Taxi Scheme we are doing harm to the taxi business."

The chief minister's representative looks flustered by what must have felt like a betrayal, even if gentle, from a government-appointed bureaucrat. The

demands of the taxi unions have laid bare the clashes of opinion as legis-
lative and bureaucratic arms of the government try to disentangle themselves for everyone to see.

The chief minister's representative does not seem happy with how the
transport commissioner is sliding into discussions of the City Taxi Scheme
to side along with the unions. He gives him a cold look of silent disapproval.
The commissioner sees this disapproval. He tries to skillfully deflect this
displeasure toward him but without losing sight of the support he needs to
provide to the transport leaders:

> Okay, okay, let's get back to the app. Who will manage the app? Making
> an app is easy, but who will manage it? Who will pay for it? I am a
> government official, but I am also a passenger in the taxi. I don't want to
> be paying a very high price for using an app and drivers also don't want
> to pay for the management of the app. I just went to Washington DC to
> learn about their taxi scheme. Washington DC municipality put in
> 20 percent for their app and the taxi associations put in 80 percent. But
> the app still does not work and people still mostly call for or hail their
> taxis. So we should not just jump on an app—Washington DC spent a
> total of one million dollars—what is that, six crores? That is a lot. We can't
> waste our money if the app does not work.

The chief minister's representative feels himself losing this battle but valiantly goes on, "The app can get rid of the business uncertainty of where
we can pick up rides."

Mr. T the leader of a newer taxi union says, "But first we have to be able
to compete. So, first implement the City Taxi Scheme."

The chief minister's representative gets impatient, "We are not discussing the City Taxi Scheme. We are discussing the app. Stick to that only."

Suddenly two men burst into the office with trays loaded with small cups
of tea. The conversation stops abruptly as the tea is served.

I take advantage of the lull to write in my notebook: "More *app-talk*, lots
of app-talk." This is becoming a central theme around which union struggles are being fought and an object of technical expertise that haunts the
taxi trade. *App-talk*, like the kind repeatedly encountered in the meeting,
circulates a great deal in taxi circles even beyond the official spheres. It is
no accident that conversation at this meeting keeps circulating back to apps.
While app-based taxis like Ola-Uber are seen as competition, the resistance
to that competition is also articulated through this technological devil

known as the "app." At this meeting there is talk about development of an app for kaalipeeli taxis and auto-rickshaws, *and* refusal to talk about it. Even outside this meeting, I observed several fragmented efforts on the part of individual union leaders trying to adopt the correct app. While they denigrate the app in front of government officials here, many union leaders spend their time attending meetings or talking on the phone with technology firms who try to woo them with different apps.

Yet after years of hearing this app-talk, I noticed that no app was adopted for the taxi industry. This failure of adoption was significant to taxi politics. As I heard more and more app-talk from union leaders, I realized that unions were not opposed to technological tools. Rather, the "app" operates as a metaphor, a heuristic for each union to carve out spaces of independent action and the possibility of separating themselves from others. If they were to agree to it collectively, here at Mantralaya, that could diminish possibilities for individual negotiations. If the jaalu operates as metaphorical togetherness that materializes as thick sociality for drivers and mechanics, in the world of unions, the app has become a technological metaphor and thing to talk about at meetings about the future that may never be intended to materialize at all.

The tea servers strut out of the room pocketing a few tips from everyone. The commissioner starts to look at his watch. It is almost lunchtime. The meeting has gone on too long. He assures everyone that if there were to be an app, the government would bear the burden of the cost of setting it up.

The chief minister's representative feels that the battle for an app is worth one more try before adjournment. He looks beseechingly at the representative from Sun Telematics. The technology consultants have not fully had their say. The young man catches his desperation and jumps in to add, "Yes, the app will be developed by us and the government. It will be just an add-on to your meters. Think of it as when you go to a *Udipi* restaurant [restaurant serving food from the Southern regions of India] and you order *idli* or *dosa* and you get *sambhar* and chutney at no extra cost.[9] That is how the app will be for you. You keep running your business and the app will be added on to help you."

No one seems to be listening to him as they rustle up papers and drag chairs to get up and leave.

Only Mr. Q raises his eyebrows at this comment and turns to Mr. S of the taxi association, "What is this *idli-dosa-sambhar*-chutney nonsense? What taximan is sitting in a restaurant? He is sitting on the roads. Talk about what is happening on roads for God's sake!"

Mr. S laughs and concurs and both men walk out of the meeting. Nothing much has been settled. Everyone now has a better idea about where they are in the tangle and a sense of the potential for future alliance.

While these various maneuvers over political position in the taxi-union environment reach into the trade and cater to different needs and differentially positioned people, and where app-talk has taken on a life of its own, the last few years have also given rise to other forms of "help" to drivers. This help is couched in the narrative of safety—road safety, in particular—and targets the production of the "good" driving subject.

I move now to discussing one particular initiative called "Safer Roads, Safer You."

SAFER ROADS, SAFER YOU

One afternoon in the summer of 2016, when I am at the offices of the Taximen's Union, a young man dressed in a buttoned-down shirt and tie walks into the office. He is accompanied by Salim, who runs the union's mechanics and spare parts shop. Salim is a mediator between many in the outside world and the union offices. Mr. Q is away from Bombay attending a family wedding in Mangalore. His desk is deserted and his chair empty. While he is away, people like Salim step in. The young man with him works for the Institute of Road Traffic Education (IRTE). The IRTE is based in Delhi. With the sponsorship of major tire manufacturer Goodyear Tyres, they are running road-safety trainings for taxi drivers in various Indian cities. They want the union's help to get the word out and to recruit drivers to attend. Their incentive for drivers who attend the day-long training is free lunch, tea, and snacks. Those who stay all day are promised a hundred rupees. The IRTE representative hands a wad of flyers to Salim and walks out without much more ceremony. I run after him, introducing myself, and ask if I could also attend and observe the training. He agrees easily and tells me to come to the Byculla Police Station the next morning where the training will be held.

Throughout the day, Salim sits behind the counter at the union office passing out flyers to drivers who come in, telling them that he knows the man who runs the training, explaining the incentives, and encouraging them to attend. Several drivers take flyers and cynically say that they cannot afford to drive all the way to Byculla Police Station and to give up a whole day of fares for lunch and a hundred rupees. They ask if this is a union event, and Salim nods his head vaguely and says, "Yes, yes, it's the union only."

Most of the drivers don't quite believe him and toss the flyers back onto the counter. Salim smiles resignedly and goes back to his shop downstairs.

I report to the Byculla Police the next morning. The police station is located in a large, historic structure. I ask for the training room and am directed to take the elevator up to the third floor, which houses the traffic police training institute. Several men who look like taxi drivers also step into the elevator with me, looking rather confused. We all make our way toward a bright, airy room set up much like a classroom with rows of desks facing a podium, blackboard, and projection screen. A big poster is on an easel outside the door that says "Safer Roads, Safer You."

Two men who introduce themselves as trainers greet us. Both are dressed in Western, business-casual wear. One of them is an older turbaned Sikh with a thick, gray beard, while the other is the younger clean-shaven man I had met at the union office the previous day. The drivers are all either dressed in their white uniforms or in plain clothes.

I sit at a desk at the back of the room while drivers sit awkwardly at desks closest to where they walked in. It is 10:00 a.m.; there is some murmuring among the drivers that the training was supposed to begin at 9:30. The trainers overhear this and inform us we need to wait for more drivers. I count nine drivers in attendance. We are told that the IRTE mandate is to have twenty drivers present in order to begin. When one more driver comes in a few minutes later to make a count of ten they decide to proceed. At around 10:30 four more drivers slip in bringing attendance to a total of fourteen—below what they needed, but the trainers are unruffled. They focus on pulling up PowerPoint presentations on the projection screen. We wait in awkward silence. I get the sense that drivers are unsure what they are here for. The walls of the room are plastered with posters related to traffic safety. On my right are posters with messages about seatbelts and helmets; on my left are posters warning drivers about the dangers of texting, use of mobile phones, overtaking, and drunk driving. On a wall behind me are posters warning drivers to slow down for children. This room dedicated to traffic safety covers it all; and yet it feels to me, and must feel to these men who spend their lives on the road, rather disconnected from the actual labor of the roads, nakas, ditches, and dust of Mumbai's roads.

The PowerPoint is up; the trainers are clearing their throats—it is time to begin. The older of the two trainers, Mr. Taig Singh, introduces the project. He begins by asking, "Tell me this, how does anyone first learn about a country?" No one responds.

Unperturbed, Mr. Singh continues, "They learn about a country from drivers, from taxi drivers like you. Foreigners see you and get picked up by you at the airport when they first come to India. If you greet one of them in a clean car and say hello, then the *angrez* [Englishman] will say 'Yes, this is a good country.' But if you break the rules the *gora* [white person] will say 'This is not a good country.'"

Tying good national citizenship to good road behavior has become an overarching strategy for driver training programs in contemporary India (Annavarapu 2019). However, as Mr. Singh begins his speech, for a moment it is unclear what language he is speaking. The drivers also look confused. The taxi trade in Mumbai is a truly multilingual space, but the Delhi-speak is confusing. Things start to make a little more sense when he hands out forms with traffic signals. He tells drivers that they must take a test by identifying what each sign means. I look at the form and see that it is set up as a multiple-choice test in English. One driver raises his hand to say he does not read English. The trainer says, "Don't worry, I'll review all the answer options and then you just pick the answer that looks the most right to you; even if you can't read, that's no problem, just pick something." Most of the drivers don't do anything at all.

The trainer jumps through most questions and settles on a question in the middle of the test, which is a question about blood alcohol levels. There are three options: fifty milligrams, one thousand milligrams, and thirty milligrams. "What is the correct answer?" he asks. Nobody responds. In a rather sinister and reprimanding way, the trainer goes on, "Okay you don't know the answer, but do you know what the punishment is for drinking and driving?" Nobody responds. With a gleam in his eye, he looks around the room and clutches at his neck dramatically before he says, "Yes, you get *phaansi*, you will be hanged." The drivers seem unruffled by this punishment. They are all trying to make sense of the form. One raises his hand and says, "I really don't know any of this, and I don't know what to write." The trainer is starting to lose his patience, "Just write your name on the form then; leave the rest, we will fill it out together." Everyone is happy to hear that they are off the hook for his test; those who can, scribble their names onto the first page. Two drivers who admit that they cannot read or write sit still. The trainer then tells each driver what answer to tick, they dutifully obey, and he collects the forms.

After this ritual of the test is complete he goes on to introduce himself to the drivers as "Mr. Taig Singh, representative of IRTE. Repeat after me, I-R-T-E." The drivers grudgingly oblige. He then delves into a history of the organization and its founding in 1991. He then pulls up a PowerPoint slide of the sponsor of today's event, Goodyear Tyres. A second slide pops up on the screen with logos of Goodyear and IRTE sitting side by side. No one seems interested. Instead they are watching the clanking of the setup of tea and biscuits in the corridor outside.

"Why do we drive?" asks Mr. Singh. Nobody answers. He prods, "We drive for our family, don't we? So that we can do the dekh-bhal of our family. So what happens if you have an accident?" One driver tentatively responds, "We die?" Mr. Singh is thrilled with this response: "Yes, now why do so many in China not die in accidents even through there are more people in China? In India we have more accidents because we have a *dalali* system. Anyone can get a license through a *dalal* (middleman/broker). So we don't get trained how to be safe."

His moves to his next question: "What is a safe driver?"

Several drivers raise their hands in response. "One who follows rules?"

"Very good, very good," says Mr. Singh excitedly. "And medical checkups are very important. There was one driver who died of a heart attack on the road and had an accident."

I am getting the sense that Mr. Singh has a fascination for morbid aspects of the road and sees roads as places of death rather than life. He goes through the slide show rapidly. This does not matter, as the slides are in English and none of the drivers appear to be literate in English. It is an interesting signal of how many of these road-safety initiatives are intended to satisfy not just a literate audience, but an English-literate audience of technocrats.

When he gets to a slide about traffic jams and images of cars stuck in traffic, many drivers sit up in recognition. The embodied experience of sitting in traffic is something they immediately recognize. But then Mr. Singh says, "See, jams are all the fault of the drivers. We have traffic jams because drivers do not follow rules."

Drivers slump back into their seats. This is something they hear all the time.

"What about taxi safety? How many of you know about deaths in taxis? Do you know that 3,644 people traveling in taxis died on the road in 2014?" The PowerPoint slides show a series of graphic images of people injured and bleeding and of dead bodies strewn along the sides of a road.

"And what about treating *ladies* with respect?" The show moves to a series of slides that show newspaper headlines about women and girls being abducted or sexually harassed by taxi drivers. Recent reports of rapes of female passengers by taxi drivers have meant that traffic safety and the safety of women have coalesced in India (Amrute 2015; Annavarapu 2019; Punit 2018).

One driver answers his ringing cell phone and begins to chat unashamedly. The trainers look at him angrily and insist he turn his phone off. He responds sheepishly that he cannot understand the slides so he is not sure why he is here.

Mr. Singh retorts rather skillfully, "See, that is the whole thing about language and not being able to understand this language. The language of the road is blind and dumb. *Batti* [light], *Patti* [lanes], *Board* [signboard]—the language of the road is different in different places, so you have to learn these symbols of the road and treat the road itself as blind and dumb. That is what makes a good driver."

CONCLUSION

Mr. Singh's declaration of what makes a good driver is a good example of the competing forms of knowledge that circulate through Mumbai's taxi trade. Interactions between drivers and union leaders and between union leaders and state representatives illustrate these socialities and competing forms of knowledge. Here the tension between legal, bureaucratic, and technological forms of knowledge is vital. A focus on the driver-training program led by Mr. Singh suggests that it is not simply that the union and technocratic spheres represent competing forms of knowledge but rather that even what it means to "know" something about the city is irreconcilable across these worlds. Taxi unions and new initiatives targeting driver education in Indian cities make up a dynamic world of politics, bureaucracy, and technocracy. These worlds and their legal, political, and bureaucratic knowledge and practices exist alongside the sensory, somatic spheres of driving and mechanics. The discursive and material connections between good and bad roads and good and bad drivers are vital to how the tensions over driving work and rights to the road's surfaces in contemporary Mumbai play out.

If taxi unions have played a central part in both historical and contemporary debates over taxis in Mumbai, their work has been accompanied by others like the IRTE initiative. These efforts are connected to private and NGO sectors. These, in turn, are connected to shifting transnational mandates from infrastructure funders like the World Bank and the IMF; these provide funding for roadbuilding but tie this funding to guarantees of changed behavior. These are competing forms of knowledge that shape various claims to the road and mark different understandings of the road itself. As Mr. Singh's well-rehearsed declaration about the language of the road as dumb and blind marks the road as inanimate, a priori, and brought to life only through norms and rules, labor unions see roads as political entities to demarcate political domains. For drivers the roads are experiential, material, and embodied—these distinctions are central to the crossroads that the taxi trade finds itself in today.

CONCLUSION

Crossroads

THIS BOOK HAS MOVED BETWEEN THE SENSORY, CAR, AND KIN worlds, the jaalu of taxi driving and auto-repair work, and the broader environmental, political, and bureaucratic spheres that the taxi trade encounters and shapes. In 2017, Mr. L, a leader in Mumbai's Taximen's Union spoke with me about this complexity:

> Everyone talks about roads, bad roads in Mumbai; yes, taxi trade has to function in this context of bad roads, congested nakas, all this. But in the taxi trade itself we are standing at our own naka just now. When I say naka, I mean we are at a crossroads; but it is two kinds of crossroads—one is the crossroads of the trade and we don't know where the trade is going; but then there is a second crossroad, a crossroad of leadership. Who will keep fighting for taxi drivers once we are all too old? Who will come out of this crossroad to fight for the people on the road?

In this travel between these worlds and surfaces of the taxi trade, Mr. L's declaration that the trade stands at a naka, or at a crossroads, is significant. He speaks wistfully of this crossroads over a cup of tea on a rainy monsoon afternoon in his flat in a middle-class housing society, about a kilometer from Pathanwadi. He looks first at me and then out onto the lush, drenched, potted plants on his small balcony. This talk of the naka, the crossroads, and the uncertainty of the future of the joona trade, clearly worry him.

His invocation of the naka as a threshold, or place of crossing over to something else, is significant for several reasons. For one, a crossroads is a temporal metaphor—it presents a way for Mr. L to reflect on the present but in terms of the past and the future—a particular expression of the off-modernity of the current state of Mumbai's taxi trade. But it brings me back to the central puzzle that I began with on my drive with Rashid, which is to ask how drivers and workers are living at the crossroads of change everywhere. Taxi drivers in practically every part of the world are experiencing upheavals. The taxi industry is also where global debates over the future of work and economic disruption are taking place. Critical understandings of work in the current economic era focus on the proliferation of either meaningless work—what anthropologist David Graeber's (2018) bestselling book calls *bullshit jobs*—or else on work that is fundamentally exploitative, precarious, and hopeless. However, the expansions of social, sensory, and mechanical expertise in Mumbai's taxi dhandha teach us that even under conditions of upheaval, change, and struggle, urban workers can and do imagine other ways of flourishing; and they continue to engage in what they feel to be dignifying work. As for Mumbai's chillia drivers and mechanics, even when conditions are outside their control, it is still possible for working classes to refuse compliance, to navigate a variety of ethical and temporal claims, and to play an active role in countering and shaping understandings of urban modernity.[1]

Further, for chillia, the jaalu of kin, technological expertise, politics, and generation of capital through hereditary networks are what make automobility legible as a key form of urban sociality and political engagement. In many parts of the world, automobility and roadbuilding went hand-in-hand. The expansion of automobility was tied to development of speed, smoothness, order, and enforceable legal systems rather than to the relations that automobiles produce to sustain social systems of value.[2] Recent scholarship on driving and automobilities outside the Western world pushes against understandings of automobile life as a purely systemic or legal realm.[3] The kaalipeeli taxi trade, the worlds that it encounters, and the socialities that it engenders could be seen as a specific, emplaced, and singularly unique *car culture* (Miller 2001). However, Mumbai's taxi trade and driving in India broadly unfolded within the more universal proliferation of automobiles and roadbuilding worldwide throughout the twentieth century. Therefore, while I have committed fully to an ethnographic engagement with Mumbai's taxi trade, the working-class culture of cars, driving, and repair that I describe here, the economic and social institutions of automobilization in India are not historically separate things. It is precisely these specific and emplaced car cultures and the sensory and social labors that surround them that allowed the automobile to take on broader social meaning and use among Indian drivers. This is what has produced what I call *Indian automobility*.

The taxi dhandha is a life of driving but it is also a life surrounded by automobiles and a variety of urban ecologies. The relationships between chillia and these objects and ecologies illustrate how Indian automobility emerged both out of projects of roadbuilding and processes of making "auto-mobile" lives in the city. As this book has illustrated, this making engaged diverse practices of dwelling, caring, sensing, and performing ongoing maintenance and repair between roads, nakas, and cars. What I call Indian automobility seen through the lens of the taxi trade unfolds through sensory, embodied, and political domains of driving work. It is labor where people who drive for a living collectively cultivate relationships to cars, technology, repair, driving, the material and ecological environment, and to the surfaces, topographies, and ecologies of the city.

In South Asia what counts as an automobile has expanded far beyond cars to other vehicles such as auto-rickshaws, motorcycles, and scooters. These are the automobiles that are expanding most rapidly in India and are also central to the expansion of other kinds of mobile work like food delivery and courier services. These have their own sensory relations to other automobiles, to each other, and to the surfaces they move through. They drive on open roads alongside cars and with non-motorized commuters, such as pedestrians and cyclists. But they also travel through other topographies. Many see them as wheels that belong to life on nakas and streets rather than to movement with smooth, open traffic. A key debate on automobility in India is about who belongs on the open road and who belongs in other places like the naka. This debate also mirrors the enduring questions about who belongs in a modern city. While automobile traffic is privileged in the mixed use of Indian roads, once all these wheels converge, the road is not a universal or equal space for all. Rather, different kinds of automobility and different drivers are differentially positioned on roads and have different capacities to stake political and sensory claims on the road's surfaces. It is in this tangle between differentially positioned automobilities and the spillage between nakas and roads that the off-modern (Boym 2017) world of Indian automobility unfolds.

Further, as drivers and their automobiles travel through urban ecologies, they fully inhabit the city. Through this they make surfaces and relations rather than (infra)structures, claim these with others, labor on and through them with others, and finally share the city's driving surfaces as kin. This collective and intersubjective approach to driving work and to life lived and sustained around the automobile moves us from an individuated to a collective and kin-like sensing of urban, automobile life. Indian drivers fully submit to the reality that the road is full of sociality and obligations. They also submit to, participate in, and shape this automobile life through the malleability of senses, topographies, and technologies of automobility. These obligations are not the same thing as road rules or what driver education initiatives call "road sense," which is closely related to what officials call "road safety." As the discussion of the Safer Roads, Safer You campaign illustrates in chapter 6, this narrative of safety casts roads in terms of epidemiology, as places of accident and death (Jacob 2018; Sayantan 2018) rather than as places of life. The work of driving, the capacity to maneuver around surfaces and to engage with the work of technicity and repair, even if it takes place in contexts of breakdown, destruction, and temporal uncertainty, is a way of claiming a malleable, collective urban life.

ROADS, CROSSROADS, AND NAKAS

A key impasse and crossroad within the taxi trade is between the kaalipeeli drivers and the app-based Ola-Uber. The expansion of Ola-Uber in India has been a boon to the Indian automobile industry because it has bumped up an allegedly slumping new-car market. People in Mumbai, including taxi drivers, feel that this expansion has created more traffic congestion and competition. For kaalipeeli taxi drivers this expansion feels like a threat to their livelihoods. As Mr. L suggests, the naka is the existential crossroads through which the taxi trade is moving; it is a state where drivers and unions are waiting for a way to participate in the modern city with others who drive and compete with them for space on the road. With the entry of fleets and now app-based taxis like Ola-Uber, the contemporary taxi trade is at a crossroads because of several new possibilities for what the taxi industry could look like. This is a crossroads that we see globally. The crossroads that Mr. L refers to is a place of waiting and repair, what anthropologist François Laplantine calls, the faded blurry, gradations (Laplantine 2015, 49) between urban surfaces and between different temporalities of driving work. The established taxi trades are standing at this crossroads in many parts of the world as they face the mobility and transport revolution.

In August 2015, I am sitting in the office of the Swabhiman (self-respect) Taxi Union. This is a newer union established to help new migrants into Mumbai who have less access to permits and support. Mr. T, himself a north Indian migrant from the state of Uttar Pradesh, is the leader. His soft-spoken tone notwithstanding, Mr. T, in his own words, is a *krantikari*, a revolutionary. Like many *krantikaris* in India, he works through a political party as the righthand man for a prominent politician. As we sit in his crowded, bustling office, he tells me about plans for a possible taxi strike to protest the app-based companies Ola-Uber. One of

Mr. T's associates, who accompanies him to various events, nods in agreement and periodically interjects with his own opinion on Ola-Uber's capture of the taxi market. Throughout our conversation, Mr. T attends to his jingling mobile phone. When the jingling pierces through our conversation for too long, Mr. T decides it must be attended to. He answers but says very little on the phone. Instead he nods vigorously, and responds to the person on the other end with encouraging agreements of "Yes, okay, okay, okay." He hangs up and tells me that the call is from members of his union, a group of both kaalipeeli taxi and auto-rickshaw drivers who are assembled on the road outside an Ola driver-recruitment center. They report that they have surrounded the Ola cars and captured and broken about twenty of their mobile devices, the devices that are the primary connection between Ola drivers and their livelihoods. "They want me to come and see what they have done and to come as protection since the police have been notified. There is going to be *kranti* [revolution] on these roads as we fight this battle, just you wait and see," says Mr. T, gleefully, as he gets up hurriedly and rushes into his waiting car. I follow him out and jump into the car with him.

In fifteen minutes we get to the Ola recruitment center. A line of kaalipeeli cabs are parked in an area with a Taxi Stand sign while a line of Ola cars are double-parked alongside them. A group of men surround the Ola cars. One Ola driver is sitting in his car, begging the kaalipeeli drivers to return his smartphone, which they wave menacingly around his window. "If we take away your phone then you will never come back on this road and your dhandha is *khallaas* [finished]," they chide him. "Take it," he says rather defiantly. "You think I can't get a new mobile? Is this your road? It's not. You can't keep me off it. You think you have a right to be here because you are joona. Okay, you do; but so do I. Now I am a new driver but one day I will also be joona. Then what?"

This assertion from the Ola driver is important. Here is a man surrounded by people trying to literally smash both his technology and his rights to a livelihood. At the same time he confronts men whom he admits have joona rights to the city's roads, but claims that he, too, has a right because he too will soon be joona in the future. As we saw in chapter 3, joona, in the world of driving, is a claim to the city made in terms of malleable jumbles of time and deep urban knowledge. This temporal jumble also unfolds at sites of topographic malleability as political claims to city surfaces, to the nakas, roads, and taxi stands of the city. It is easy to read tension between these different transporters as one fought between different spheres of capital, or over what kinds of taxis or taxi drivers belong most legitimately in a modern city. Passengers regularly make value claims based on whether a taxi is old or new, modern or obsolete. These competing claims of value are certainly at stake here and they permeate every discussion about taxis and urban transport more broadly. However, these also land violently as temporal and topographic jumbles as they do at taxi stands and at nakas where drivers either fight over who belongs in time, wait at the naka to sense what other surfaces and politics might materialize, or else encounter places of both collision and cooperation along the way.

COLLISION/COOPERATION

At 4:00 p.m. on a busy Thursday afternoon, the chillia driver, Maliq, stops his kaalipeeli to let off his passenger on a congested road in a busy business district in Central Mumbai. I am sitting in the front passenger seat. The passenger, a young man, dressed in "business casual," has not looked away from his phone for the entire drive from Andheri to Lower Parel. This is a drive of less than ten miles but it has taken us almost an hour. We have encountered plenty of traffic, pedestrians, processions, and policemen—all the people who make up moving things in Mumbai's traffic. However, we have also maneuvered around the enormous barricades that mark where construction for the new Mumbai metro is taking place. These barricades snake into the road haphazardly, making their way around existing buildings, bridges, and flyovers, often taking up almost entire swaths of the road.

This infrastructure of underground transport promises to revolutionize Mumbai's problems of mobility. The metro will open one day, but for now, the underground sprouts like a colony of red-and-yellow barricades into the dull black and gray of the ground above it—onto the urban road. For months, the barricades have been appendages, resolute parts of the road. They are upright, vertical, plastic, rather than reclining, concrete matter. The dexterity and the different tempos of clutch, break, and accelerator that drivers have to apply in order to maneuver through and around this upright appendage of the road is significantly different from the maneuvers on the smooth, horizontal road. Moreover, the thrashing monsoon has settled as small lakes into the ditches along the way. These have all become part of the everyday tangle of *auto-space* (Freund and Martin 1993). In this tangle of sprouting underground and urban lakes, what do we call a road and who gets to claim it?

Maliq's passenger pays and, without moving his eyes off the WhatsApp videos on his phone, swings open the taxi door. Just behind us, a motorcyclist, delivering for Uber's food delivery service Uber Eats, is pushed by a large truck toward the line of barricades on the passenger side of the taxi. To avoid the barricades, the motorcyclist catapults himself onto the footpath. In Mumbai, for two-wheelers, the footpath behaves like a simulated road. But if the open road has its appendages, this simulated road has its limits. The motorcyclist encounters a line of flower sellers crouched along the footpath stringing together *gajras* (hair garlands) out of perfumed jasmine flowers. The motorcyclist launches himself back onto the barricaded road again, straight into the swing of the door of Maliq's taxi. As Maliq's passenger inattentively exits, the motorcyclist is caught in the door and horrifyingly launched through the barricades toward the footpath. His helmet ricochets over the top of the taxi and into the moving traffic on the other side. The passenger gives him a momentary, disinterested look, turns away quickly, and keeps walking into the corporate building in front of him.

Maliq and I both dart out of his taxi to help. Three other taxi drivers who have also just dropped off passengers and see what happened also leave their cars on one side of the road and dash around the traffic toward the motorcyclist. Two of them are Ola drivers. Maliq and all three of these men are competitors in a strictly economic sense with the Uber Eats driver who has been injured and with each other. However, as laboring subjects who share the road, they lift the man and his bike off the road and onto the footpath while one of them runs into the traffic to recoup his helmet. The motorcyclist is shaken but, other than some scratches on his elbows and shins, he is miraculously okay. He thanks the men and tells them that he has to run because he has to keep working. He has food to deliver and the app is beeping away in the clip at his waist; the drivers have passengers to pick up. They all dissolve into the city to earn their keep just like the passenger who kindled the mishap but dissolved into his office without a second look. Maliq, the kaalipeeli driver, the Ola drivers, the Uber Eats deliveryman, the passenger—these are all men who seem to be fighting each other in the economic sense, but in truth, perhaps they are embroiled in a contest over who gets rights to the city's road space and infrastructure.

As the lives of the taxi drivers in this book illustrate, what a road *is* shifts in the course of driving work. In Mumbai it moves between mud, slush, dust, and ditches; it also alternates between naka, road, and gully, each of which shapes the road claims and practices that are possible. Further, for those who spend the most time driving, the road imprints itself on their clothes, their feet, their cars, their bodies; it does so through the callouses on their feet, the thoks on their cars, the quivers of their worn-out suspensions, the twitches and jerks of their neurological systems, the hammering pain on their bodies, and the deposits in their kidneys from sitting too long in traffic.

The taxis, too, are imprinted by the stamps of incessant road travel—these are cars that move along the roads, but that are also moved by them as they shake, shudder, and break down. Often the consuming middle classes show both bewilderment and contempt at taxi drivers' noncompliance with various kinds of modernization. I heard many times, "If we want a modern city, we cannot have these dirty, old, rickety cars on the road. New cars have GPS, they have everything you need. Passengers are willing to pay, why is [the driver] not willing to drive [the new cars]?" This sentiment reflects a tension between those who see their citizenship in the modern city through their position vis-à-vis the technologies of modern capital, new cars, and free-flowing roads, and those who see it through equally modern registers of skilled labor, relational economies of the jaalu, mutuality, and everyday technological knowledge. The taxi is located within these conflicting social, spatial, and material landscapes of roadmaking as a *disconnecting experience* (Anand 2006) and roadmaking as an entangled and relational domain of rights, or *haq*, and socialities. The owner-operated, chillia taxi trade, the fleet taxi trade owned by corporate fleets, and Ola-Uber, are all different articulations of local and global capital; however, they are also shared materializations of life on the road but with different claims to a life of dignifying labor.

◆   ◆   ◆

What do we make of these everyday disputes over the road and what do they tell us about Indian automobility? As the anthropologist Kathleen Stewart (2014) has observed, roads are *registers* of life, they are places where lives coexist and are co-constituted. On Mumbai's roads, and for Mumbai's taxi drivers, staking individual claims to the road, and sitting and waiting at the naka, go together with giving into, recognizing, (and not recognizing) the claims of others. The work of driving for a living in Indian cities is a way of fully inhabiting the city and living sensorially within its broader ecologies and landscapes. It is also about actively shaping these ecologies and landscapes in the course of driving work. Therefore, what I call Indian automobility is both a universal experience of automobilization and a specific sensory, embodied, and political domain where people who drive for a living collectively cultivate relationships to cars, technology, repair, the material and ecological environment, and the road. Tensions at the crossroads might pit nostalgic pasts against hopes for a new technological future, and the slippages between nakas and roads; and the debates over old and new taxis point are also arguments over order and disorder. However, I suggest that these frictions are all signals of what automobility does in the life of the city and of how driving work produces both sensuous persons and malleable landscapes in Mumbai.

As Rashid the chillia driver wisely says,

See, if there is one thing about being a joona driver in *Bambai* it is this—you have knowledge of roads and of politics and you have dignity because your feet are on the ground. Ola-Uber can manipulate the software to send their drivers to the moon but joona drivers are here on the roads and city. The roads are jammed and painful, but I will take the city rather than be manipulated to fly to the moon any day.

GLOSSARY

aadat habit
aas-paas close by; local
abba father
azaan Muslim call to prayer

Bambai colloquial term used for the city otherwise known as Bombay or
   Mumbai
baobab Indian species of tree; also known as the upside down or bottle tree
bhai brother
bharosa trust
bombil fish, also known as Bombay duck

chacha paternal uncle
challan traffic ticket
CNG compressed natural gas

dalal broker
dekh-bhal care, looking after
dhandha business
dhooli dust
dum life, strength
dupatta long women's scarves

gharry horse-drawn cab
gharrywallah gharry driver
ghulami slavery

haath hands; related to hands and touch
haq rights
hathaura hammer

jaalu/jaal web/webs
joona old; original
julaha professional weaver caste

kaalipeeli black-and-yellow taxi
karanj Indian Beech tree
khandani dhandha family business
khul extrajudicial divorce

maal commodity
madrassa religious school
malmal soft cotton
mantralaya offices of the state government
masjid mosque
momin faithful believer; Muslim caste category

naka where roads meet; crossroads
nalla fake, useless
namaaz Muslim prayer
niqab veil

pandal raised pavilion
peepal Indian fig tree

ramzaan holy month of the Muslim calendar; also Ramadan
riba interest paid on financial loans

sarkar government

taalim teaching and instruction of the Koran
taxiwallah taximan
thok bump or scrape
tongawallah tonga driver

zakat alms or charity to the poor

NOTES

INTRODUCTION

1. Bombay was renamed Mumbai in 1995. I use *Bombay* when referring to the pre-1995 period and *Mumbai* when referring to the post-1995 period. When quoting directly from my informants I also use the colloquially used term *Bambai*.
2. On vibration as a sensory experience, see Eidsheim (2015).
3. On aspiration of the poor for a better life, see Appadurai (2004).
4. I use sensory and sensorial interchangeably. I use sensuous as Stoller (1997) does to describe my experiences as the sensing ethnographer.
5. I am aware of debates in sensory anthropology (see Howes 2011; Ingold 2011b) over direct vs. mediated experience and between individual and collective perceptions. I see all these dynamics in play for my interlocutors and avoid taking theoretical sides here.
6. I depart from Illich (1992) who applies the term to a past, vernacular living counterpoised to "modern" life.
7. On automobility, see Urry et al. (2005) and Sheller and Urry (2006).
8. On technological expertise outside the Western world, see Mavhunga (2014) who uses the term "African technology" to describe technological innovation in Africa.
9. The Padmini has its gearbox and gearshift connected to the steering.
10. On the intertwined relationships between men and women, see Strathern (1988, 2020).
11. On connections between domestic work and capital accumulation, see Besky (2017); Federici (2004); Rofel (1999); and Yanagisako (2002).
12. On enmeshment, see Lefebvre ([1974] 1991b) and Ingold (2011a).
13. For ethnographic work on urban driving, see Melly (2017); Monroe (2017); Sopranzetti (2017); and Thrift 2004.
14. On a discussion of the different worlds that make up social life, see de la Belacasa (2017) and de la Cadena (2015).
15. On how people shape their relations with capitalism to make valuable lives, see Garcia (2020).
16. The term Bollywood refers to the Hindi film industry based in Mumbai.
17. On sound in South Asia, see Brueck et al. (2020) and Kunreuther (2018).
18. On sound, music, and driving see Hirschkind (2006) and Hansen (2006).
19. See Laet and Mol (2000) on what they call "fluid technologies."
20. Here "service" refers to waged employment. For drivers, these are jobs that garner monthly rather than daily incomes.

1. *DHANDHA*

1. For a discussion of surfaces, see Amato (2013).
2. On early India's automobile industry, see Bedi (2016).
3. On economic shifts in India, see Ahmed (2014) and Kohli (2006).
4. On fragmented urban governance in Mumbai, see Weinstein (2014).
5. In 2017 permit applications were opened for short windows.
6. For a discussion of the most recent Motor Vehicle Act, see Annavarapu and Joshi (2019).
7. Loosely calling on cultural narratives of Hindu communities, Indian Muslim caste has its own distinct history and politics.
8. On a history of Momin political mobilization, see Ghosh (2008).
9. For discussions of caste among Muslims, see Ahmad (1973); Mines (1973); and Momin (1973).
10. See Ezekiel (1976) and Irani and Sharma (2004) on "Irani" restaurants owned by families who trace their origins to Persia.
11. Indian Parsis follow Zoroastrianism and trace their origins to Persia. See Ganesh (2008) and Luhrmann (1996).
12. On the circulation of images of untrustworthy, dangerous Muslims, see Devji (2013).
13. On Mumbai politics, see Bjorkman (2014); Hansen (2001); and Patel (2003).
14. On the relations between Hindu majorities and Muslims in India, see Appadurai (1986); Gayer and Jaffrelot (2012b); Hansen (2000); and Seabrook and Siddiqui (2011).
15. Talk by chillia men of having no other economic choice plays into Hindu majoritarian and global, political-economic tropes of terrorism, particularly focused on cross-border terrorism between India and Pakistan.
16. With gratitude to Aditi Aggarwal for this insight.
17. Characteristics often associated with sex work.
18. See Anjaria (2011) on how street hawkers must constantly engage in similar negotiations.
19. On kinship, see Bamford (2004) and Strathern (2005).

2. ECOLOGIES

1. On urban ecologies in South Asia, see Rademacher and Sivaramakrishnan (2013).
2. See Howe and Pandian (2017) for an ecological lexicon of the Anthropocene.
3. Many of Mumbai's routes take one along or close to the coast of the Arabian Sea.
4. On the experience of the morning city, see Anjaria (2019).
5. See Yi Fu Tuan (1995) on sensuous geography.
6. On surfaces, see Joseph A. Amato (2013); also Sara Ahmed and Jackie Stacey, eds. (2001) on surface encounters.
7. On archaeological discussions of ancient roads, see Hendrickson (2010) and Forbes (1964).
8. On the social skin, see Turner (2012) and Gros (2019).
9. For anthropological studies of contemporary road infrastructures, see Anand (2006); Dalakoglou (2017); Harris (2018); and Masquelier (2002).

10. With thanks to Thomas Blom Hansen for this insight.

11. On relations between the environment and bodies, see Agard-Jones (2016); Roberts (2017); and Solomon (2016).

12. The Bohra housing society is a Gujarati Muslim community prominent in business and trading. See Engineer (1993) on Bohras. It is common for housing societies to be dedicated to housing particular ethnic groups. See a discussion of such societies in Rao (2013).

13. "Flag-ups" refers to the refusal of drivers to pick up passengers, which requires them to put the flags of their (then) manual meters down.

14. For an excellent discussion of the naka as a vital urban space and the possibilities for working-class labor that develop around it, see Shah (2014).

3. JOONA

1. For a discussion of these temporal struggles, see Bedi (2020).

2. On urban anachronisms, see Finklestein (2019).

3. On antipollution activism see Devidayal (2002) and Kulkarni-Apte and D'Souza (1998).

4. A chief complaint is that kaalipeeli drivers "refuse" to take their passengers where they want to go.

5. Marathi is spoken in the state of Maharashtra.

6. With thanks to Nasser Mufti for this literary insight.

7. On brokers in Mumbai, see Björkman, ed. (2021).

8. Drivers refer to this contraption by this English term.

4. JAALU

1. On social life as mixture, see Mol and Law (1994, 60).

2. On the relationship between dependence and personhood, see Ferguson (2013, 2015).

3. Meru is one of the first fleet taxi companies in India.

4. During the 2020 COVID–19 lockdown, new fleet companies reliant on apps, and dedicated just to transporting people to hospitals, were founded. It is too soon to gauge their effectiveness or what will happen to them.

5. In Gujarati, *utarri* means to be brought down a notch, to have one's standing "removed" (*uttar*).

6. On care, see Belacasa (2017) and Mol (2008).

7. On the workings of equity-based finance in Muslim societies, see Lawal (2010) and Rudnyckyj (2018).

5. DEKH-BHAL

1. See Laet and Mol (2000) on fluid technologies.

2. On the provincial, see Chakrabarty (2000); on provincializing of technology specifically, see Mavhunga (2014).

3. On the city in Bollywood films, see Mazumdar (2007).
4. On transient objects and value, see Sheller (2014) and Urry (2004).
5. On feminist ethics of care, see Barad (2010); Belacasa (2017); Mol (2008); and Tronto 1992.
6. On surfaces, see Amato (2013).
7. On the activation of one sense through the other, see Howes (2003).
8. For the pleasurable aspects of mastery, see Tuan (1985, 37).
9. On car parts and secondhand economy, see Cholez and Trompette (2020).

6. POLITICS

1. On early labor unions, see Gupte (1981); Hensman (2011); and Janardhan 2007.
2. As everyone in the taxi industry used this hyphenated term, I follow this term of reference too.
3. For a discussion of *Aadhaar*, see Cohen (2019) and Nair (2018).
4. Meru is one of the first major fleet taxi companies to enter the Indian market.
5. For discussions of *riba*, see Kuran (1997) and Lawal (2010).
6. A considered discussion of state corruption is beyond the scope of this book. But see Anjaria (2011); Rajan (2020); Jauregui (2014); and Gupta (2012).
7. For a discussion of the legal debates over the City Taxi Scheme, see Srivastava (2017).
8. Mantralaya houses the administrative headquarters of the Maharashtra State Government.
9. *Idli* (steamed rice cake) and *dosa* (pan-fried rice and lentil fritter) served with *sambhar* (spicy lentils) and coconut chutney, originally from the southern Indian state of Tamil Nadu, are popular and inexpensive foods in much of India.

CONCLUSION

1. See Millar (2018) for a recent analysis of labor and life-making in Brazil.
2. On the systems of automobility, see Urry (2004) and Urry et al. (2005).
3. For recent studies of automobility and driving in the Global South, see Agbiboa (2018); Gopakumar (2020); Melly (2017); Monroe (2016); Small (2018); Sopranzetti (2017); and Zhang (2019).

REFERENCES

Agard-Jones, Vanessa. 2016. "Episode 35." *Cultures of Energy* (podcast). Accessed February 17, 2021. http://culturesofenergy.com/ep-35-vanessa-agard-jones.

Agbiboa, Daniel E. 2018. "Informal Urban Governance and Predatory Politics in Africa: The Role of Motor Park Touts in Lagos." *African Affairs* 117 (466): 62–82.

Aggarwal, Aditi, and Tarini Bedi. Forthcoming. "Dhandha and the Making of Valuable Livelihoods in Contemporary Mumbai." *South Asia: Journal of South Asian Studies.*

Ahmad, Imtiaz, ed. 1973. *Caste and Social Stratification among the Muslims.* Delhi: Manohar Book Service.

Ahmed, Sara, and Jackie Stacey, eds. 2001. *Thinking through the Skin.* London; New York: Routledge.

Ahmed, Waquar. 2014. "The Political Economy and Geopolitical Context of India's Economic Crisis, 1990–91." *Singapore Journal of Tropical Geography* 35 (2): 179–96.

Ali, Syed. 2002. "Collective and Elective Ethnicity: Caste among Urban Muslims in India." *Sociological Forum* 17 (4): 593–620.

Amato, Joseph A. 2000. *Dust: A History of the Small and the Invisible.* Berkeley: University of California Press.

———. 2013. *Surfaces: A History.* Berkley: University of California Press.

Amrute, Sarita. 2015. "Moving Rape: Trafficking in the Violence of Postliberalization." *Public Culture* 27 (2): 331–59.

Anand, Nikhil. 2006. "Disconnecting Experience: Making World-Class Roads in Mumbai." *Economic and Political Weekly* 41 (31): 3422–29.

———. 2017. *Hydraulic City: Water and the Infrastructures of Citizenship in Mumbai.* Durham, NC: Duke University Press.

Ange, Olivia, and David Berliner. 2015. "Anthropology of Nostalgia—Anthropology as Nostalgia." In *Anthropology and Nostalgia*, edited by O. Ange and D. Berliner. New York; Oxford: Berghahn Books.

Anjaria, Jonathan Shapiro. 2009. "Guardians of the Bourgeois City: Citizenship, Public Space, and Middle-Class Activism in Mumbai." *City and Community* 8 (4): 391–406.

———. 2011. "Ordinary States: Everyday Corruption and the Politics of Space in Mumbai." *American Ethnologist* 38 (1): 58–72.

———. 2016. *The Slow Boil: Street Food, Rights and Public Space in Mumbai.* Stanford, CA: Stanford University Press.

———. 2019. "Surface Pleasures: Bicycling and the Limits of Infrastructural Thinking." *South Asia: Journal of South Asian Studies* 43 (2): 267–80.

Annavarapu, Sneha. 2019. "Risky Routes, Safe Suspicions: Gender, Class, and Cabs in Hyderabad, India." Paper Presented at the Gender and Sexuality Studies Workshop, University of Chicago.

Annavarapu, Sneha, and Bhoomika Joshi. 2019. "Driver-Citizens and Technical Safety in India: Traffic Violations and Penalties in the Motor Vehicle Act 2019." *Platypus: The CASTAC Blog.* Accessed February 17, 2021. http://blog.castac.org/author /snehaa91/.

Appadurai, Arjun. 1986. "Theory in Anthropology: Centre and Periphery." *Comparative Studies in Society and History* 28: 356–61.

———. 2004. "The Capacity to Aspire: Culture and the Terms of Recognition." In *Culture and Public Action*, edited by V. Rao and M. Walton, 59–84. Stanford, CA: Stanford University Press.

Athukorala, Prema-Chandra, and C. Veeramani. 2019. "From Import Substitution to Integration into Global Production Networks: The Case of the Indian Automobile Industry." *Asian Development Review* 36 (2): 72–99.

Aulino, Felicity. 2019. *Rituals of Care: Karmic Politics in Aging Thailand.* Ithaca, NY: Cornell University Press.

Bamford, Sandra. 2004. "Embodiments of Detachment: Engendering Agency in the Highlands of Papua New Guinea." In *Women as Unseen Characters: Male Ritual in Papua New Guinea*, edited by P. Bonnemère, 34–56. Philadelphia: University of Pennsylvania Press.

Barad, Karen. 2007. *Meeting the Universe Halfway: Quantum Physics and the Entanglement of Matter and Meaning.* Durham, NC: Duke University Press.

———. 2010. "Quantum Entanglements and Hauntological Relations of Inheritance: Dis/continuities, SpaceTime Enfoldings, and Justice-to-Come." *Derrida Today* 3 (2): 240–68.

———. 2012. "On Touching—The Inhuman That Therefore I Am." *Differences: A Journal of Feminist Cultural Studies* 23 (3): 206–23.

Baron, Ava, and Eileen Boris. 2007. "'The Body' as a Useful Category for a Working-Class History." *Labor: Studies in Working-Class History of the Americas* 1 (2): 23–43.

Bauman, Zygmunt. 2014. *Wasted Lives: Modernity and its Outcasts.* Cambridge: Polity Press.

Baviskar, Amita, and Raka Ray, eds. 2011. *Elite and Everyman: The Cultural Politics of the Indian Middle Classes.* New Delhi; New York: Routledge.

Bear, Laura. 2014. "Doubt, Conflict, and Mediation: The Anthropology of Modern Time." *Journal of the Royal Anthropological Institute* 20 (1): 3–30.

Beckmann, Jorg. 2001. "Automobility: A Social Problem and Theoretical Concept." *Environment and Planning D: Society and Space* 19 (5): 593–607.

Bedi, Tarini. 2016a. *The Dashing Ladies of Shiv Sena: Political Matronage in Urbanizing India.* Albany, NY: SUNY Press.

———. 2016b. "Taxi-Drivers, Infrastructures, and Urban Change in Globalizing Mumbai." *City and Society* 28 (3): 387–410.

———. 2020. "Thinking through Urban Obsolescence: Tinkering, Repair, and the Politics of *Joona* in Bombay/Mumbai's Taxi Trade." *International Journal of Urban and Regional Research*, November 17, 2020. https://doi.org/10.1111/1468-2427.12948.

Belacasa, Maria Puig de la. 2017. *Matters of Care: Speculative Ethics in More Than Human Worlds*. Minneapolis: University of Minnesota Press.

Bellucci, Stefano, Larissa Rosa Corrêa, Jan-Georg Deutsch, and Chitra Joshi. 2014. Special Issue 22: "Introduction: Labour in Transport: Histories from the Global South (Africa, Asia, and Latin America) c. 1750–1950." *International Review of Social History* 59: 1–10.

Bennett, Jane. 2009. *Vibrant Matter: A Political Ecology of Things*. Durham, NC: Duke University Press.

Berlant, Lauren. 2011. *Cruel Optimism*. Durham, NC: Duke University Press.

Berntsen, Rita Maxine. 1982–83. "Marathi Teaching Materials." *Digital Dictionaries of South Asia*. New Delhi: American Institute of Indian Studies.

Besky, Sarah. 2017. "Fixity: On the Inheritance and Maintenance of Tea Plantation Houses in Darjeeling, India." *American Ethnologist* 44 (4): 617–31.

Beteille, Andre. 1997. "Caste in Contemporary India." In *Caste Today*, edited by C. J. Fuller, 150–79. Delhi: Oxford University Press.

Bhabha, Homi. 1997. "Of Mimicry and Man: The Ambivalence of Colonial Discourse." In *Tensions of Empire: Colonial Cultures in a Bourgeois World*, edited by F. Cooper and L.A. Stoler, 152–60. Berkeley: University of California Press.

Bhayana, Neha. 2007. "The Mumbai Project: Changing Mumbai's Taxi's Singapore Style." *Hindustan Times*, December 15, 2007.

Björkman, Lisa. 2015. *Pipe Politics: Contested Waters, Embedded Infrastructures of Millennial Mumbai*. Durham, NC: Duke University Press.

———. 2020. *Waiting Town: Life in Transit and Mumbai's Other World-Class Histories*. New York: Columbia University Press.

———, ed. 2021. *Bombay Brokers*. Durham, NC: Duke University Press.

Boek, Filip de, and Sammy Baloji. 2017. "Positing the Polis: Topography as a Way to De-centre Urban Thinking." *Urbanisation* 2 (2): 142–54.

Bonnemère, Pascale. 2018. *Acting for Others: Relational Transformations in Papua New Guinea*. Translated by N. Scott. Chicago: HAU Books.

Borg, Kevin L. 1999. "The 'Chauffeur Problem' in the Early Auto Era: Structuration Theory and the Users of Technology." *Technology and Culture* 40 (4): 797–832.

———. 2007. *Auto Mechanics: Technology and Expertise in Twentieth-Century America*. Baltimore, MD: Johns Hopkins University Press.

Boym, Svetlana. 2001. *The Future of Nostalgia*. New York: Basic Books.

———. 2017. *The Off-Modern*. New York: Bloomsbury.

Brueck, Laura, Jacob Smith, and Neil Verma, eds. 2020. *Indian Sound Cultures, Indian Sound Citizenship*. Ann Arbor: University of Michigan Press.

Budhiraja, Bakul, Girish Agrawal, and Prasad Pathak. 2020. "Urban Heat Island Effect of a Polynuclear Megacity Delhi: Compactness and Thermal Evaluation of Four Sub-cities." *Urban Climate* 32 (June 2020): 100634. https://doi.org/10.1016/j.uclim.2020.100634.

Cadena, Marisol de la. 2015. *Earth Beings: Ecologies of Practice across Andean Worlds*. Durham, NC: Duke University Press.

Callon, Michael, ed. 1998. *The Laws of the Markets*. Oxford, UK: Blackwell.

Callon, Michael, and Vololona Rabeharisoa. 2003. "Research 'in the Wild' and the Shaping of New Social Identities." *Technology in Society* 25 (2): 193–204.

Carsten, Janet. 1997. *The Heat of the Hearth: The Process of Kinship in a Malay Fishing Community*. Oxford, UK: Clarendon.

———. 2000. "Introduction: Cultures of Relatedness." In *Cultures of Relatedness: New Approaches to the Study of Kinship*, edited by J. Carsten, 1–36. Cambridge, UK: Cambridge University Press.

———. 2004. *After Kinship*. Cambridge, UK: Cambridge University Press.

Carsten, Janet, Sophie Day, and Charles Stafford. 2018. "Introduction: Reason and Passion: The Parallel Worlds of Ethnography and Biography." *Social Anthropology* 26 (1): 5–14.

Caturvedi, Mahendra. 1970. *A Practical Hindi-English Dictionary*. Digital Dictionaries of South Asia. Delhi: National Publishing House.

Chakrabarty, Dipesh. 2000. *Provincializing Europe: Postcolonial Thought and Colonial Difference*. Princeton, NJ: Princeton University Press.

Chandavarkar, Rajnarayan. 1994. *The Origins of Industrial Capitalism in India: Business Strategies and the Working Classes in Bombay 1900–1940*. Cambridge, UK: Cambridge University Press.

Cholez, Celine, and Pascale Trompette. 2020. "A Mundane Infrastructure of Energy Poverty: The Informal Trading of Second-Hand Car Batteries in Madagascar." *Journal of Material Culture*. https://journals.sagepub.com/ doi/10.1177/1359183519895048.

Chua, Beng Huat. 2011. "Singapore as Model: Planning Innovations, Knowledge Experts." In *Worlding Cities: Asian Experiments and the Art of Being Global*, edited by A. Roy and A. Ong, 30–54. West Sussex, UK: Wiley Blackwell.

Classen, Constance. 1993a. *Inca Cosmology and the Human Body*. Salt Lake City: University of Utah Press.

———. 1993b. *Worlds of Sense: Exploring the Senses in History and Across Cultures*. London; New York: Routledge.

———. 1997a. "Engendering Perception: Gender Ideologies and Sensory Hierarchies in Western History." *Body and Society* 3 (2):1–19.

———. 1997b. "Foundations for an Anthropology of the Senses." *International Social Science Journal* 49 (153): 401–12.

Cohen, Lawrence L. 2019. "The Social De-duplicated: On the Aadhaar Platform and the Engineering of Service." *South Asia: Journal of South Asian Studies* 42 (3): 482–500.

Craven, Thomas. 1893. *The Royal Dictionary: English and Hindustani and Hindustani and English*. Lucknow: Methodist Pub. House.

Crowell, Maddy. 2015. "In Wake of Uber Rape, Women-Only Car Services Emerge in India." *Christian Science Monitor*, October 20, 2015.

Dalakoglou, Dimitris. 2017. *The Road: An Ethnography of (Im)mobility, Space, and Cross-Border Infrastructures in the Balkans*. Manchester, UK: University of Manchester Press.

Davis, Mike. 2004. "Planet of Slums: Urban Involution and the Informal Proletariat." *New Left Review* 26: 5–34.

Devidayal, Namrata. 2002. "Polluting Vehicles are the Enemy for this Crusader." *Times of India*, September 30, 2002.

Devji, Faisal. 2013. *Muslim Zion: Pakistan as a Political Idea*. Cambridge, MA: Harvard University Press.

Dey, Adrija. 2019. "'Others' Within the 'Others': An Intersectional Analysis of Gender Violence in India." *Gender Issues* 36 (4): 357–73.

Dickens, Charles. 1894. *Sketches by Boz: Illustrative of Every-Day Life and Every-Day People*. Boston; New York: Houghton Mifflin.

Dorsch, Sebastian, and Jutta Vinzent. 2018. *SpatioTemporalities on the Line: Representations-Practices-Dynamic*. Berlin, Germany: De Gruyter Oldenbourg.

Dwivedi, Sharada, and Rahul Mehrotra. 1995. *Bombay: The Cities Within*. Bombay: India Book House.

Edgerton, David. 2007. *The Shock of the Old: Technology and Global History Since 1900*. London; New York: Oxford University Press.

Eidsheim, Nina Sun. 2015. *Sensing Sound: Singing and Listening as Vibrational Practice*. Durham, NC: Duke University Press.

"End of Strike Ordeal Hailed by Disputants." 1960. *Sunday Standard*, Sunday, January 3, 1960.

Engineer, Ashgar Ali. 1993. *The Bohras*. New Delhi: Vikas Publishing House.

Ezekiel, Nissim. 1976. "Irani Restaurant Instructions." *Journal of South Asian Literature* 11 (3/4): 106.

Fallon, S. W., D. Fakir Chand, and R. Carnac Temple. 1886. *A Dictionary of Hindustani Proverbs: Including Many Marwari, Panjabi, Maggah, Bhojpuri and Tirhuti Proverbs, Sayings, Emblems, Aphorisms, Maxims and Similes*. Banaras: Banaras Medical Hall Press.

Fanon, Frantz. (1963) 1965. *The Wretched of the Earth*. New York: Grove Press.

———. 1965. *A Dying Colonialism*. New York: Grove Press.

Federici, Sylvia. 2004. *Caliban and the Witch: Women, the Body, and Primitive Accumulation*. New York: Autonomedia.

Ferguson, James. 2013. "Declarations of Dependence: Labour, Personhood, and Welfare in South Africa." *Journal of the Royal Anthropological Institute* 19 (2): 223–42.

———. 2015. *Give a Man a Fish: Reflections on the New Politics of Distribution*. Durham; London: Duke University Press.

Finkelstein, Maura. 2019. *The Archive of Loss: Lively Ruination in Mill Land Mumbai*. Durham, NC: Duke University Press.

Fisch, Michael. 2018. *An Anthropology of the Machine: Tokyo's Commuter Train Network*. Chicago: University of Chicago Press.

Fisher, Berenice, and Joan C. Tronto. 1990. "Toward a Feminist Theory of Caring." In *Circles of Care*, edited by E. K. Abel and M. Nelson. Albany, NY: SUNY Press.

Forbes, Duncan. 1857. *A Dictionary, Hindustani and English: Accompanied by a Reversed Dictionary, English and Hindustani*. London: W. H. Allen.

Forbes, Robert James. (1934) 1964. *Notes on the History of Ancient Roads and Their Construction*. Amsterdam: Adolf M. Hakkert.

Foucault, Michel. 2007. *Security, Territory, Population*. New York: Palgrave Macmillan.

Franz, Kathleen. 2005. *Tinkering: Consumers Reinvent the Early Automobile*. Philadelphia: University of Pennsylvania Press.

Freund, Peter, and George Martin. 1993. *The Ecology of the Automobile*. Chicago: University of Chicago Press.

Gandhi, Mahatma. (1938) 1944. *Hind Swaraj*. Ahmedabad: Navajivan.

Ganesh, Kamala. 2008. "Intra-community Dissent and Dialogue: The Bombay Parsis and the Zoroastrian Diaspora." *Sociological Bulletin* 57 (3): 315–36.

Gayer, Laurent, and Christophe Jaffrelot, eds. 2012. *Muslims in Indian Cities: Trajectories of Marginalisation*. London: Hurst.

Ghertner, Asher D. 2015. *Rule by Aesthetics: World-Class City-Making in Delhi*. New York: Oxford University Press.

——. 2020. "Airpocalypse: Distributions of Life amidst Delhi's Polluted Airs." *Public Culture* 32 (1): 133–62.

Ghosh, Papiya. 2010. *Muhajirs and the Nation: Bihar in the 1940s*. New Delhi: Routledge.

Gilbertson, Amand. 2018. "Between Inclusivity and Feminist Purism: Young Gender Justice Workers in Post-Nirbhaya Delhi." *Women's Studies International Forum* 67: 1–9.

Gopakumar, Govind. 2020. *Installing Automobility: Emerging Politics of Mobility and Streets in Indian Cities*. Cambridge, MA: MIT Press.

Gould, S. J. 1985. *The Flamingo's Smile: Reflections in Natural History*. New York: Norton.

Graeber, David. 2018. *Bullshit Jobs*. New York: Simon and Schuster.

Green, Nile. 2011. *Bombay Islam: The Religious Economy of the West Indian Ocean 1840–1915*. Cambridge, UK: Cambridge University Press.

Gros, Stéphane. 2019. "Surfacing." Theorizing the Contemporary series, *Fieldsights*, September 30, 2019. https://culanth.org/fieldsights/surfacing.

Gupta, Akhil. 1995. "Blurred Boundaries: The Discourse of Corruption, the Culture of Politics, and the Imagined State." *American Ethnologist* 22 (2): 375–402.

——. 2012. *Red Tape: Bureaucracy, Structural Violence, and Poverty in India*. Durham, NC: Duke University Press.

Gupte, Vasant. 1981. *Labour Movement in Bombay: Origin and Growth upto Independence*. Bombay: Insititute of Worker's Education.

"Hackney Carriages in Bombay." 1897. *Times of India*, January 4, 1897.

Hansen, Thomas Blom. 1999. *Saffron Wave: Democracy and Hindu Nationalism in Modern India*. Princeton, NJ: Princeton University Press.

——. 2000. "Predicaments of Secularism: Muslim Identities and Politics in Mumbai." *Journal of the Royal Anthropological Institute* 6 (2): 255–72.

——. 2001. *Wages of Violence: Naming and Identity in Postcolonial Bombay*. Princeton, NJ: Princeton University Press.

——. 2006. "Sounds of Freedom: Music, Taxis, and Racial Imagination in Urban South Africa." *Public Culture* 18 (1): 185–208.

Harris, Andrew. 2013. "Concrete Geographies: Assembling Global Mumbai through Transport Infrastructure." *City* 17(3):343–360.

———. 2018. "Engineering Formality: Flyover and Skywalk Construction in Mumbai." *International Journal of Urban and Regional Research* 42 (2): 295–314.

Harvey, David. 2000. *Space of Hope*. Berkeley: University of California Press.

Haynes, Douglas, and Tirthankar Roy. 1999. "Conceiving Mobility: Weavers' Migrations in Pre-colonial and Colonial India." *Indian Economic and Social History Review* 36 (1): 35–67.

Heatherington, Kevin. 2004. "Secondhandedness: Consumption, Disposal and Absent Presence." *Environment and Planning D: Society and Space* 22 (1): 157–73.

Hendrickson, Mitch. 2010. "Re-Appraising a Myth of the Angkorian Period Road System (Ninth to Fifteenth Centuries CE)." *Aseanie* 25: 83–109.

Hensman, Rohini. 2011. *Workers, Unions and Global Capitalism: Lessons from India*. New York: Columbia University Press.

Hirschkind, Charles. 2006. *The Ethical Soundscape: Cassette Sermons and Islamic Counterpublics*. New York: Columbia University Press.

Hochschild, Arlie Russell. 1983. *The Managed Heart: The Commercialization of Human Feeling*. Berkeley: University of California Press.

Hodges, Graham Russell Gao. 2007. *Taxi! A Social History of the New York City Cabdriver*. Baltimore: Johns Hopkins University Press.

Horta, Gerard. 2019. "From Peripatetic Anthropology to the Ethnography of Roads and Motorisation in Africa." *Cadernos de Estudos Africanos* 37: 213–33.

Howe, Cymene, and Anand Pandian, eds. 2017. *Anthropocene Unseen: A Lexicon*. Earth, Milky Way: Punctum Books.

Howes, David. 2003. *Sensual Relations: Engaging the Senses in Culture and Social Theory*. Ann Arbor: University of Michigan Press.

———. 2011. "Reply to Tim Ingold." *Social Anthropology* 19 (3): 328–31.

———. 2019. "Multisensory Anthropology." *Annual Review of Anthropology* 48 (17): 17–28.

Howes, David, and Constance Classen. 2014. *Ways of Sensing: Understanding the Senses in Society*. New York: Routledge.

Hull, Matthew. 2012. *Government of Paper: The Materiality of Bureaucracy in Urban Pakistan*. Berkeley: University of California Press.

Illich, Ivan. 1992. *In the Mirror of the Past: Lectures and Addresses 1978–1990*. London, UK: Marion Boyars.

Ingold, Timothy. 2000. *The Perception of the Environment: Essays on Livelihood, Dwelling and Skill*. London: Routledge.

———. 2007. *Lines: A Brief History*. London: Routledge.

———. 2011a. *Being Alive: Essays on Movement, Knowledge and Description*. Abingdon, UK: Routledge.

———. 2011b. "Worlds of Sense and Sensing the World: A Response to Sarah Pink and David Howes." *Social Anthropology* 19 (3): 313–17.

———. 2015. *The Life of Lines*. Abingdon, Oxon; New York: Routledge.

Irani, Berzin, and Vikas Sharma, dirs. 2004. *Aur Irani Chai*. Mumbai.

Jackson, Stephen J. 2014. "Rethinking Repair." In *Media Technologies: Essays on Communication, Materiality, and Society*, edited by T. Gillespie, P. J. Boczkowski, and K. A. Foot. Cambridge, MA: MIT Press.

Jacob, Jabin T. 2018. "The China-Pakistan Economic Corridor and the China-India-Pakistan Triangle." In *China's Maritime Silk Road Initiative in South Asia: A Political Economic Analysis of Its Purposes, Perils, and Promise*, edited by J.-M.F. Blanchard, 105–36. Singapore: Palgrave Macmillan.

Janardhan, V. 2007. "Depoliticisation of Labour Unions: The Need of the Hour?" *Labor File* 5 (1–2): 34–38.

Jauregui, Beatrice. 2014. "Provisional Agency in India: Jugaad and the Legitimation of Corruption." *American Ethnologist* 41 (1): 76–91.

Joshi, Chitra. 2008. "Histories of Indian Labour: Predicaments and Possibilities." *History Compass* 6 (2): 439–54.

Kafer, Alison. 2013. *Feminist, Queer, Crip*. Bloomington: Indiana University Press.

Khanolkar, G. D. (1969) 2007. *Walchand Hirachand: Man, His Times, and His Achievements*. Bombay: Walchand.

King, Tiffany Lethabo. 2016. "The Labor or (re)Reading Plantation Landscapes Fungible(ly)." *Antipode* 48 (4): 1022–39.

Kohli, Atul. 2006. "Politics of Economic Growth in India, 1980–2005." *Political and Economic Weekly* 41 (13): 1251–59.

Kopytoff, I. 1986. "The Cultural Biography of Things: Commoditization as Process." In *The Social Life of Things: Commodities in Cultural Perspective*, edited by Arjun Appadurai, 64–91. Cambridge, UK: Cambridge University Press.

Kulkarni-Apte, Vaijayanti, and Mignonne D'Souza. 1998. "9,000 Diesel Taxis Leave Mumbaites Gasping." *Times of India*, October 9, 1998.

Kunreuther, Laura. 2018. "Sounds of Democracy: Performance, Protest, and Political Subjectivity." *Cultural Anthropology* 33 (1): 1–31.

Kuran, Timur. 1997. "The Genesis of Islamic Economics: A Chapter in the Politics of Muslim Identity." *Social Research* 64 (2): 301–38.

Laet, Marianne de, and Annemarie Mol. 2000. "The Zimbabwe Bush Pump: Mechanics of a Fluid Technology." *Social Studies of Science* 30 (2): 225–63.

Lakshmi, Rama. 2014. "India's Quest to Build Modern Toll Roads Hits a Pothole." *Washington Post*, March 23, 2014.

Lambert, Helen. 2000. "Sentiment and Substance in North Indian Forms of Relatedness." In *Cultures of Relatedness: New Approaches to the Study of Kinship*, edited by Janet Carsten, 73–89. Cambridge, UK: Cambridge University Press.

Laplantine, François. 2015. *The Life of the Senses: Introduction to a Modal Anthropology*. London: Bloomsbury.

Latour, Bruno. 1996. *Aramis, or the Love of Technology*. Translated by C. Porter. Cambridge, MA: Harvard University Press.

———. 2005. *Reassembling the Social: An Introduction to Actor-Network Theory*. Oxford, UK: Oxford University Press.

———. 2012. "Love your Monsters: Why We Must Care for Our Technologies as We Do Our Children." Breakthrough Institute (Spring 2012). https://thebreakthrough.org/journal/issue-2/love-your-monsters.

Lawal, Y. O. 2010. "Islamic Economics: The Cornerstone of Islamic Banking." *Journal of Economics and Engineering* 4: 95–99.

Leder, D., and M. W. Krucoff. 2008. "The Touch That Heals: The Use and Meanings of Touch in the Clinical Encounter." *Journal of Alternative and Complementary Medicine* 14 (3): 321–27.

Lefebvre, Henri. (1974) 1991. *The Production of Space*. Translated by D. Nicholson-Smith. Cambridge, MA; Oxford, UK: Blackwell.

Leonardo, Michaela di. 1987. "The Female World of Cards and Holidays: Women, Families, and the Work of Kinship." *Signs: Journal of Women in Culture and Society* 12 (3): 440–53.

Luhrmann, Tanya M. 1996. *The Good Parsi: The Fate of a Colonial Elite in a Postcolonial Society*. Cambridge, MA: Harvard University Press.

Lutgendorf, Philip. 2012. "Making Tea in India: Chai, Capitalism, and Culture." *Thesis Eleven* 113 (1): 11–31.

"The Making of Naya Daur." 2017. *Eastern Eye*, January 27, 2017.

Manning, Erin. 2006. *Politics of Touch: Sense, Movement, Sovereignty*. Minneapolis: University of Minnesota Press.

Marriot, McKim. 1976. "Hindu Transactions: Diversity without Dualism." In *Transactions in Meaning*, edited by Bruce Kapferer. Philadelphia: ISHI Publications.

Masquelier, Adeline. 2002. "Road Mythographies: Space, Mobility, and the Historical Imagination in Postcolonial Niger." *American Ethnologist* 29 (4): 829–56.

Mass, Alon Y., David S. Goldfarb, and Ojas Shah. 2014. "Taxi Cab Syndrome: A Review of the Extensive Genitourinary Pathology Experienced by Taxi Cab Drivers and What We Can Do to Help." *Reviews in Urology* 16 (3): 99–104.

Mathew, Biju. 2005. *Taxi! Cabs and Capitalism in New York City*. New York: New Press.

Maurer, Bill. 2005. *Mutual Life, Limited: Islamic Banking, Alternative Currencies, Lateral Reason*. Princeton, NJ: Princeton University Press.

Mavhunga, Clapperton Chakanetsa. 2014. *Transient Workspaces: Technologies of Everyday Innovation in Zimbabwe*. Cambridge, MA: MIT Press.

Mazumdar, Ranjani. 2007. *Bombay Cinema: An Archive of the City* Minneapolis: University of Minnesota Press.

Mbembe, Achille. 2015. "Decolonizing Knowledge and the Question of the Archive." Public Lecture. Wits Institute for Social and Economic Research (WISER), University of Witwatersrand, Johannesburg.https://wiser.wits.ac.za/system/files /Achille%20Mbembe%20-%20Decolonizing%20Knowledge%20and%20the%20 Question%20of%20the%20Archive.pdf.

McAuliffe, Jane Dammen. 2002. *Encyclopedia of the Quar'an*. Vol. 2. Leiden, The Netherlands: Koninklijke Brill.

McFarlane, Colin. 2008. "Governing the Contaminated City: Infrastructure and Sanitation in Colonial and Postcolonial Bombay." *International Journal of Urban and Regional Research* 32 (2): 415–35.

Mehrotra, Rahul. 2012. "An Interview With Rahul Mehrotra: Between Equity and Impatient Capital: Making Indian Cities." *Journal of International Affairs* 65 (2): 133–37.

Melly, Caroline. 2017. *Bottleneck: Moving, Building, and Belonging in an African City*. Chicago: University of Chicago Press.

Millar, Kathleen M. 2018. *Reclaiming the Discarded: Life and Labor on Rio's Garbage Dump*. Durham, NC: Duke University Press.

Miller, Daniel, ed. 2001. *Car Cultures*. New York: Berg.

Mines, Mattison. 1973. "Social Stratification among Muslim Tamils in Tamilnadu, South India." In *Caste and Social Stratification among the Muslims*, edited by I. Ahmad, 61–71. Delhi: Manohar.

Mirza, Shireen. 2019. "Cow Politics: Spatial Shifts in the Location of Slaughterhouses in Mumbai City." *South Asia: Journal of South Asian Studies* 42 (5): 861–79.

Mohiuddin, Momin. 2002. *Muslim Communities in Medieval Konkan (610–1900 A.D.)*. New Delhi: Sundeep Prakashan.

Mol, Annemarie. 2008. *The Logic of Care: Health and the Problem of Patient Choice*. London; New York: Routledge.

Mol, Annemarie, and John Law. 1994. "Regions, Networks and Fluids: Anemia and Social Topology." *Social Studies of Science* 24: 641–71.

Molesworth, J. T. 1857. *A Dictionary, Marathi and English*. Digital Dictionaries of South Asia. Bombay: Bombay Education Society Press.

Mom, Gijs. 2003. "Costs, Technology, and Culture: Propelling the Early Taxicab 1900–25." *Journal of Transport History* 24 (2): 199–221.

Momin, A. R. 1973. "Muslim Castes in an Industrial Township of Maharashtra." In *Caste and Social Stratification among Muslims in India*, edited by I. Ahmad, 117–140. New Delhi: Manohar.

Monroe, Kristin. 2016. *The Insecure City: Space, Power, and Mobility in Beirut*. Rutgers, NJ: Rutgers University Press.

Munn, Nancy D. 1992. *The Fame of Gawa: A Symbolic Study of Value Transformation in a Massim (Papua New Guinea) Society*. Durham, NC: Duke University Press.

Nadri, Ghulam A. 2009. *Eighteenth-Century Gujarat and the Dynamics of Its Political Economy, 1750–1800*. Leiden; Boston: Brill.

Naik, Navami. 1995. "Navalkar Declares War on Polluting Vehicles." *Times of India*, August 18, 1995.

Naipaul, V. S. 1979. *A Bend in the River*. New York: Knopf.

Nair, Vijayanka. 2018. "An Eye for an I: Recording Biometrics and Reconsidering Identity in Postcolonial India." *Contemporary South Asia* 26 (2): 143–56.

National Taxi Association. 2010. *We Are One*. Singapore: NTUC Media Co-Operative Limited.

Neve, Geert De. 2008. "'We are all Sondukar [relatives]!': Kinship and Its Morality in an Urban Industry of Tamil Nadu." *Modern Asian Studies* 42 (1): 211–46.

Orr, Julian E. 1996. *Talking About Machines: Ethnography of a Modern Job*. Ithaca, NY: Cornell University Press.

———. 2006. "Ten Years of Talking About Machines." *Organization Studies* 27 (12): 1805–20.

Pandey, Gyanendra. 1990. *The Construction of Communalism in Colonial North India*. Delhi: Oxford University Press.

Peck, Jamie 1992. "Labor and Agglomeration: Control and Flexibility in Local Labor Markets." *Economic Geography* 68: 325–47.

———. 1996. *Workplace: The Social Regulation of Labor Markets*. New York: Guildford Press.

Polanyi, Michael. 1966. *The Tacit Dimension*. Garden City, NY: Doubleday.

Powell, John. 1995. *The Survival of the Fitter: Lives of Some African Engineers*. London: Intermediate Technology.

Prasad, Durga M. 1890. *The English-Urdū Translator's Companion, in the Roman Character*. Benares, India: Medical Hall.

Punit, Itika S. 2018. "Panic Buttons Won't Fix Ola and Uber's Sexual Assault Problem." *Quartz India*. June 26, 2018. https://qz.com/india/1298182/why-ola-and-ubers-measures-for-womens-safety-is-just-not-working/.

Rademacher, Anne, and K. Sivaramakrishnan, eds. 2013. *Ecologies of Urbanism in India: Metropolitan Civility and Sustainability*. Hong Kong: Hong Kong University Press.

Rajan, Sudhir Chella. 2020. *A Social Theory of Corruption: Notes from the Indian Subcontinent*. Cambridge, MA: Harvard University Press.

Rao, Nikhil. 2013. *House but No Garden: Apartment Living in Bombay's Suburbs, 1898–1964*. Minneapolis: University of Minnesota Press.

Rao, P. D. P. Prasada. 1972. *Strikes in India (1860–1970)*. Hyderabad, India: Ravi and Brothers.

Rofel, Lisa. 1999. *Other Modernities: Gendered Yearnings In China After Socialism*. Berkeley: University of California Press.

Roy, Nobhojit, V. Murlidhar, Ritam Chowdhury, Sandeep B. Patil, Priyanka A. Supe, Poonam D. Vaishnav, and Arvind Vatkar. 2010. "Where There Are No Emergency Medical Services—Prehospital Care for the Injured in Mumbai, India." *Prehospital and Disaster Medicine* 25 (2): 145–51.

Rudnyckyj, Daromir. 2018. *Beyond Debt: Islamic Experiments in Global Finance*. Chicago: University of Chicago Press.

Russell, Andrew L., and Lee Vinsel. 2018. "After Innovation, Turn to Maintenance." *Technology and Culture* 59 (1): 1–25.

Sahlins, Marshall D. 2012. *What Kinship Is—And Is Not*. Chicago: University of Chicago Press.

Salve, Prachi. 2019. "Overworked and Underpaid, India's 'Gig Workers' Are Survivors of a Flawed Economy." *Scroll.in* (blog), June 7, 2019. https://scroll.in/article/926146/overworked-and-underpaid-indias-gig-workers-are-survivors-of-a-flawed-economy.

Sangaji, S., and J. Shakespear. 1899. *A Handy Urdu-English Dictionary Based on Shakespear and the Best Modern Authorities*. Madras: S.P.C.K. Press.

Sastri, Kasirama Kesavarama. 1976–81. *Brhad Gujarati Kosa—Comprehensive Gujarati Dictionary*. Amadavada: Yunivarsiti Granthanirmana Borda, Gujarata Rajya: Vitaraka, Balagovinda Bukaselarsa.

Sayantan, Haldar. 2018. "Mapping Substance in India's Counter-strategies to China's Emergent Belt and Road Initiatives: Narratives and Counter-Narratives." *Indian Journal of Asian Affairs* 31 (1–2): 75–90.

Schiller, Frederich von. 1965. *On the Aesthetic Education of Man: In a Series of Letters*. Translated by R. Snell. New York: Frederick Ungar.

Seabrook, Jeremy, and Imran Ahmed Siddiqui. 2011. *People without History: India's Muslim Ghettos*. New Delhi: Navayana.

Seiler, Cotton. 2008. *Republic of Drivers: A Cultural History of Automobility in America*. Chicago: University of Chicago Press.

Shah, Svati. 2014. *Street Corner Secrets: Sex, Work, and Migration in the City of Mumbai.* Durham, NC: Duke University Press.

Sheller, Mimi. 2004. "Automotive Emotions: Feeling the Car." *Theory, Culture, and Society* 21 (4–5): 221–42.

Sheller, Mimi, and John Urry. 2006. "Introduction: Mobile Cities, Urban Mobilities." In *Mobile Technologies of the City,* edited by M. Sheller and J. Urry, 1–17. London: Routledge.

Shulman, David D. 2009. *Spring, Heat, Rains: A South Indian Diary.* Chicago: University of Chicago Press.

Simone, AbdouMaliq. 2004. "People as Infrastructure: Intersecting Fragments in Johannesburg." *Public Culture* 16 (3): 407–29.

———. 2014. "Relational Infrastructures in Postcolonial Worlds." In *Infrastructural Lives: Politics, Experience, and the Urban Fabric,* edited by S. Graham and C. McFarlane, 17–38. London: Routledge.

"Six Taxi Drivers Go on Fast." 1960. *Indian Express,* Friday, January 29, 1960.

Small, Ivan V. 2018. *Currencies of Imagination: Channeling Money and Chasing Mobility in Vietnam.* Ithaca, NY: Cornell University Press.

Solomon, Harris. 2016. *Metabolic Living: Food, Fat, and the Absorption of Illness in India.* Durham, NC: Duke University Press.

Sonneveld, Nadia, and Erin Stiles. 2019. "Khulʿ: Local Contours of a Global Phenomenon." *Islamic Law and Society* 26 (1/2): 1–11.

Sopranzetti, Claudio. 2017. *Owners of the Map: Motorcycle Taxi Drivers, Mobility, and Politics in Bangkok.* Berkeley: University of California Press.

Srivastava, Jyoti. 2017. "Maharashtra and The City Taxi Rules 2017 and the Court Case." Indian Law Watch. Delhi. June 16, 2017. https://indianlawwatch.com/practice/maharashtra-city-taxi-rules-2017-court-case/.

Steele, Anne. 2014. "India Rape Case: Does Uber Know Who's Driving?" *Christian Science Monitor,* December 8, 2014.

Stengers, Isabelle. 2005. "Introductory Notes on an Ecology of Practices." *Cultural Studies Review* 11 (1): 183–96.

Sterne, Jonathan. 2003. *The Audible Past: Cultural Origins of Sound Reproduction.* Durham, NC: Duke University Press.

Stewart, Kathleen. 2014. "Road Registers." *Cultural Geographies* 21 (4): 549–63.

Stoller, Paul. 1989. *The Taste of Ethnographic Things: The Senses in Anthropology.* Philadelphia: University of Pennsylvania Press.

———. 1997. *Sensuous Scholarship.* Philadelphia: University of Pennsylvania Press.

Strathern, Marilyn. 1988. *The Gender of the Gift.* Berkeley: University of California Press.

———. 2005. *Kinship, Law, and the Unexpected: Relatives Are Always a Surprise.* New York: Cambridge University Press.

———. 2020. *Relations: An Anthropological Account.* Durham, NC: Duke University Press.

Suchman, Lucy A. 1987. *Plans and Situated Actions: The Problem of Machine-Human Communication.* Cambridge, UK; New York: Cambridge University Press.

Surie, Aditi. 2018. "Are Ola and Uber Drivers Entrepreneurs or Exploited Workers?" *Economic and Political Weekly* 53 (24).

"Taxi Drivers' Co-Ops: M.L.A's Suggestion." 1959. *Times of India*, September 16, 1959.

"The Taxicab in Bombay: Regular Service Begun, Description of Cars, Chauffeurs and Meters." 1909. *Times of India*, December 21, 1909.

"Taxicabs for Bombay." 1909. *Times of India*, May 25, 1909.

Terra, Paulo Cruz. 2014. "Free and Unfree Labour and Ethnic Conflicts in the Brazilian Transport Industry: Rio de Janeiro in the Nineteenth Century." *International Review of Social History* 59: 113–32.

Thompson, E. P. 1963. *The Making of the English Working Class*. New York: Vintage.

Thompson, M. 1979. *Rubbish Theory*. Oxford, UK: Oxford University Press.

Thrift, Nigel. 2004. "Driving in the City." *Theory, Culture, and Society* 21 (4/5): 41–59.

Tronto, Joan C. 1992. *Moral Boundaries: A Political Argument for an Ethic of Care*. New York: Routledge.

———. 2013. *Caring Democracy: Markets, Equality, and Justice*. New York: New York University Press.

———. 2016. *Who Cares? How to Reshape a Democratic Politics*. London: Cornell Selects.

Tuan, Yi Fu. 1995. *Passing Strange and Wonderful: Aesthetics, Nature, and Culture*. Tokyo; New York: Kodansha International.

Turner, Terence. 2012. "The Social Skin." *HAU: Journal of Ethnographic Theory* 2 (2): 486–504.

Urry, John. 2004. "The "System" of Automobility." *Theory, Culture and Society* 21 (4/5): 25–39.

———. 2007. *Mobilities*. Cambridge, UK: Polity Press.

Urry, John, N. J. Thrift, and Mike Featherstone, eds. 2005. *Automobilities*. London: Sage.

Vatuk, Sylvia. 1969. "Reference, Address, and Fictive Kinship in Urban North India." *Ethnology* 8: 255–72.

———. 2019. "Extra-Judicial Khulʿ Divorce in India's Muslim Personal Law." *Islamic Law and Society* 26 (1/2): 111–48.

Verrips, Jojada, and Birgit Meyer. 2001. "Kwaku's Car: The Struggles and Stories of a Ghanaian Long-Distance Taxi-Driver." In *Car Cultures*, edited by D. Miller. New York: Berg.

Virilio, Paul. 1986. *Speed and Politics*. New York: Semiotext(e).

Von Uexküll, Jakob. 1957. "A Stroll through the Worlds of Animals and Men: A Picture Book of Invisible Worlds." In *Instinctive Behavior: The Development of a Modern Concept*, translated by Claire H. Schiller (ed.), 5–80. New York: International Universities Press.

"Walk or Ride? Our Public Conveyance Problem." 1918. *Times of India*, May 29, 1918.

Weinstein, Liza. 2014. *The Durable Slum: Dharavi and the Right to Stay Put in Globalizing Mumbai*. Minneapolis: University of Minnesota Press.

Weston, Kath. 2017. *Animate Planet: Making Visceral Sense of Living in a High-Tech Ecologically Damaged World*. Durham, NC: Duke University Press.

Yanagisako, Sylvia Junko. 2002. *Producing Culture and Capital: Family Firms in Italy*. Princeton, NJ: Princeton University Press.

Zhang, Jun. 2019. *Driving Toward Modernity: Cars and the Lives of the Middle Class in Contemporary China*. Ithaca, NY: Cornell University Press.

INDEX

A

Abdul (chillia man), on the genealogy
of chillia, 37
aggregators. *See* Ola-Uber
Ali, Syed, on caste among Indian
Muslims, 38
Altaf (chillia taximan): compensation for
maal work by his daughters Naseem
and Halima, 136; khandani dhandha
as incompatible with joining Ola-Uber
explained by, 54–55; Rashid and
Tariq's car driven by, 21
Amato, Joseph A.: on dust, 73; on
surfaces, 70
Amira (chillia woman): Momin husband
of, 125–26. *See also* Benazir (chillia
woman); Bilal (chillia taximan); Bisma
(chillia woman); Noori (chillia woman)
Anjaria, Jonathan Shapiro, on surfaces, 70
Appadurai, Arjun, on aspirational claims, 4
app-based taxis. *See* Ola-Uber
Aulino, Felicity, on "rituals" of care, 15
automobile ownership: dekh-bhal
used for the financing of, 21, 51–52;
externalities of, 100, 109; pooling of
resources to purchase vehicles, 44;
repair expenses as a factor, 145
automobility and the automobile
industry: transience and durability
of automobiles, 146. *See also* modern
mobility
auto-rickshaws: Mumbai Auto-Rickshaw
Drivers Association, 172; platform-
based auto-rickshaws proposed by

Ola-Uber, 171, 182, 185; resistance by
drivers to Ola, 196; and transportation
in Mumbai, 12, 40, 64, 78, 83, 194
Ayesha (chillia woman): family life of,
128–29, 136–37, 139. *See also* Hamid
(chillia driver)

B

Barad, Karen: on relations of obligations,
130; on touch and relatedness, 136
Bear, Laura, 87
Benazir (chillia woman): family life
of, 126–27, 136, 137; maal work by,
133–35; vegetable shopping with
the author, 131–32. *See also* Amira
(chillia woman); Bilal (chillia
taximan); Bisma (chillia woman);
Farid (chillia taximan); Hamid
(chillia driver); Noori (chillia
woman)
Besky, Sarah, on "fixity," 16
Bhabha, Homi, 31
Bilal (chillia taximan): family of, 122–23;
and the relational economy of the
chillia trade, 57, 79. *See also* Amira
(chillia woman); Benazir (chillia
woman); Bisma (chillia woman); Noori
(chillia woman)
Bisma (chillia woman): khul (extrajudicial
divorce) of, 125. *See also* Amira (chillia
woman); Benazir (chillia woman);
Bilal (chillia taximan); Farid (chillia
taxi man); Hamid (chillia driver);
Noori (chillia woman)

GLOBAL
SOUTH
ASIA

Padma Kaimal
K. Sivaramakrishnan
Anand A. Yang
SERIES EDITORS

GLOBAL SOUTH ASIA takes an interdisciplinary approach to the humanities and social sciences in its exploration of how South Asia, through its global influence, is and has been shaping the world.